Winner of the Jules and Frances Landry Award for 2007

INVISIBLE ACTIVISTS

WOMEN OF THE LOUISIANA NAACP AND THE STRUGGLE FOR CIVIL RIGHTS, 1915–1945

LEE SARTAIN

LOUISIANA STATE UNIVERSITY PRESS
BATON ROUGE

Published by Louisiana State University Press
lsupress.org

Copyright © 2007 by Louisiana State University Press
All rights reserved. Except in the case of brief quotations used in articles or reviews, no part of this publication may be reproduced or transmitted in any format or by any means without written permission of Louisiana State University Press.

Louisiana Paperback Edition, 2023

DESIGNER: Amanda McDonald Scallan
TYPEFACE: Trump Mediaeval

Library of Congress Cataloging-in-Publication Data
Sartain, Lee.
Invisible activists : women of the Louisiana NAACP and the struggle for civil rights, 1915–1945 / Lee Sartain.
  p. cm.
Includes bibliographical references and index.
ISBN 978-0-8071-3221-0 (cloth : alk. paper) | ISBN 978-0-8071-8042-6 (paperback) | ISBN 978-0-8071-3576-1 (pdf) | ISBN 978-0-8071-4919-5 (epub)
1. African American women civil rights workers—Louisiana—History—20th century. 2. African American women political activists—Louisiana—History—20th century. 3. African Americans—Civil rights—Louisiana—History—20th century. 4. National Association for the Advancement of Colored People—History—20th century. 5. Civil rights movements—Louisiana—History—20th century. 6. Louisiana—Race relations—History—20th century. I. Title.
 E185.93.L6S27 2007
 323.1196'0730082—dc22

2006024807

Parts of this work have appeared previously in slightly different form as "'Local Leadership': The Role of Women in the Louisiana Branches of the National Association for the Advancement of Colored People in Louisiana, 1920–1939," *Louisiana History* 66, no. 3 (Summer 2005): 311–31; and "'We Are but Americans': Miss Georgia M. Johnson and the National Association for the Advancement of Colored People in Alexandria, Louisiana, 1941–1946," *North Louisiana History* 35, nos. 2–3 (Spring–Summer 2004): 108–34.

This book is dedicated to:
  My wife, Sam, and daughter, Róisín Eve
    My dad, Ron, sister, Paula, and my niece, Honey
      Especially to my mum, Yvonne
And, crucially, to Professor Kevern Verney of Edge Hill University, whose skilled and insightful guidance and unwavering encouragement and optimism at every stage of the process permitted this book to be written.

CONTENTS

Introduction / 1

ONE
Weapons of the Utmost Value:
NAACP Organizational History, 1909–1945 / 15

TWO
The Sympathy of Women:
Black Women's Involvement in Louisiana
Civil Rights up to 1920 / 39

THREE
Destined to Bring Splendid Results:
NAACP Women's Auxiliaries and
Networks, 1921–1945 / 57

FOUR
God's Valiant Minority:
Teachers and Civil Rights / 82

FIVE
Leaders Who Persevere:
Elected Officials / 99

SIX
We Are but Americans:
Miss Georgia M. Johnson / 120

Conclusion / 137

Appendixes / 145
Notes / 157
Bibliography / 189
Index / 205

INVISIBLE ACTIVISTS

INTRODUCTION

Black women have been doubly victimized by scholarly neglect and racist assumptions. Belonging as they do to two groups which have traditionally been treated as inferiors by American society—Blacks and women—they have been doubly invisible. Their records lie buried, unread, infrequently noticed and even more seldom interpreted.

To research African American women's roles in the civil rights struggle before 1945 is, in part, a deductive exercise. The few first-hand accounts of the time only hint at women's roles. Such a case in point is Rev. John H. Scott's *Witness to the Truth: My Struggle for Human Rights in Louisiana,* an account of the author's time as president of the Transylvania branch of the National Association for the Advancement of Colored People (NAACP) in the 1930s and the East Carroll (Lake Providence) branch in the 1940s. There is very little expressly said about women, yet their presence is felt in subtle ways. In one example, after many East Carroll branch members attempted to register to vote, Scott was asked to stay to talk to the registrar. Feeling "uneasy about not having witnesses, I told the ladies who were with me, 'Don't leave that door. When you go out, you stay right at the door until I come out. I don't know what she [the registrar] wants.'" In other recollections of voter registration attempts Scott only mentions male associates, mainly other ministers. This brief glimpse of local female activists reveals that they were seen as being integral to the NAACP. Indeed they were often on the front lines of the civil rights battle, particularly in asserting their right to vote. However, it was men who received the publicity and who are named in such accounts. Women remained anonymous, albeit as an army of activists behind the generalship of men such as Reverend Scott.[1]

In the extensive and fastidiously documented NAACP archives there is ample evidence of women at the branches writing annual reports and letters to the national office in New York. They illustrate the expectations and activities of women in an integrationist civil rights association during the first half of the twentieth century. Although historians have frequently used this source, it has been untapped in researching women's unique experiences. It is virtually impossible to read the files of the Louisiana branches of the NAACP without becoming familiar with the names of Mrs. D. J. Dupuy (Baton Rouge chapter vice-president, 1929–1934; secretary, 1935–1939, 1942–1944), Miss Georgia M. Johnson (Alexandria chair of the legal redress and legislation committee, 1941–1944), Mrs. H. W. Johnson (Monroe vice-president, 1936–1938), and a host of other women. They ran the branches throughout the interwar years and into World War II. Their letters describe the tribulations that beset the early NAACP and how they attempted to overcome the problems of racial segregation in the Deep South. Seen through the paradigm of prevailing gender patterns, these personal communications also give invaluable insight into the motivation of women at the grass roots during the civil rights struggle.[2]

Commentators on the period have mostly ignored these women for various reasons, but primarily because women were not prominent in media reporting of the dramatic events of the early civil rights struggle. In Louisiana they did not serve as elected branch presidents, and this has tended to put them out of historical sight. Yet the day-to-day work of keeping a branch alive in difficult social and economic conditions was mainly the activity of women, as individual leaders and as collective activists who undertook fundraising events, entertainments, and youth education projects, as well as general campaigning on civil rights issues.

Historians have traditionally defined the role of women in the local civil rights movement in the United States as one in which men were the public leaders and women were the anonymous organizers in the background. Specific accounts of the NAACP have often suggested that women had little control or authority over local branches. Men were understood to be the leaders of local civil rights groups while women were more concerned with community networking, with church and charity groups, and contributing to local membership support. The strict definition of "leadership" within the NAACP, in its narrow sense of a high public profile or a prominent official title, has concealed women's wide-ranging participation in the organization. Indeed, the apparently overriding issue of race for the early civil rights movement has invariably disguised other areas of social discrimination, namely, sexism. Yet, as this study reveals, women did hold important official posts in the NAACP and were an indispensable part of the membership that kept the organization active in Louisiana in the interwar period.[3]

Manning Marable, in a Marxist critique of U.S. society, argues that historians have ignored African American women for a variety of reasons: "Black social history . . . has been profoundly patriarchal. The sexist critical framework of American white history has been accepted by Black male scholars; the reconstruction of our past, the reclamation of our history from the ruins, has been an enterprise wherein women have been too long segregated. Obligatory references are generally made to those 'outstanding sisters' who gave some special contribution to the liberation of the 'Black man.' Even these token footnotes probably do more harm than good, because they reinforce the false belief that the most oppressed victim of white racial tyranny has been the *Black man.*"[4] Marable claimed that black women historically "carried the greatest burden in the battle for democracy" in America, and while they were the "foundation of Black culture and society . . . their contributions have been generally ignored, or relegated to second-class status by most Black male activists, historians, and social scientists." Likewise, historian Paula Giddings, in her influential *When and Where I Enter*, sees black women as being "perceived as token women in Black texts and as token Blacks in feminist ones." Giddings's study stretches from the National Association of Colored Women (NACW) to the NAACP, although with little focus on NAACP women in the 1940s. Although black women were acknowledged to be important to historical analysis, they have not constituted more than a passing mention or reference in major texts, certainly not an entire study devoted to their activities and contribution to the early modern civil rights struggle. Most historians who write about the civil rights movement have begun with a focus on African American men with only an occasional nod toward female involvement as being necessary in some indefinable way.[5]

Modern historical texts, of course, have increasingly examined women's roles in the civil rights struggle of the twentieth century. For example, a collection of essays edited by La Frances Rodgers-Rose has given a broader appreciation of the role of women in African American communities and within the early civil rights movement. The articles credit black women with being intimately involved in a variety of local and national organizations, such as black churches and social groups, yet sexism was a central factor in suppressing a full utilization of women in the political sphere, which was seen as primarily a male preserve. Moreover, African American women participated in social and political clubs just as black men did, and such voluntary community work was customarily seen as being a professional activity that would lead to general racial uplift. Women's work in local NAACP branches, it is argued, should be studied as professional, though unsalaried, occupations.[6]

The very latest research into the civil rights struggle has mainly focused on studies at the state and city level, which has been particularly illuminating for the study of African American women. Many books have covered the 1950s and 1960s as being the apogee of the civil rights movement, the era of Martin Luther King Jr., yet historians have correspondingly recognized that this phase of the struggle for political and civic rights had its roots in the first half of the twentieth century. Scholars have challenged the idea that men led the civil rights struggle and women simply followed certain male leaders and organized to implement their plans. And it has become increasingly uncertain as to which role was seen as the more important or where authority within certain organizations necessarily rested. In many cases black women's efforts kept local civil rights afloat during trying times, such as the economic depression of the 1930s, when membership was at a low level. During these times, women obviously were leaders *and* organizers of the NAACP, often within the limits of what was traditionally expected of them, although particular individuals were not always entirely constrained by these stereotypes.[7]

A highly influential study of the civil rights struggle that elicits some of these points is Charles Payne's book on Mississippi, *I've Got the Light of Freedom*, which appreciates that black women had a long history of social and religious community activism, which gave them invaluable experience to bring over into the civil rights struggle. Payne discounts the idea that women were merely able to participate in civil rights campaigns due to some *differential-reprisal* interpretation that they were less likely than men to suffer from violent or economic retribution from the white community for their political involvement. Women lost their jobs, suffered physical abuse, and placed their families at risk because of their activities. Payne also explores the explanations that women themselves gave for joining the civil rights struggle as an interplay of factors deriving from their religious beliefs and their longstanding involvement in established kinship networks.[8]

In addition, Payne suggests that women naturally had an antibureaucratic and antihierarchical leaning that involved them acting outside the *normal* structures of a male-dominated hierarchy. In particular, women acted as social-network operatives who mobilized existing social groupings around general political objectives. Their affiliations with many interrelated organizations, through crossover membership and common interests, enabled them to work for various social and political appeals on a local and national scale. Such women had a myriad of roles, such as mediating conflicts, keeping a flow of information to group members, coordinating activities, and creating and sustaining "good relations and solidarity among co-workers." Such experience, responsibility, and dependability ensured that women took control of civil rights organizations in their localities, albeit not always in the highest and most visible leadership roles. The invisibility of women in the standard story of the civil rights struggle, Payne maintains, is mainly due to an overemphasis of dramatic moments over the more mundane activities that paved the way to such confrontations. The everyday work of the organizations that involved women's dedication and perseverance over years and decades was obscured by shorter term, albeit spectacular, moments that were etched into contemporary media images and historical accounts.[9]

Similarly, historian Bernice McNair Barnett argues that while black women looked to men as leaders of the movement, it was often women who did most of the work of civil rights groups and that this was due to the church tradition of male ministers. Many black women felt obliged to work behind the scenes as they "did not want to be leaders in the traditional sense of public spokes-person or central figure." Barnett suggests that due to the triple constraints of race, class, and gender, black women were restrained from being recognized as primary articulators of the movement, especially by the media, even though women performed essential leadership functions. The roles that women were to accept, at the grassroots level or behind the scenes, represented "profiles in courage and suggest that they were *leaders* in their communities, [and] *leaders* in the day-to-day fight against forms of oppression."[10]

Belinda Robnett, in her analysis of African American women in their fight for political rights, argues plainly that black women were "Leaders, Not Just Organizers." She portrays them as "community bridge leaders" who provided "much of the emotional work needed to persuade the masses to join the movement and to act." Such women, individually and collectively, were trusted within their communities and worked to build group cohesion and sustain momentum in a unified movement with specific goals. These bridge leaders were "well known as solid, outspoken, and trustworthy individuals who often took the initiative during community crises."[11]

Such studies attempt to delineate the broader definitions of what local black leadership actually meant in the period before the civil rights movement of the 1950s and 1960s. The dichotomy that men were leaders and women were simply backroom followers appears too simplistic when scrutinized carefully. Accordingly, recent historical studies have followed this trend of reappraising leadership definitions and have focused in detail on local civil rights campaigns and organizations in the pre–World War II period, with some emphasis on the NAACP.

Dorothy Autrey's "Can These Bones Live?" a study of the NAACP in Alabama, 1918–1930, is one such study that examines the relationship between local, state, and national organization. Autrey argues that mass membership was elusive for the NAACP in the Deep South in particular, as it required "some degree of economic independence. For the easily intimidated and for working-class blacks, dependent upon whites for their economic livelihood, NAACP membership may have been temporarily accepted but was not usually maintained." The active membership was principally middle class throughout this period, which led the organization to demonstrate little concern for a program involving the black masses, or for seriously challenging local white-power economic structures. As Autrey suggests, just belonging to the NAACP represented a serious social and economic risk, so membership seems to have been inspired by genuine concern with the wider problems of the local black community. The principal aim of the pre-1930 NAACP in Alabama was for social and political rights rather than economic emancipation, a fact that particularly attracted the middle classes to its cause. However, it was difficult to keep branches in the Deep South alive through the 1920s, and it was this core group of mostly middle-class blacks who kept the NAACP in existence throughout their communities.[12]

Northern branches of the NAACP reflected similar social trends in membership. In Chicago, according to Christopher R. Reed, the NAACP proved an ideal channel for a middle-class, professional agenda, namely, of attaining the American Dream. The Chicago membership was small in the 1920s and 1930s, much as in the South, and Reed specifically recognizes the essential civil rights work of women in the local branch. He depicts the distinctive work undertaken by middle-class black women as "quiet leadership" that existed "with widespread social and civic support." Black women's social and political "networks of solidarity" were essential in providing informal structures (or "micro-mobilization," as Reed describes it) enabling a branch to survive through intricate personnel and organizational links. Though women did not dominate the hierarchical structures or elected positions of the branch, they were a component voice in the planning and organizing stages of the Chicago NAACP due to their social networks. However, gender inequality meant that women did not have full access to the formal decision-making structures of the branch, as they were restrained to activities seen as exclusively female concerns.[13]

Nonetheless, the men in the Chicago branch fully acknowledged that the NAACP in the city would lapse without the invaluable contribution of its female members. Reed observes that this role tended to be at the grassroots level rather than in any comprehensive policy-deciding capacity. It was mainly in fundraising that women played a vital role within the branch and therefore secured its long-term survival. Each year hundreds of women were recruited for work as "taggers on street corners as well as for sponsors of tables at the annual tea held annually each Spring."[14]

Academic works that have focused on individuals have added to the detail of women's roles in the NAACP, as many of them forged leadership positions for themselves in local branch hierarchies. In her book on Lula B. White of Houston, Texas, Merline Pitre points out that the NAACP was one of the few organizations that accepted both male and female members and also allowed women to gain valuable leadership skills. Through the local NAACP, White forged a political power base by which to interact with the black and white power structures of Texas and with the national NAACP officers in New York.[15]

Lula White worked hard to create a serious and influential role for herself in the NAACP in Texas, something that was also to involve her marriage to a man of status. As Pitre explains, marriage for a black woman, while potentially being portrayed as a reduction of personal power, may also be seen as a route to maintain respectability (or, indeed, to a rise in social standing) and thus to gain access to further aspects of authority. As the wife of an activist within the local NAACP and the wider community, Lula White tapped into important social and political networks that could help alter the position of blacks in Texas.[16]

Pitre claims that Lula White clearly understood the correlation between race and gender and that political action was clearly directed toward altering the disadvantageous status of both blacks and women. Yet her activity was done within the framework of what was considered the feminine sphere of influence. For instance, Lula White's home was a place for conventional fraternal female meetings where traditional aspects of femininity and club women's groups were enacted, such as embroidery, book reviews, and social work concerns.[17]

Another major figure in the NAACP during the early 1940s was Ella Baker, field secretary from 1941 to 1943 and national director of branches from 1943 to 1946. Baker held a radical view of women in the organization and was an unvarying critic of the bureaucratic nature of the NAACP. Baker criticized egos within civil rights organizations and objected to most groups' undemocratic structures, and in particular was disapproving of a civil rights movement based solely on middle-class attitudes. The faith of Baker's organizing lay in her encouragement of local people to campaign in their own neighborhoods on issues that concerned them and with leadership being a democratic and community affair. Ella Baker saw that women in the NAACP were indispensable to its functioning, that local branches maintained viability by their familial and personal relationships, but that they went largely unappreciated by official channels. Women's major contributions at the local level rarely translated into official positions in the branches. Historian Barbara Ransby designates Baker's ideals as a "radical democratic vision" by which individuals with the respect and trust of their communities would organize the civil rights struggle in their own areas, rather than be dictated to by a bureaucratic hierarchy. This was particularly relevant for the movement in the Deep South, which had to confront various cultural concerns that the New York–based NAACP could not practically have imagined.[18]

In 1969, at the Institute for the Black World, in Atlanta, Ella Baker gave a speech entitled "The Black Woman in the Civil Rights Struggle." Tellingly, Baker saw the civil rights struggle as one not entirely consumed by gender issues:

> I have never been one to feel great needs in the direction of setting myself apart as a woman. I've always thought first and foremost of people as individuals . . . [but] whenever there has been struggle, black women have been identified with that struggle . . . [Yet, there was] an assumption that those who were trained [as leaders] were not . . . to be *part* of the community, but to be *lead-*

ers of the community. This carried with it the false assumption that being a leader meant that you were separate and apart from the masses . . . and that your responsibility to the people was to *represent* them. This means that the people were never given a sense of their own values . . . Later, in the 1960s, a different concept emerged: the concept of the right of the people to participate in the decisions that affected their lives.[19]

Nevertheless, gender cannot be totally disregarded from the debate on civil rights and leadership. Indeed, Baker was confronted with questions of gender and class on many occasions and was often exasperated by such issues in the local NAACP branches, exemplified by the Baltimore branch under the leadership of socialite Lillie Jackson. The branch in Baltimore was run entirely by women, and Baker found her own ideas of radical democracy at odds with Jackson's class-conscious, bureaucratic elitism based on typical gender stereotypes and an eye to social events.[20]

Glenda E. Gilmore's seminal study, *Gender and Jim Crow*, takes the debate even farther, seeing the concept of gender disparity within society as the essence of the modern civil rights cause. These ideas were based on the defense of black female integrity, or in Gilmore's phrase the "Best Man ideal." Black men had to constantly affirm their "manhood" by protecting black female integrity while aspiring for their family units to achieve a white middle-class ideal, "even if they could never prove it to whites' satisfaction." Such an ideal held that women should not work outside the domestic sphere and that men should be the sole wage earners for their family. Black women, while being aware of this gender issue, saw their role as sustaining the civil rights battle on male political terms and subordinated personal citizenship to the idea of "group progress." Although women were on the front line of the NAACP battle in the Deep South, they saw themselves as having to fight for the full rights of black male citizenship rather than for a doctrine of female liberation.[21]

Rosa Parks's recollection of her early experiences in the NAACP in Alabama gives us some insight into the daily routines of local branches in the Deep South in the early 1940s. Participation in local branches gave women different kinds of experience, ranging from practical skills in a professional context, extended social networks, personal fulfillment (intellectual and psychological), and a raised social and political consciousness. Rosa Parks saw self-respect as an essential requirement for being a socially dynamic black woman, and this issue was directly related to the acquisition of the ballot. The vote would protect black women as being both black and being female. The two issues were irrevocably linked.[22]

The gender issue manifests itself in Rosa Parks's autobiography often as an undercurrent of southern chivalry from her husband. Raymond Parks initially discouraged his wife from joining the NAACP in the early 1940s because he believed it was far too dangerous for her as a woman to be involved in the organization. When she finally joined in 1943 she soon found that there was an expected organizational role for women: "I paid my membership dues, and then they had the election of officers. I was the only woman there, and they said they needed a secretary, and I was too timid to say no. I just started taking minutes . . . There was no pay, but I enjoyed the work." In this manner, deeply ingrained gender categorization defined many local NAACP branches and the practical roles expected to be undertaken by women and men. Parks was familiar with the role that men and women performed in society at large and, by extension, how this affected their roles in social and political groups. For her, the idea of political rights rested on a concept of a truly civilized society based on middle-class social attitudes and courteous manners. Indeed Rosa Parks, famed for not giving up her seat on a Montgomery bus and thus starting the city's public transport boycott, described her general indignation at white men not giving up their bus seats to women, black or white: "It did not seem proper, particularly for a woman to give her seat to a man."[23]

As secretary, Rosa Parks ran the local NAACP office alongside branch president E. D. Nixon, and when he was out of town she managed it entirely. Familial relationships were very important to membership of a branch and in strengthening bonds of trust; Parks's husband often served as her political educator. Before meeting Raymond Parks, Rosa Parks had never discussed racial issues with another black person outside her family circle. Furthermore, she was motivated to join when her brother, Sylvester, was drafted into the army. The reality of her brother fighting for American democracy yet being denied the vote at home was an important crossroads in Rosa Parks's life and had an effect on her internal convictions as a black American. The NAACP was a place to reaffirm these personal beliefs and expand her knowledge of racial issues beyond the immediate hometown or state. As Rosa Parks stated, "The more I became involved with the NAACP, the more I learned of discrimination and acts of violence against blacks, such as lynchings, rapes, and unsolved murders. And the more I learned about these incidents, the more I felt I could no longer passively sit by and accept the Jim Crow laws. A better day had to come."[24]

The lives of individual women through autobiography and historical accounts are important to understanding their personal motivation in joining the NAACP and their subsequent civil rights careers. Adding to this level of detail are recent academic works on the civil rights movement and the NAACP at the state and local levels, including several critical analyses of Louisiana. New Orleans, naturally, takes more attention than other towns and cities due to its central role in the state's history and culture and the lack of resources readily available outside the Crescent City. Historian Adam Fairclough has specifically claimed the importance of southern states to the history of the civil rights struggle, as "future researchers may well find that in states like Louisiana and South Carolina the NAACP formed the backbone of the civil rights movement." Indeed, Fairclough claims that by the 1940s in Louisiana "the NAACP served as the locomotive of black protest and political activity."[25]

In Louisiana civil rights progress tended to occur earlier than in other states in the South. For example, by 1948 all of Louisiana's black teachers had gained equal pay with white educators; by 1949 New Orleans had its first black policeman since 1900; by 1950 Louisiana State University had admitted its first black graduate student; in 1953 citizens of Baton Rouge undertook a bus boycott on the scale of the Montgomery protests; and by 1954 New Orleans had integrated its public libraries, and two black city councilors were elected in Crowley. Significantly, by 1956 the state's black electorate totaled 160,000, overtaking the official figures of 1896, before Louisiana had brought in disfranchisement laws. Yet these breakthroughs did not appear owing to any overnight radical protest; indeed, the issues were carefully structured and worked through by decades of gradual assertion and organizing. The NAACP was an important element of black protest continuity for many communities in Louisiana, with its core membership belonging to the organization over several decades.[26]

In *Race and Democracy*, Fairclough highlights women as central activists to Louisiana's civil rights progress between 1915 and 1972. He claims that "women of great courage and integrity . . . [were] the bedrock . . . of the civil rights movement. They deserve more than footnotes."

Fairclough's subsequent work, *Teaching Equality,* published in 2001, with a profile of teachers in Louisiana, confirms women's central contribution to the NAACP in the 1930s.[27]

According to Fairclough, the New Orleans NAACP branch was a common vehicle for those opposing racial discrimination up to World War II. Its decision-making body, the executive committee, read like a "who's who of the black bourgeoisie." Such groups tended to be wealthy and highly cultured in the European tradition and were not so much middle class as essentially upper class in their perceptions and outlook. However, this elite group fostered the NAACP through its formative and most precarious years in Louisiana. While New Orleans was the largest and most visibly active branch in the state, other cities had particular social settings that affected branch interests and dynamics in various ways. For example, Baton Rouge was highly industrialized after World War I, with Standard Oil being a major employer, and Shreveport and Alexandria were the principal areas of military training for the whole United States. In such diverse settings branches might focus on antilynching campaigns or on getting jobs in major industries for black people or, as was the case in Alexandria, trying to achieve equity for African American soldiers suffering from racial injustices. Yet campaigning was not merely a parochial concern, as the New York national office also had its own bureaucratic requirements that anticipated women in certain roles, such as the organizing of NAACP women's auxiliaries and their involvement in youth groups.[28]

These studies indicate that the idea of leadership in the NAACP needs to be modified to represent the reality of female participation in local branches. Some women did hold hierarchical positions in the branches that gave them a form of traditional leadership, such as making speeches and chairing executive committees, while others were public advocates for particular issues, notably the voter registration and antilynching campaigns. In both roles, women served as the local leaders of the NAACP and could be seen as the embodiment of its values and hopes. Indeed, women in the local branches organized and led in major campaigns; yet how did this reflect in branch dynamics and in the decision-making process?

The role of black women in the NAACP and the early civil rights struggle has generally been ignored, or at best given cursory acknowledgment. Only recently have studies begun to detail the role and gender expectations of women in the organization. Such scholarship has focused on state and local analysis for an understanding of these questions, and Louisiana has followed this trend. However, black women have not been fully included in this approach, with an analysis of gender roles and how they relate to civil rights organizing.

This work will analyze African American women's activities in the Louisiana NAACP within the context of their comprehensive social and political networks. These include family, career, church, fraternal affiliations, and, importantly, women's charitable work in organizations other than the NAACP. What emerges is a more complete picture of women's conceptual world, allowing us to appreciate better their ideological and philosophical beliefs.

Women associated with the early NAACP did not leave complete historical biographies. They did, however, leave fragments of clues as to their diverse social world in newspapers, NAACP records, membership lists of various organizations, campaigning pamphlets, and personal letters. Assembled, these fragments provide a reasonable picture of women's complex and integrated lives as social reformers and political activists. These reconstituted biographies bring to light women whose civil rights work would have otherwise been lost, despite the occasional frustrating gap in their stories. Geographical disparities compounded these research challenges. Areas with more severe racial oppression, such as Shreveport and New Iberia, did not have as complete branch records as cities like New Orleans and Baton Rouge.

This section has undertaken an examination of the recent historiography and issues of leadership surrounding African American women in the early civil rights struggle. Chapter 1 covers the history of the development of the NAACP from its organization in 1909, examining the evolution of its institutional growth and the contributions of its major figures such as Mary White Ovington, W. E. B. Du Bois, and Walter White. Because the NAACP was such a bureaucratic and hierarchical organization, it is necessary to appreciate its structural history and campaigning methods at the national level and its correlation with local branches. Chapter 2 looks at women's civil rights activity in Louisiana prior to the establishment of the NAACP. This activity was shaped by the concept of spheres of influence, which was firmly established for men and women in this period, and by the idea that group probity was at the forefront of political and civic advancement for African Americans. With the founding of the first stable chapter of the NAACP in the state in New Orleans, the centrality of community morality and, by extension, women's roles in organizing, is evident in examples from the local branch's newspaper, *The Vindicator*.

Chapter 3 examines the role of women's auxiliaries in the Louisiana

NAACP branches from 1920 through to 1945. The general campaigning that emerged during this period highlights the expectation of women activists at the state level, as well as decrees from the central office in New York, and how gender roles were integral to the civil rights struggle. Women's social networks provide a broader picture of how they viewed their own political activities and how sophisticated concepts emerged to confront racism and segregation in the localities, as well as ideas of how to live with, and possibly defeat, Jim Crow in Louisiana. Chapter 4 takes this a step further by focusing on a pivotal professional grouping for the NAACP in the Deep South. Teachers had a vital role within African American communities as local leaders and youth mentors, and had a developed concept of how to foster general group uplift. Indeed, the development of the NAACP as a statewide organization in the early 1940s was due, in part, to the campaign to equalize black teachers' salaries with those of white educators.

Chapters 5 and 6 give extensive coverage of women in their elected roles in the branches of the NAACP from 1917 to 1945, and attempts to understand their formal leadership positions and influence within the local organizations. Two case studies illustrate the positions of individual female leaders and the essential role women played in the stability and growth of the NAACP in Louisiana. Chapter 5 examines the numerous elected posts occupied by Mrs. D. J. Dupuy in Louisiana's state capital, Baton Rouge, and showcases her as a woman who used gender concepts to carve a powerful position for herself in the NAACP. Miss Georgia M. Johnson of Alexandria, the subject of Chapter 6, was generally at variance with the gender propriety of the times and struggled to maintain her position in the NAACP in her city because of it.

Women played multifarious roles in the local branches of the Louisiana NAACP, both collectively and as individuals. Their roles were pivotal in membership drives, fundraising, and campaigning, and they often had great responsibilities, though not with matching official authority or rank within the organization. Some women stand out as leaders in their own right, even though men took the greater part of the publicity for campaigns and were presidents of the branches. Women played many different parts in the NAACP in Louisiana and at various levels of authority and responsibility. In the words of historian Mark Robert Schneider, "As the narrative unfolds, many of these characters will emerge as the local heroines they were."[29]

ONE

WEAPONS OF THE UTMOST VALUE
NAACP Organizational History, 1909–1945

The Association's branches are weapons of the utmost value and importance. Did we not have them, we should be forced to invent them.

ORGANIZED in 1909 the NAACP developed its organizational structures and campaigning techniques over time. The group's specific issues and concerns directly affected these structures, but they also reflected the social background and personalities of its personnel. The broad and varied elements of the NAACP—its legal department and many local branches and youth councils—made it a multifaceted organization functioning and interacting at various levels within the American social, political, and judicial system in its aim to bring greater civic opportunities to African American people.

The idea of the NAACP originated in 1908 with the race riots in Springfield, Illinois, and socialist William English Walling's subsequent newspaper article, "The Race War in the North." Walling called for the setting up of a biracial national organization of "fair-minded whites and intelligent blacks" to combat the growing racial divisions in the whole of the United States, arguing that the problem was not just a sectional one. The essay was read by social worker Mary White Ovington who, along with Walling and others, was inspired to issue "The Call" for a national conference to renew the struggle for black civil rights. This pronouncement brought together eminent black and white liberals who wished for urgent progress on the race issue. Later, the Amenia Conference of August 1916, held on the property of Joel Spingarn, an influential white supporter of the NAACP, would bring together black leaders of all ideological persuasions in a further attempt to unify the cause within the African American intellectual community. However, this was largely a superficial accord, as many southern black people were only too aware of the physical hazards of open political agitation.[1]

The emphasis of events such as "The Call" and the Amenia Conference was on the civil and political rights of African Americans, rather than their economic concerns, which secured the focus of the NAACP throughout the coming decades. Many perceived it as a direct challenge to the long-term professed ideals of Booker T. Washington that had placed economic progress before promotion of suffrage rights. According to the new organization, African Americans could not enjoy any economic or social aspects of being Americans without simultaneously having the protection of their fundamental political rights.

The NAACP was to develop structures of command and decision-making that grew over its early decades and into World War II, which made it a rather bureaucratically led group controlled from a central headquarters in New York City. At its inception the national organization had thirty members on its board of directors, which grew to thirty-five in 1919, and forty-eight by 1936. The NAACP constitution stated that the directors were to have "control and government" to "exercise all such powers and do all such acts and things as may be exercised by or done by the Association." This board of directors could employ executive officers as were required. A president was to preside over meetings of the full Association, such as the annual conference, and oversaw board meetings in the absence of the chairman. The chairman was also to have "full authority over all officers and employees." Furthermore, the chairman had to make annual reports to the board "covering the status" of the NAACP and its activities. A secretary was to "coordinate and integrate the work of the several divisions, branches, departments and bureaus, and shall aid and cooperate in the work of all committees." This complex, top-heavy structure became dominated by key figures, and in time the executive secretary became the focus of national and political leadership of the NAACP.[2]

One of the most important early appointments took place when W. E. B. Du Bois was employed to direct the propaganda wing of the NAACP. Du Bois founded and became editor of the NAACP's monthly publication *The Crisis: A Record of the Darker Races* and as such was also the only paid staff member on the executive committee. *The Crisis* first went to print in November 1910 and sought to redress the negative press that black people received in the mainstream white media. The magazine had such features as "Along the Color Line" (news), "Opinion" (editorial articles from other newspapers), "Men of the Month" (which also included women), poetry and short stories by black writers,

"The Burden" (a catalogue of lynchings across the nation), "What to Read," and national and local NAACP news.[3]

The Crisis addressed the issues of the day in an uncompromising manner. The August 1915 issue was given over entirely to the female suffrage question, and it was to be a recurring theme well beyond the ratification of the Nineteenth Amendment in 1920 in fighting for the enfranchisement of black women. Leading black female activists wrote articles for the periodical, such as the vice-president of the National Association of Colored Women (NACW), Mary Talbert, and Tuskegee Woman's Club member Adella Hunt Logan. In February 1916 the publication was devoted exclusively to New Orleans and its most influential black residents. With such an approach, provincial branches of the NAACP could be encouraged in their local efforts and their morale strengthened in fighting for political rights, as well as pursuing new members, which was a constant struggle.[4]

In the early days of the NAACP white people were vital at the national level as they procured money, prestige, and political connections for the organization. For example, Moorfield Storey, a noted jurist, had connections with the nineteenth-century abolitionist movement, and served as president of the NAACP from 1910 to 1929. Joel Spingarn, poet, academic, and publisher, was president from 1930 to 1939, and was influential from the group's inception. His brother, Arthur, a lawyer, succeeded him as president and remained in the post until 1967. White members were important political symbols of the NAACP, but by the early 1920s the greater part of the membership was black. This symbolism of having white officers proclaimed the NAACP's long-held philosophical stance for integration and the hope of working with white America to meet these ends.[5]

Mary White Ovington held many of the executive positions, including executive secretary (1911–12), acting chairman of the board (1917–18), treasurer (1932), and she was a long-time member of the board of directors and a reliable fundraiser. Ovington was one of the few white people in the organization to have links with important black reformers, such as W. E. B. Du Bois, Mary Church Terrell, and Ida B. Wells-Barnett. Indeed, mainly due to Ovington's influence, more than a third of the signers of "The Call" in 1909 were women. However, she became increasingly marginal by the late 1920s as more black members took over the hierarchy. Indeed, Ovington said that she had become "not much use except as a cheerer on" and fully recognized that Walter White's ascendancy to the executive secretary's post in 1931 was an important turning point for the organization.[6]

While the racial composition of the board of directors was not strictly a constitutional matter, there was recognition within the organization that it ought to be balanced between its black and white members. In 1920 there were nineteen blacks and sixteen whites. By 1929 there were still nineteen black board members out of thirty-seven. Initially, the NAACP was directed, though not numerically dominated, by a white-controlled board of directors who held the key financial posts. According to historians Elliot Rudwick and August Meier, it took two decades for the NAACP to change to a "black secretariat." In contrast to the national organization, however, at the grassroots level the NAACP always appealed to a greater number of blacks than whites. In 1947 Ovington admitted that "We used to pride ourselves on never knowing how many white members we had and how many colored— we do still. It would be correct, however, to say that more board work was done at this time by white than by colored. In the field, the situation was the reverse."[7]

Rudwick and Meier pinpoint 1920 as the year that national executive positions changed from white to black officers, notable because of James Weldon Johnson's appointment as executive secretary with Walter White as his assistant. They stated that the NAACP had been organized when "black protest had proven ineffective, and this interracial organization had been founded just because the wealth and prominence of sympathetic whites were needed. Yet in less than a decade the NAACP discovered that it would have to base its income and membership primarily on the black community." Indeed as early as 1914 the executive secretary, Mary Childs Nerney, had suggested replacing herself with a black person, as this would "absolutely eliminate the race issue. That is the . . . only way this Association is to come into its own—under a colored leader . . . who has the . . . confidence of the colored people. The colored people will never come into their own until they do it for themselves." Despite such counsel the board selected another white person to replace Nerney, Roy Nash, and John Shillady replaced Nash in 1918.[8]

However, most of the secretarial work in this period was increasingly delegated to James Weldon Johnson and Walter White. Johnson, who became permanent executive secretary in 1920, was a writer, poet, diplomat, Republican Party supporter, and a field secretary for the NAACP, and he realized that black strength lay with uniting under black leadership, rather than relying on a few white people's goodwill and sponsorship. Johnson's strength lay in the fact that his affiliations were not as unambiguous as Du Bois's had been at the start of the twentieth century with regard to Booker T. Washington's stance of accommodating Jim Crow. In fact, Johnson had been a Washingtonian and still retained some affiliation with the Tuskegee organization, while Du Bois had been a vociferous detractor of Washington. Under Johnson's organizational and inspirational leadership, the NAACP membership was 95 percent black by 1921. However, the white members of the board and the executive committee retained the organization's financial control and continued to authorize expenditure.[9]

Walter White took over much of Johnson's workload as the 1920s progressed, and in 1931 he finally took on the executive secretary's office. This was a time of severe financial crisis and membership decline for the NAACP, and White asserted his authority over the organization to reflect his personality and concerns. By the early 1930s many of the early dominant figures were departing from the NAACP or were declining in influence. Du Bois was to resign as editor of *The Crisis* in 1934 over his controversial editorial declaring that segregation was not always an absolute evil, which was at odds with the proclaimed policy of the NAACP. He also claimed that the Association was antidemocratic in its decision-making structures and was not adapting itself toward an economic agenda, especially with the damage the Great Depression was inflicting upon black Americans. The journal came under White's administration until he replaced himself with Roy Wilkins, editor of the *Kansas City Call*, the following year. Ovington resigned as chairman in 1931 because she felt that White was not consulting her over business. By this time Joel Spingarn was also in partial retirement. Arthur Spingarn made himself available for legal advice to the officers of the NAACP, but he only responded to the issues the black secretariat brought forward and did not direct policy.[10]

With the initial limitations on staffing and finance levels the NAACP undertook campaigns that had to attract media headlines and disseminate the organization's underlying philosophy in potentially popular and cost-effective methods. Carefully orchestrated operations were selected to elicit general white sympathy, generate membership, and produce financial resources. (During the Great Depression it would be even more vital to focus on pivotal issues, as fiscal restraints were severe.) One of the NAACP's first public-relations issues was the attempt to highlight stereotyped racism in the media by campaigning against D. W. Griffith's film *Birth of a Nation* (1915), which depicted African Americans as politically immoral and sexually lascivious creatures. Calling for a boycott of the movie, the NAACP picketed cinemas in major cities. However, the censorship issue was antithetical to many white liberals who otherwise may have been attracted to the organization. The campaign failed to have the film nationally censored or banned, although there was a temporary ban in Illinois.[11]

Similarly, James Weldon Johnson attempted to highlight and protest lynching and mob violence against blacks in the United States by leading a silent parade of approximately 15,000 people down New York's Fifth Avenue on July 28, 1917. The demonstrators advocated that the government initiate and pass antilynching legislation in Congress to make such crimes a federal offense, thus attaining central government powers to protect black people's constitutional rights (criminal law being a constitutional prerogative of individual states). Such protest exemplified NAACP campaigning techniques by highlighting a relevant issue, catching the media's attention, and projecting the NAACP as a well-organized and mannerly group, while also raising its profile among the black and white populations, and, vitally, among politicians.[12]

The antilynching campaign became one of the most important battles over the first three decades of the NAACP. In one sense it could be assessed as a failure, as it never secured legislation making lynching a federal offense. However, James Weldon Johnson was to assert, with regard to the Dyer Anti-Lynching Bill in the Senate in the early 1920s, that while it "did not become a law . . . it made the floors of Congress a forum in which facts were brought home to the American people as they had never been before." Historian Robert Zangrando argues that it was "the NAACP's great service . . . [which] facilitated lynching's decline." The NAACP secured House of Representatives passage of such bills in 1922, 1937, and 1940, although the Senate filibustered the measures and ensured their defeat. However, the campaign was vital in encouraging black communities to organize for civil rights activities and educated the American people to the NAACP's social and political agenda. With the failure to pass legislation, however, the Association had to reprioritize its campaigning, and some supporters believed it ought to focus on equality in education or on some form of economic policy to reinforce the political program. However, Walter White continued to focus on the Costigan-Wagner antilynching bill in the 1930s.[13]

Such NAACP campaigns were run alongside other high-profile political matters, such as the 1930 battle to keep Judge J. Parker, who was perceived to be a racist, from being appointed to the U.S. Supreme Court. Such a case was not only a matter of publicity and an attempt at national moral suasion; it was also a subject of deep social concern as it was believed that the fabric of American life could be changed by the laws of the land. The campaign against Judge Parker was successful, thanks in part to the aid of organized labor's opposition. Although the campaign lasted only six weeks, it was, in historian Kenneth W. Goings words, "instrumental in solidifying the position of the organization in the eyes of black and white America . . . Besieged by critics, black and white, and sapped of money and membership by the Great Depression, the campaign against Parker became a rallying point for the Association that reinvigorated it after the aimlessness following the collapse of its efforts in support of the Dyer Anti-Lynching Bill."[14]

To defeat Parker's nomination, the NAACP had to rely on its local and state branch networks. Kenneth Goings describes this campaign, which entailed extensive letter writing by the local branches across the nation, as instrumental in expanding the role of the local chapters and for creating statewide conferences and cooperation. Indeed the NAACP annual report of 1930 saw that "The Branches of the Association played an indispensable part in the fight to prevent the confirmation of Judge Parker as associate justice of the United States Supreme Court. They sent numbers of telegrams and letters to their respective senators, urging that they oppose the confirmation, and aroused other organizations and individuals to do the same. They held many meetings to arouse sentiment in this matter. It was their faithful work which enabled the National Office to unite the colored people of the country in this fight."[15]

Moreover, the NAACP saw that the closeness of the U.S. Supreme Court decision in its legal action *Nixon v. Condon* (1932), a white primary case in which blacks were refused participation in a Texas Democratic convention, "demonstrated the wisdom of the Association's fight in 1930 against the seating of Judge John J. Parker." Five Supreme Court Justices voted in favor of the case, with four voting against. With Parker on the bench the decision could have easily gone against the NAACP.

The Association followed up Parker's defeat by attempting to unseat congressmen who had voted in favor of appointing the North Carolinian judge to the Supreme Court.[16]

A central and growing criticism of the NAACP during the Great Depression was that there was no strategy to help poorer black people and that its focus on civil rights was mainly a black middle-class preoccupation. This coincided with fears that there could be a communist insurgency in the 1930s and that many African Americans might see extreme political action as preferable to the Association's mainstream and legalistic methods. Indeed the NAACP found itself in direct rivalry with the Communist Party over a struggle to control the Scottsboro Case. The Scottsboro Boys were nine black men and boys, aged between twelve and twenty, who had been falsely convicted of raping two white women in Alabama in March 1931 and had been sentenced to death. The case became a nationwide propaganda battle yet was prolonged in the courts due to the rivalry between the Communists and the NAACP. Walter White had not immediately taken the case, as the NAACP tended to take up causes that were eminently winnable and which showed blacks in the best possible light to the rest of America. The Scottsboro Boys, in contrast, were unemployed, illiterate, and had undesirable reputations as drifters. The Communist Party of the USA, conversely, made the insightful argument that the NAACP was simply not interested in the fundamental problems of black Americans' lives, essentially their economic welfare and prospects. In part because of their divided defense, the acquittal and release of all the Scottsboro Boys took until 1950. The NAACP's focus on African American economic rights in the 1930s, therefore, was to be largely a defensive measure that included broader political arguments for blacks to join trades unions and to be included on federal government aid programs of the New Deal and World War II defense jobs.[17]

The NAACP was active in monitoring government relief work on the Mississippi River throughout the 1920s and 1930s. This was a particularly high-profile effort for the organization after the Mississippi flooded in 1927, displacing thousands of people from their homes and workplaces. Walter White used the fact that black refugees did not receive equal federal aid as powerful political propaganda against President Calvin Coolidge. Black refugees were held in relief camps by national guards and were forced to work on the river's levees in work gangs. At other camps food and shelter were dispensed unequally to black people and white. The federal government set up a Colored Advisory Commission for relief aid, under secretary of commerce Herbert Hoover's auspices, without any NAACP representatives. Subsequently, Du Bois regularly criticized the commission in *The Crisis* for making "no real effort to investigate the desperate and evil conditions" in the levee camps.[18]

In 1932 Joel Spingarn, as board chairman, personally commissioned and paid for a study to help him understand the structures of the NAACP and to evaluate its cost-effectiveness and efficiency. The Lonigan report saw the need for the NAACP to diversify its program to include the economic rights of a wider black constituency. It was suggested that "an elaborate study of the relief situation by each local branch and of the local employment and industrial difficulties among the colored people" be instigated in the first instance, thus utilizing local skills and membership and making the Association relevant at the regional level. The Lonigan report regarded W. E. B. Du Bois as the person to "build up a valuable body of specific information about Negro life" using *The Crisis* as a foundation for this work. Furthermore it advised that the economic program could not be a mere "paper scheme," as

> every member of the Association's staff talked about the need for an economic program . . . [and] all were very vague about it . . . There can be no question that there exist economic problems of the greatest importance to the Negro that involve the same militant attitude that the Association stands for in politics . . . It is important, however, because it would tie in with a significant world-wide tendency to improve the living standards of workers as a far more important service than merely raising wages . . . Even after the depression is over I expect a serious unemployment problem will remain. That may permanently affect the economic openings for the Negro. A knowledge of the situation, city by city, and the planning of a program to meet it, are important but difficult tasks for the Association.[19]

The report advised the NAACP to turn "its full intellectual energies upon this question of an economic program" and then it would "do fine pioneer work in the next ten years." By so doing, this "could solve the serious problem of how to use the Association's appeal to the more intellectual colored people for the benefit of poorer and less intelligent Negroes. It could offset the intellectualist, separatist tendencies created by the highly specialized technical nature of the Association's present work, and the inevitable gap between the better educated and the less educated people everywhere." Therefore, the Lonigan report saw that it was expedient to utilize the organization's current strengths, such as the preponderance of a middle-class membership, for the task of improving the lives of African Americans who were less fortunate.[20]

The NAACP acknowledged that it needed to address such issues, albeit tepidly. At the Second Amenia Conference in 1932, young black leaders were invited to offer their opinions on an economic program for the NAACP. Juanita Jackson, who would later be NAACP youth director, was invited on account of her organizational activities with black youth in Baltimore and the hope that she would have ideas of how to increase the Association's membership base. Indeed Roy Wilkins, NAACP assistant executive secretary, understood that the Depression "added a new level of complexity" to civil rights work: "By tradition, the N.A.A.C.P. was a political organisation preoccupied with civil rights; but the times were full of radical new economic theories, and it was obvious that we had to take up issues like unemployment. I was no Communist or rabble-rouser; but I felt for a long time that the N.A.A.C.P. needed to pay less attention to brokers of power and more to its own people down where poverty and discrimination were the most severe."[21]

The 1932 annual report announced that the NAACP had "broadened its program to include militant and specific attacks upon the economic barriers in the path of the Negro." Yet in 1934 the black economist Abram L. Harris chaired a committee for the NAACP and urged the organization to be more involved with black economic issues rather than just the civil and political spheres. The Harris report continued to be critical of the middle-class dominance of the NAACP and argued that the leadership ought to be much more radical in its aims and methods. Walter White was not wholly responsive to the report, as his inclinations leaned toward political campaigns for educational equality and antilynching legislation.[22]

The NAACP may have missed a valuable opportunity to broaden its membership base during the 1920s and 1930s by not fully embracing a radical economic agenda. The Universal Negro Improvement Association (UNIA) was formed by Marcus Garvey in Jamaica during 1914 with an agenda to appeal specifically to poorer and dispossessed black people. Garvey founded the Harlem branch of the UNIA in 1917 on the ideas of self-help and black pride. The organization became a persistent critic of the NAACP for failing to address the true needs of the black community. Many communities the NAACP could not hope to reach formed UNIA branches. Indeed the immediate contrast with Louisiana's NAACP chapters and membership is apparent. New Orleans was seen as a "Mecca for Garveyites" during the 1920s and 1930s, and in 1936 had three UNIA branches. The first poorly organized UNIA branch had no more than 300 members in 1921, but this number rose rapidly to 5,000 in 1922. During 1924 there was somewhere in the region of 3,000 members in New Orleans, contrasting dramatically with the mere 206 in the city's NAACP branch. One reason for the disparity was black labor groups, such as the International Longshoremen's Union, joining the UNIA in the 1920s. The NAACP only began to approach such unions seriously for membership in the late 1930s but with little success.[23]

The economic separatism of the UNIA penetrated rural areas where the NAACP had no foundation at all, where Garveyism was perceived as being not such a threat as a political and integrationist organization. In 1929 the UNIA had branches in such isolated rural areas in Louisiana as Violet (124 members), Algiers (101), White Castle (150), Rosemount (164), and Lockport (192). During 1929 the NAACP could only muster 109 members in New Orleans, one of its main southern branches. The only other functioning branch in the state during that year, Baton Rouge, had a mere 67 members. As a racial separatist organization, the UNIA was less threatening to local white power structures; plus, it had a potentially wider membership base in Louisiana as a working-class- and rural-poor-centered organization.[24]

By the 1940s the NAACP developed its strategy further to take account of economic justice for blacks within a war context. It fought to make permanent the Fair Employment Practices Committee (FEPC), which enforced black representation in national defense jobs after President Roosevelt's Executive Order 8802 of June 1941. The attempt to get black people into wartime industries was an uphill struggle; the FEPC met with fierce white resistance. It could only investigate discrimination of an industry if a complaint was brought to it and could neither impose sanctions nor file court cases. While it did highlight significant issues of racism, aided by publicity and complaints by the NAACP,

Charles Houston, a NAACP attorney, resigned from the FEPC because it lacked any real authority.[25]

It could be argued that the focus on civil rights gave the NAACP a strong philosophical base and an identity that allowed it to survive longer than many other black groups, such as the UNIA. The NAACP central office was highly focused on political and social redress through the American legal system from its very inception, which tended to mitigate any impetus toward wholesale organizational democracy and wider economic concerns. Indeed in 1930 the NAACP hired Nathan Margold, a distinguished New York lawyer, to develop a consistent tactic that would advance civil rights issues in the court system by setting important legal precedents, rather than using its limited resources in varied and disjointed legal issues. Margold recommended that the NAACP focus its funds on confronting segregation directly, rather than trying to equalize separate but equal facilities with those of white institutions. While this was increasingly the method of NAACP legal teams, the recurring debate within the organization during the 1930s was for greater internal organizational democracy.[26]

The genesis of the Association's legal work was dependent on white men such as Moorfield Storey and acclaimed lawyer Clarence Darrow. As Walter White noted, "We knew that for many years to come there would be certain types of cases in which there would be an advantage in having a white lawyer in preference to a Negro attorney, but our real objective was to hasten the time when an attorney's color in a court of law would be of no importance and where the only criterion would be his ability." Change came only gradually as black civil rights lawyers increased in expertise and numbers, and a separate legal department of the NAACP was eventually created. Charles Houston, special counsel for the NAACP from 1935 to 1939, has been recognized as the man who undertook the groundwork for the Association's legal attack on segregation and who educated and inspired a generation of black constitutional lawyers. Houston restructured the law department at Howard University, in Washington, D.C., and taught that black lawyers were social engineers and therefore responsible for interpreting black group objectives. In so doing, according to Houston, they had to be "not only good but superior [to white lawyers], and just as superior in all respects as time, energy, money and ability permit."[27]

The NAACP judicial focus was not to make it a mere legal aid society, however, but a carefully orchestrated program of specialized cases that would fundamentally change the law as it stood following the 1896 U.S. Supreme Court decision allowing "separate but equal" facilities between the races (*Plessy v. Ferguson*). For a case to be considered applicable for the NAACP legal department, it was necessary for the action to highlight discrimination along racial lines.[28] As the 1920 annual report of the NAACP noted: "Much of the time one of the executives is given to the task of deciding, in conjunction with the Legal Committee, which of the many cases that come to the National Office from the branches and individuals should be undertaken. Two considerations enter into such decisions. First, is the case one in which race prejudice has undoubtedly prevented a colored person from receiving justice? Second, will active participation by the N.A.A.C.P. and the gaining of a favorable decision establish a principle or precedent in that community which will raise or strengthen the civil status of the colored people?"[29]

Eventually it became apparent that there was a need for a nonprofit educational and legal aid agency that could, for the purposes of funding, be given charitable status (which it could not achieve as a political body being part of the NAACP). In 1939 this was established as the NAACP Legal Defense and Educational Fund (which became simply known as the Inc. Fund) and was distinctly separate from the propaganda arm of the main NAACP organization.[30]

There were three main symbolic victories that established the NAACP on a legal route to enforce black civil rights. The "grandfather clause" in Oklahoma, which excluded potential voters from taking a literacy test if they could prove a clear lineage of voters within a family all the way back to January 1, 1866, was defeated by the NAACP-assisted action *Guinn v. US* (1915). Only white people, of course, were exempt from such a clause. The NAACP's president, Moorfield Storey, presented the case to the Supreme Court, and it was the first time that the court had ever struck down a disfranchising law. Two years later, the Louisville segregation case *Buchanan v. Warley* (1917) saw the Supreme Court throw out a housing segregation ordinance that prevented blacks from moving into certain residential districts. Meanwhile, the peonage case *Moore v. Dempsey* (1923) exposed the economic exploitation of black workers in Arkansas and saved the lives of twelve men condemned to death for their alleged role in a riot. The Supreme Court overturned the death penalty in the case because the original trial had lasted only forty-five minutes and had exempted blacks from serving on the jury. The Court decided that the trial had been dominated by mob rule rather than the principles of justice.[31]

The NAACP began to concentrate its legal approach specifically on segregated facilities in the 1930s. It focused on the education system, where black people were worst affected by separation and where it might have a good chance of success. The strategy was to use the dual system of education against itself. By insisting on legal mandates to enforce the separate but equal rule, the NAACP hoped to make the system financially insupportable. Furthermore, the focus on education—an area that had immediate relevance and emotion—helped enlist more local community support.[32]

The NAACP undertook many different types of cases in the equality of education battle. First was an attempt to desegregate graduate and professional schools and colleges, invariably focusing on university law departments. Second, there were attempts in the late 1930s and early 1940s to equalize salaries between black and white teachers and to adjust the imbalance of the physical facilities at segregated elementary and secondary schools. To redress these inequalities would make the system of segregation impossible to maintain in the long term and, therefore, make integration of educational facilities appear as a serious and practical consideration. The immediate goal, however, was to gain more spending on black facilities, thus mobilizing black communities toward the NAACP integrationist objectives at some future date.[33]

One of the more important cases in the education campaign was *Gaines v. University of Missouri* (1935) in which the Supreme Court ruled on the University of Missouri having a law school for white students only. Although the court did not integrate the facilities, it did order that if the state provided a legal education for white students then it had a duty to provide such opportunities for blacks. It was declared, therefore, that sending black students out of Missouri to be educated was discriminatory. However, the results of the decision were not all positive. In response to the ruling, the state closed down a white journalism department in 1942 rather than open up a black college with equal facilities or admit black students to its courses.[34]

By late 1939 the legal program had replaced the antilynching legislation struggle as the NAACP's chief campaign. However, the drawback to a largely law-oriented agenda was that it only required a minimal reliance on mass support or a high public profile. It took many years for a case initiated at the local level to be pushed through the various state and federal courts, and sustaining public excitement for this gradualist approach to civil rights was to prove troublesome. As Roy Wilkins observed, "We tended to be isolated in New York and out of touch with the very people we needed most to serve. I knew very well that the N.A.A.C.P.'s strategy of carefully selecting lawsuits and political issues and working on high in Congress and the Supreme Court had produced many tangible benefits, but from the vantage of those muddy camps on the Mississippi, such tactics looked less meaningful than they did from the snug offices at 69 Fifth Avenue."[35]

Very early on the NAACP saw the need for local organizations to take its message to the people to "form local groups, to which may be referred questions of race discrimination or injustice arising from race prejudice, and thus to prepare the ground work for vigilance committees." They were to act as "bureaus of information as to race relations in their communities and keep the National Office informed of such conditions throughout the country . . . [and to] . . . stimulate the cultural life of colored people and to better their opportunities. In addition the Branches furnish the larger part of the National Budget." Furthermore, the function of these branches was "to conduct propaganda against injustices accorded the Negroes by white people in the immediate community where it is located." It was understood that issues would arise that could not be covered by a national organization alone, and by using the power base of a local branch, the NAACP could serve communities large and small. Even so it was understood that in the Deep South "membership in the Association still carries with it a possibility of physical hardship and reprisals."[36]

The NAACP organized the United States into seven districts in which to undertake sectional work and co-ordinate its programs. Louisiana fell under the auspices of the Southwest regional office based in Dallas (which at one time had been based in New Orleans), a headquarters that also served Texas, Arkansas, New Mexico, and Oklahoma. A regional secretary and special counsel allowed for quick and effective processing of legal cases and coordination of propaganda and campaigning within the area. Similarly, state conferences allowed coordination of activities between all NAACP branches within a single state and gave smaller chapters the opportunity to gain experience from large city branches.[37]

The original constitution and by-laws for the branches of the NAACP clearly saw local organizations as subordinate units of the Association "subject to the general authority and jurisdiction of the Board of Directors." Each branch was to elect a president, vice-president, treasurer, and secretary and was to hold monthly and special meetings with an aim to initiate local civil rights programs. The president of a branch was its chief executive who would preside at general meetings and chair an executive committee and appoint its working committees. Vice-presidents were simply to "perform all the duties of the President in his absence or disability."[38]

The role of the secretary of a branch, while sounding routine, was actually a pivotal organizational function. They were to "act as secretary of the branch and of the Executive Committee . . . [and t]o keep a card index, or other record, of all branch members and their dues." Additionally the secretary was required to "aid, coordinate and integrate the work of the several committees and divisions of the Branch." Significantly, the secretary had "to forward to the National Office . . . a report of branch activities for the preceding month; and an annual report of the work of the branch . . . [and to] keep the Secretary of the National Association informed of all events affecting colored people in the vicinity of the branch."[39]

Consequently, the secretary was the central figure in nearly all of a chapter's affairs and was the person who identified and reported on main issues and campaigns. Such diligence was vital to a branch, as an absence of reports for "a period of four consecutive months" would lead to a declaration of "any or all of the offices of the Branch vacant and [the] order[ing of] a new election." By 1937 the secretary was also an ex-officio member of all committees and as a result became the figure that had the broadest perspective of branch activities. The role was significantly expanded in that year, in "conjunction with the President, to sign requisitions for disbursements from the Branch treasury and to maintain a file of receipts." This expansion into the financial sphere had the consequence of giving the position more status within a branch hierarchy.[40]

The formal policy-deciding component of a chapter was the executive committee, as long as its judgments remained in accordance with national policy, and by 1946 its agenda was to be endorsed by the entire branch. The executive committee was to comprise the major officers of the branch and included elected members as well as the chairpersons of all the standing committees, and presidents of the youth council and college chapters. While this may have seemed democratic in principle, it was to transpire in many of the local branches that a dedicated core of members were to dominate the executive committee and the elected branch posts, while determining the direction of local policy. However, in a small branch or during hard economic periods, when the dollar membership fee may have seemed an extravagance, such a dedicated cadre kept the name of the NAACP and its values alive in a community.[41]

Women's roles in the local branches of the NAACP tended to conform to established practices in the nation, as well as to idiosyncrasies of local communities and regions. Women were not officially excluded from holding any offices or chairmanships. Nevertheless, they were seen, as a group, to have unique talents that could be utilized via a subordinate body to the main structure. This view was a social expectation rather than an official requirement of a chapter, as the branch constitution simply claimed that "Branches of the Association may organize a Woman's Auxiliary." The twentieth annual report also stated that "the idea of organizing the women of the Association into groups to work under their own leaders, while at the same time retaining their full identity with the branch, these groups being called Woman's Auxiliaries, has spread widely throughout the country and has been most successful."[42]

Women were seen as traditional and necessary sources of fundraising. This work was central to a branch's efforts, as "failure of any branch to raise a minimum of $50 per year for national work may be deemed . . . sufficient reason for the revocation of its charter." In addition to fundraising, the auxiliary acted "as the Committee on Entertainments and the Committee on Junior Work where the Branch so decides." Women's indispensable role, it appeared, was as foot soldiers who planned entertainments for branch fundraising and undertook general campaigning and who had some influence over youth and student organizing.[43]

Indeed, youth councils and college chapters were seen as an enlightening way of "training . . . children . . . [and] college students in Association methods and ideals" and of teaching "young people the history of the Negro." Prior to 1936 minors and college students could hold general NAACP membership, although the Association eventually felt that by doing so it was not utilizing black youth effectively. The NAACP made a conscious attempt during 1936 to develop a specific mass movement of young people. Youth councils and college chapters were established with the explicit aim to draw young people into the civil rights movement, cultivate future leaders, and cooperate with the adult branches to implement NAACP policy.[44]

The youth movement of the NAACP reflected the Depression-era intention for young people to find direction and purpose and direct their energies away from Communist Party involvement. Juanita Jackson, special assistant to the NAACP secretary, led the attempt to build up such a mass movement among young people by calling an NAACP youth conference in 1936. She subsequently organized youth auxiliaries and college chapters throughout the country.[45] In 1935 an NAACP pamphlet announced the ideal arrangement for the youth groups:

> The Youth Council is a most important adjunct to our branch structure. Here we have the new blood that is so necessary to keep alive the ever-changing spirit and growth of our organization. Here we have the future members of the senior branch. Here we have energy, faith, and the will to do . . . And what do they work on? Why, the program of the N.A.A.C.P.—physical security, equality in educational opportunities, the use of the ballot, economic equality, health, and civil rights . . . [working] within the framework of the N.A.A.C.P. as provided for in the constitution and by-laws for branches. They are not separate and apart; they are one with the whole . . . *Neither* are they parallel to the senior branch. Such an existence would be inconceivable as it would deprive the Youth Council of the wisdom of the more experienced members of the branch and at the same time deprive the senior branch of the faith, enthusiasm and adventure of the younger members.[46]

The work undertaken by the youth councils in many ways was to complement the work of the adult branches. Youth divisions were "uniting and working," according to the NAACP youth pledge, to "secure the fundamental constitutional rights for twelve millions of American Negroes, in order that they may make a more significant contribution to the building of a more desirable social order." Yet they were also seen as cooperating with senior branches and the national office in their legal operations such as "the fight to free the Scottsboro youths." Furthermore, youth councils were assisting to "secure fair municipal recreational facilities . . . to have representation on the municipal housing committees, to eliminate segregation and discrimination in theaters, restaurants, and other public places." NAACP youth leaders offered assistance to the adult branch in drives to register black voters "and to stimulate the registered voters to use the ballot." Youth councils were to replicate much of the traditional work of the NAACP adult branches. During February 1937 Dillard University in New Orleans staged a traditional demonstration against lynching with the wearing of black armbands. The demonstration had the full approval of the main adult branch. Indeed, there was a similar shift in emphasis in all sections of the branches from mere letter writing, such as with the Judge Parker campaign in 1930, to visible group demonstrations to protest against lynching in the 1930s.[47]

Young people maintained an interest in, and helped evolve, the civil rights movement beyond their membership in the NAACP youth councils. Some youth members went on to join the adult branches, such as Miss Elsie Lenoir of the New Orleans youth council executive committee in 1935, who joined the adult branch the following year. Similarly Mr. C. D. Sartor, also of the New Orleans youth council executive committee of 1935, joined the adult branch in the city during the 1940s. He was chair of the housing committee in 1953, through which he continued the old NAACP fights by entering a "protest against plans of a segregated redevelopment project." Thelma S. Shelby, who had joined the NAACP while at Dillard University, also was involved with the adult branch, becoming its vice-president in 1939.[48]

Other students went on to various other civil rights organizations in the 1950s and 1960s after their formative training in the NAACP youth wing. Vice-president of the 1935 youth council of New Orleans, Mr. Raymond B. Floyd, went on to become a Xavier college instructor, and headed the Consumers League of Greater New Orleans during 1959, which provided an avenue for the growing radicalism of students. It organized to increase the numbers of black people in retail employment and targeted stores in predominantly black neighborhoods, most of which did not employ black checkout staff. The Consumers League was also to involve itself in the Congress of Racial Equality (CORE) sit-ins in New Orleans of 1961. The NAACP youth councils, it could be said, were an important training ground for future civil rights agitators, and this continued well into the 1960s.[49]

The bureaucratic nature of the NAACP organization and its highly centralized national executive gave W. E. B. Du Bois cause to argue that it stifled the effectiveness of many local branches across the country. Du Bois claimed that the "branches and their officials have no scientifically planned program except to raise money and defend cases of injustice or discrimination in courts. The organization fears the processes of democracy and avoids discussion." The Lonigan report identified further problems between the national office and the branches: "Every organization consists of two connected but distinct aspects, the official organization, and the living body out of which the official body grows ... The relation of the official body to the real society involves the further question of the relation between New York City and the rest of the country, and the relation of the N.A.A.C.P. to the less intellectual and non-professional classes among the colored people."[50]

During the 1930s this was a vital debate in which constitutional arrangements were put in place in the hope to instigate a greater sense of grassroots populism. The national board of directors became an elective holding, and by 1936 its forty-eight seats were up for contest for a three-year tenancy, with a third up for election every year. An annual convention, while a long-standing tradition, became more of an institutional barometer of national Association opinion, and by 1946 the NAACP constitution stated formally that it was "to establish policies and programs of action for the ensuing year." The decisions of the convention were to be binding upon the board of directors, officers, and other areas of the association, unless two-thirds of the board vetoed the proposals. Branches were to have representation at conventions proportional to their membership numbers and were to be elected at regular branch meetings the month prior to a conference.[51]

However, while the central office was extremely active on the national political scene and made gestures toward democratic structures in the organization, the local branches tended to suffer from a lack of authentic representation and appreciation by the NAACP hierarchy. The Lonigan report saw the function of the local branches as being "rather difficult to define." Indeed to "an outsider it looks as if the chief function of the branches was raising money," as they "responded to appeals [from the national office] which seemed to consist principally of the annual apportionment and requests for travel expenses."[52]

The Lonigan report saw the problem of galvanizing local communities' interest in the Association's work as a central question. The solution was, in part, to overhaul the policies of the NAACP: "The ultimate answer is an entirely new program for the branches, which I think can be found and must be found in the economic program of the branches ... The more fundamental improvement can be made only by thinking through the whole question of the aims of the organisation in a changing world. This is a program entirely dependent upon the Board."[53] This grassroots program was directed by NAACP field agents working with the local branches and the national office whose enterprise was "physically and nervously exhausting":

> The whole revolt of the local agency against the central office may be due in large part to the fact that the central office could not get supermen for field agents. It is the function of the field agent to see the branch as it sees itself, to keep open the connection between the central office which is essentially narrow and rigid in its interests and the outside association whose interests are unspecialized, unformulated and constantly changing ... The greater the need for money the greater the temptation to think of the branches as sources of supply, the more absolutely necessary is it that an emphasis can be found on something else than money. It is no question of theoretical democracy. The branches always have one weapon. They can do nothing.[54]

In this regard in the Lonigan report, national field director Daisy Lampkin was contrasted favorably with other field operatives such as Robert Bagnall and William Pickens. Lampkin was too busy to be able to contribute to the report, as she "spends all of her time in the field and has not gotten the central office point of view" and was "good at organization work." She was highly regarded in the regions, and the national office was continually inundated by requests for her help in directing local membership drives. However, most branches directed their own canvassing under local leadership due to a lack of national field workers.[55]

Sheldon Avery's book, *Up from Washington*, a study of William Pickens, field secretary from 1919 to 1927, and then director of branches until 1942, contrasts Pickens's NAACP work directly with that of Daisy Lampkin. The comparison originally arose over Walter White taking issue over Lampkin's high-level public organizational and fundraising skills against Pickens's private lecturing and supposedly more inspirational role. Lampkin was held up as a model fundraiser who was greatly appreciated by the local branches, whereas Pickens was seen as not bringing in his fair share of finances during the Depression years. Pickens's claimed that Lampkin concentrated on a few large and financially stable branches while he had to visit more than 200 branches to keep them in touch with the national office. Daisy Lampkin's response to Pickens was much more conciliatory and held up his attributes as being perfectly balanced with her own: "I think your service has been invaluable. There must be someone whose full time is given to the type of work you are doing if we hope to contact four hundred branches with only two persons in the field to do it." However, this is to neglect Daisy Lampkin's role as director of local campaigns and in motivating and inspiring members and the wider public. Lampkin was seen as a loyal functionary not able to match Pickens's supposed romantic role as orator, despite her huge popular following among local branches across the country.[56]

Ella Baker, field secretary from 1941 to 1943 and national director of branches from 1943 to 1946, exemplifies further the tension between the local chapters, the national office, and those national staff members caught in the middle. Baker often accused the NAACP executives of being more interested in enlarging its membership so as to raise organizational funds than in building mass civil rights protest. Conversely, Baker's professed ideas of leadership tended toward activists' decision-making at the local level and their own perceptions of their communities' needs rather than a centralized and bureaucratic organization simply dictating what they should be doing.[57]

Black women in the national office at New York, such as Daisy Lampkin, Juanita Jackson, and Ella Baker, tended to highlight the "personalist" nature of their political activism at this time. In such a context African American women saw race progress as occurring through interdependence and cooperation between individuals and organizations. These three women in particular were hugely popular at the grassroots level of the NAACP and they encouraged and inspired large numbers of people to become members by their methods and ideas. This relation of gender to power is revealing. Women often tended toward concepts of democratic organizing and motivation at the community level to organize civil rights activities toward local issues, while the NAACP was a strong centralized association whose more visible male leaders pursued a national agenda.[58]

In 1946 Ella Baker was to resign from the NAACP, saying that the organization had "got itself hung-up in . . . its legal success." Baker had tried to get the NAACP to allow its local branches to "take the initiative in developing leadership in all social and economic problems and problems of discrimination, job employment and the like, which confronts Negroes today." Indeed, during 1943 she had attempted to facilitate such leadership programs by proposing regional training conferences and proclaimed that different branches often had very different training requirements depending on their local circumstances. Baker went on to co-found the Southern Christian Leadership Conference (SCLC) in 1957 and to inspire the Student Non-Violent Coordinating Committee (SNCC) in 1960, very much with these ideas in mind. Daisy Lampkin, on the other hand, resigned her post as national field secretary in 1947, fatigued by her NAACP duties. However, she continued to help local NAACP branches organize membership drives when such chapters made it clear that no one else would suffice.[59]

Like Baker and Lampkin, Juanita Jackson had a strong personal commitment to local community organizing, rather than a hierarchical dictation of policy, with a particular focus on a mass movement of young people. Accordingly, she encouraged NAACP youth to undertake direct action as a method of civil rights protest, maintaining that individuals and groups could change their social setting by challenging racism and discrimination in their local communities. In Baltimore during the early 1930s she had organized with her sister, Virginia, the City-Wide Young People's Forum (known simply as the Forum). This was a broad-based community educational program that undertook high-profile political and direct action campaigns related to African American job discrimination and civil rights issues. Revealing of women's own perceptions of their role in the NAACP, Jackson's time as national youth director was short, only from 1935 to 1938, when she left to marry Clarence Mitchell. Jackson viewed supporting her husband's work in the National Urban League as part of her role as a married woman, although she returned to running and supporting her local Baltimore NAACP branch along with her mother, Lillie, who was president of the chapter.[60]

A major problem with the NAACP as a whole, including its local branches, as perceived by Ella Baker and W. E. B. Du Bois in particular, was its concern with parliamentary procedure. Indeed the NAACP often appeared committee-obsessed, which frequently led to intense internal politicking that could divide and weaken local chapters, preventing them from organizing effectively, as occurred in New Orleans in the late 1930s and the Alexandria branch, Louisiana, in 1945. For instance, in 1931 the national office urged its local branches to evaluate their districts and the proportion of official regional public expenditure spent on black groups, yet this was set out in a cumbersome planning arrangement: "[1. Form committees] to gather authoritative information as to whether or not Negroes participate in or benefit from expenditures of public tax money . . . [2. Appoint a special committee] to inquire into the distribution of funds for unemployment relief—whether raised by public subscription or appropriated from municipal, county, state, or federal sources . . . [3. Form a third committee] to present to proprietors and managers of chain stores and other businesses operating in Negro neighborhoods a request that Negroes be given employment." In this manner, the NAACP, with its attention to formal administration and procedures, particularly attracted the middle classes, although it did see its role as being relevant to all black people.[61]

The NAACP's philosophical underpinnings were to remain consistent over time, although implementing greater institutional democracy was a gradual process that met with only limited accomplishments during this period. At the Sixteenth Annual Conference, held in Denver, Colorado, in 1925, the NAACP proposed five key principles as its major aims: the complete abolition of lynching and mob law; full political freedom; industrial democracy; better education; and the absolute ending of segregation on race and color. While these aims were tied to specific programs reflecting concerns of the times, they suggested a broader focus on the political and civic freedoms of black people as Americans.[62]

In 1940 the program remained much the same. The long-term strategy was full equality for blacks as U.S. citizens with an agenda based around the pertinent issues of the day: antilynching legislation, economic emancipation from peonage and debt, the vote, abolition of legal discrimination based on race, a fair share of public funds for education for blacks, integrated trade unions, and an end to segregation. In this manner the basic tenets of the NAACP reflected the steadfast conviction that the American Dream was to be made a reality for all. As the Fifteenth Annual Conference in 1924 professed, "It is not to obtain mere benefits and privileges for the Negro that the National Association for the Advancement of Colored People is striving; it is striving to vindicate the American idea. That idea is: that every man shall have opportunity for the highest self development and that his achievements shall not be denied recognition on their merits."[63]

TWO

THE SYMPATHY OF WOMEN
Black Women's Involvement in Louisiana Civil Rights up to 1920

> Flowers in their beauty and sweetness may represent the womanhood of the world. Some flowers are fragile and delicate, some strong and hardy, some are carefully guarded and cherished, others are rough treated and trodden under foot. These last are the colored women. They have a crown of thorns continually pressed upon their brow, yet they are advancing and sometimes you find them further on than you would have expected. When woman like you, Miss Anthony, come to see us and speak to us it helps us believe in the Fatherhood of God and the Brotherhood of man, and at least for the time being in the sympathy of women.

THROUGHOUT the nineteenth century middle-class African American women and men were instrumental in organizing benevolent societies with the aim of providing welfare services and education to their members and families and, increasingly, to a wider social setting. Black women joined such groups as auxiliaries to men's organizations, yet they also created social clubs entirely of their own, by which they self-consciously strove for their own agenda, as well as that of the betterment of African Americans more generally. These interconnected ideals, pragmatism, and diverse social networking were the bedrock of the early civil rights movement in Louisiana and were to be utilized by the local branches of the NAACP during the first half of the twentieth century.[1]

The cultural background of Louisiana, with its blend of French, Spanish, and American history, gave its black population a unique standpoint in the United States that affected the racial environment throughout the nineteenth and twentieth centuries. There has been much academic debate regarding the cultural differences between ex-slaves (who were perceived as *Americanized*, Protestant, and English speaking) and creoles of color, who were said to have an interracial background and were generally not slaves before the Civil War (and were seen as French speaking,

Catholic, and more orientated toward elite European culture). The supposed maintenance of a three-caste system in Louisiana has been seen as dividing the twentieth-century civil rights crusade by class and intricate racial differences, although this analysis has not been without its critics. Joseph G. Tregle, author of *Louisiana in the Age of Jackson*, debunked the so-called creole myth, albeit admitting that no "other state seems to have been so seriously affected by ethnic cleavages as Louisiana." He does, however, dispute the existence of a stark divide between the genteel French and Spanish colonist and the culturally dissimilar Anglo-Saxon hoards from the north of state and the United States, on which historians have relied.[2]

Yet some believe that such a legacy did spread into organizations like the NAACP in the twentieth century. During 1931 the New Orleans attorney A. P. Tureaud, himself of French creole lineage, claimed that the city branch was run by its president, George Labat, with too much "French flavor," which, in his opinion, perpetuated class and minute racial distinctions within the African American community, although this was probably a generational issue as well. Historian Adam Fairclough has claimed that such differences have been generally overstated by academics and that a common oppression based on race gave both groups in Louisiana a cause by which to work closely together for a common civil rights agenda. However, cultural differences based on class did remain a source of ongoing tension that may have been the impetus for a belief in purported ethnic disparities. Moreover, class and gender concepts in this setting were intricately bound up with the long history of black women being sexually exploited by white men and by black men trying to *normalize* their family conditions to white standards. Middle-class black women, in turn, created social and reform groups to reinforce ideals of virtue to uplift the race as a whole with themselves as the key to moral and group progress. Indeed, such concepts of class and gender were to become a cornerstone of the civil rights struggle and its tactics were to project black people as decent, middle-class Americans with a shared morality with white America.[3]

Indeed, during the nineteenth century many black women organized their group occasions to involve some form of socializing and literary appreciation, although these invariably became more than just meeting places for people who shared common cultural pursuits. For example, the middle-class New Orleans Colored Female Benevolent Society of Louisiana, established in 1846, provided private insurance benefits for its members yet was also to pursue wider social concerns. In particular it sought the "suppression of vice and inculcation of virtue among the colored class—to relieve the sick and bury the dead—to alleviate the distress of widows" and also sought to help orphans.[4]

Black women frequently organized community groups with common social and structural themes. For example, the Société des Jeunes Amis, a French-speaking group, founded in 1886, and the English-speaking Ladies' Friends of Faith, founded in 1914, both reflected the status consciousness of the elite African American community of New Orleans, despite obvious cultural differences. Historian Claude F. Jacobs describes the structural constructs of such groups in New Orleans: "Some associations were exclusively for either men or women, while others were restricted by age to juveniles, young people, or older adults. In most of the men's societies, there were two types of membership. Adult males were regular members. Their wives, minor children, or parents could be enrolled as 'passive members' and also receive society benefits. Women sometimes organized 'circles' to work in conjunction with the men's groups." Such organizations provided comradeship and membership privileges, such as health insurance for a small monthly fee, which could also cover their families as nonvoting "passive members." These groups were male-led and "enabled blacks to acquire skills in running organizations—writing constitutions, keeping minutes, and learning bookkeeping . . . and were vehicles for an ideology aimed at strengthening and unifying the black population."[5]

The role of these organizations attracted and cultivated a reform-minded, middle-class female membership that analyzed the institutions and values of the social setting they lived in. However, their sphere of concern was often restricted to the social role that was invariably left to women in late nineteenth-century society: the special cultivation of the family. While middle-class groups did have a practical agenda of providing health centers for the community, schools, orphanages, and homes for the elderly, it was invariably with a focus on the general moral improvement of society. Women pursued the elusive goal of respectability within the United States, as determined by white cultural norms, while at the same time aiming for some restructuring of that society, such as in mitigating racism and ending lynching. In this manner it has been argued by political activist and feminist Angela Davis that, although "Americans did not have Victoria as their Queen, they were Victorians in their economy, industry, and culture . . . [T]hey accepted and emulated the English belief in the dual nature of womanhood, and similarly assigned the aspects of this nature to particular classes of women."[6]

Yet the Victorian Age, which espoused high-moral attributes to individuals, particularly to women who stayed within the family home, was essentially incongruous to most black women, as they were compelled to work to supplement the family income. Black women sometimes found themselves the sole or main provider for their families by working as washerwomen, domestics, and peddlers. Some were also to be found as landladies, seamstresses, hairdressers, merchants, and midwives. Black nurses were extremely popular with white people, as they were believed to be immune to yellow fever. During the Reconstruction period in particular it became an ideal for ex-slaves to withdraw females from the labor market, especially from plantation work, as it was believed that they ought to focus their lives on home and family. Conversely, middle-class black women who had to work consciously perpetuated a distinction between their occupations and that of working- and lower-class blacks. Teaching and sewing were acceptable to their sensibilities, but domestic and personal service in another person's home was frowned upon. Housework in a white family's home was considered demeaning, and there was the additional fear of sexual exploitation by white men that went alongside this perception. While all black women maintained these same fears, it was not possible for poorer woman to avoid such work completely.[7]

The focus of reform for many middle-class women who joined social groups was improving the education and health of the poorer masses. Such an emphasis was firmly placed on the moral influence of women and how they could bring feminine nurturing and understanding to a masculine world. While helping the poor was a socially accepted aspect of women's groups, black organizations did not merely imitate white society but related these issues specifically to racism and the alleviation of oppression. Women's voluntary activism became, in essence, an unpaid career that gave them a chance to express themselves in ways not possible in a strictly middle-class domestic existence. Therefore, fraternal and beneficial clubs could bestow a serious civic status within the community in which they served.[8]

Black men, in turn, were striving to counteract white society's views of them as savage and uncivilized, thus legitimizing lynching, by asserting concepts of black masculinity and the "endangered black woman."

Such an emphasis defined African American men's political rights to mean that they should be able to protect their wives, children, and communities from social inequality and racial assault. Women, meanwhile, were to support their men to these ends. In response to this linking of citizenship and manhood, women were to use ideals of respectability as a shield of protection against white male sexual aggression and as a sphere of civil rights protest of their own. This reaffirmed the civil rights agenda as having the idea of black masculinity and citizenship at its center, while women remained the defenders of mainstream morality and family norms.[9]

In many ways such goals were paradoxical: respectability was an attempt to show that black society was equal to white social standards, while black women were also fighting the inconsistencies of that white system. Women's associations, therefore, reconciled this paradox by channeling their political and social energies into improving the status of black women as a whole, thus advancing their entire community: self-improvement on an individual level would advance racial pride and lead to wider group acceptance by white society. As historian Paula Giddings has stated, black women "saw themselves not just as messengers but as living examples" of moral propriety, which they believed would lead inevitably toward a perfectly equitable American society.[10]

Female social roles in black associations, like those in white middle-class groups, were tied to appropriate spheres of the sexes. This meant nonemployed wives, a strong focus on motherhood, and a particular spiritual and moral rectitude of the individual. Anna Julia Cooper, a suffragist and proponent of female higher education, saw these attributes as the essence of womanhood and of a decent society: "Woman, Mother,—your responsibility is one that might make angels tremble and fear to take hold! To trifle with it, to ignore or misuse it, is to treat lightly the most sacred and solemn trust ever confided by God to human kind. The training of children is a task on which an infinity of weal or woe depends. Who does not covet it? Yet who does not stand awe-struck before its momentus [sic] issues!"[11]

Such a concern on group morality, however, could reinforce class prejudices and create a patronizing attitude when dealing with the poor. Focus on child health and education, which did relate directly to the poor, could bridge these class barriers, and while there was an emphasis on class predominance, there was also an infusion of general race pride and advancement in such undertakings. It was the moral imperative for middle-class women to help poorer people and by doing so to reposition African Americans as a group into being accepted by white society.[12]

With this mission in mind, the National Association of Colored Women (NACW) was created in 1896. The NACW was intended to encourage groups to be more aware and socially active in women's racial issues, and it was the first national organization in the United States to be entirely controlled by black women. The reporting of the various clubs in NACW journals, such as *Women's Era* and *National Notes*, gave both a dignity and a new direction to diverse local women's clubs. It taught more sophisticated methods of organization and undertook the formal training of local leadership. Mary Church Terrell, founding president of the NACW, saw the association as a vehicle for the betterment of the race and for black women specifically. Terrell taught classes on parliamentary procedure and effective group management and saw the organization as a way to cultivate leadership skills among women throughout the nation and at the state and local level.[13]

Nevertheless, the organization was not feminist in the late-twentieth-century sense of the term. Indeed, it was innately conservative in its concept of society and a woman's place therein. The NACW accepted women's social and domestic nature, and its aim was to make better wives and mothers while improving employment opportunities and social conditions for those forced to work, especially in the cities. Terrell saw women in her association as being an elite who would naturally lead and elevate other black women, as the NACW motto, "Lifting as We Climb," explicitly proclaimed. It was believed that the faults of any black woman affected white perceptions of the group as a whole, therefore the morality of the lowliest of women meant that those of a higher status "cannot escape the consequences of their acts."[14]

The ideology behind the NACW lay in the belief that women held a monopoly on virtue and, therefore, were the foundation for the moral advancement of society as a whole. This belief began with women's behavior in the home, where children were reared and moral and ethical standards enforced. While the group did not advocate against women's employment, it was understood that there was no substitute for a wife and mother devoting her energies primarily to the home, family, and community environment. Work was often seen as unavoidable, however, so the NACW set up kindergartens to safeguard children's moral welfare.[15]

The NACW advocated a strict, Victorian view of woman's identity in a household; as one of the organization's many dictums stated, "Homes, more homes, better homes, purer homes." Although many women in the organization may have subscribed to this fundamental tenet, another impetus for membership was to organize their clubs around public reforms that would demonstrate their potential outside the domestic sphere. Clubwomen did not believe that women existed solely to perform domestic chores or to be good wives, but they were encouraged to contribute to general community advancement. Furthermore, there was a general distancing from the rigid acceptance of Booker T. Washington's industrial tutelage for blacks and the interminable wait for social and political advances. The NACW was a fervent advocate for female political rights, although it was to argue that women would bring their unique qualities to the political forum and create a better world in their own sphere of influence, such as education, health, and childcare.[16]

The Phyllis Wheatley Club of New Orleans joined this fashion of female activism under the auspices of the NACW. It professed social welfare causes and the temperance movement under the "ideology of domestic feminism," which saw women's roles as a mother, wife, and homemaker as cornerstones to race uplift and progress. For those women who had to work, the club organized a training school for nurses in 1894. Nursing was an occupation that was acceptable for women, but opportunities for training needed to be formalized and the safety of working women, who were often single and in an urban setting, was seen as an imperative. The school opened in 1896 with five women ready to train as nurses. By 1897 University of New Orleans had taken over the majority of the funding for the project, though the Phyllis Wheatley Club still contributed money toward the school. The facilities were entrenched in both a moral code of training and securing a safe profession for young women, alongside the American concept of individual hard work and eschewing charity except in extremely disadvantageous circumstances.[17]

In 1930 the club had a mention in the *Who's Who in Colored Louisiana*, stating that the "colored women undertook, in a small way, to serve the needs of their race by providing hospital facilities for those who could afford to pay something for the services, and therefore ought not to accept charity, and the training of colored girls in the profession of nursing. They were given the use of one of the rooms in the college building for a sanitarium, where the nurse training started with only seven beds for patients and five nurses." By 1901 the club had also established kindergartens and day nurseries for working women's children. This social work was also extended to the political sphere, as the Flint-Goodridge Nurses' Alumni Association had club membership in the NAACP in the 1930s. Mrs. Eola Lyons-Taylor, one of the first graduates of the training school and later directress of nurses at the Flint-Goodridge Hospital, was also a member of the New Orleans NAACP branch in the late 1930s and held a seat on its executive committee in 1938.[18]

However, there was the expectation that women, while having an active social role, were to be kept back from the political battlefield, or at least to be kept back from its front line. The organizing in New Orleans of the Comité des Citoyens, which sought to test the constitutional validity of the state segregation law of 1890 on public transport, saw the male membership opposed to using a woman in any potential legal case as it might place them in a position of physical danger. Louis Martinet, editor of the newspaper *Crusader*, claimed that it "would be quite difficult to have a lady *too* nearly white refused admission to a 'white' car. There are the strangest white people you ever saw here." However, this was due more to a chivalrous attitude rather than simply an acute regard for the light coloring of certain black women. It was believed that such vanguard action was best done by men in the name of the entire community, especially in protecting their women and children from insult and danger. The test case was eventually undertaken by Homer Plessy and resulted in the U.S. Supreme Court decision giving legal sanction to "separate but equal" facilities between blacks and whites.[19]

Women were not to be totally excluded from the political sphere in the latter part of the nineteenth century, however, even though the franchise in the United States was a male preserve. Throughout the period the African American community in Louisiana and across the South tended to look in the direction of the Republican Party, as the political home of Abraham Lincoln and emancipation, with the hope for further social justice for black people. This political belief included equity for black women with white social norms even though policy, of course, was for black male suffrage only. But both women and men could participate in political gatherings with the intent that Republican Party values would bring the widest benefits to their communities. The ballot had a "sacred and collective character" in which women had much at stake, and they could be involved in the process by advocating to those who did have the vote the causes for which they were concerned, such as the family and education or the prohibition of alcohol.[20]

Nevertheless, women's organizations, like the Phyllis Wheatley Club of New Orleans, did become important centers of the black suffrage movement, particularly as white women's groups, both within the state and nationally, were beginning to argue for the enfranchisement of white women. At the end of the nineteenth century, the black poet Frances E. W. Harper visited New Orleans specifically to lecture on women's political rights and used as her argument that the ballot for women was an essential tool in protecting the entire black community. She claimed that women gaining the vote would also help restore and reinforce the franchise of black men as well as empowering women both socially and politically.[21]

Meanwhile, black women were under no illusions as to the stance that white female suffragists took to African American civil rights. White women of Louisiana saw black female suffrage as inherently problematic and tended to appease racists by the rhetoric of the Bloody Shirt. In this fashion Mrs. Wilton McHenry, leader of the Louisiana Suffrage Party in Ouachita Parish, invoked "the black shadow that imperilled the South during the period of Reconstruction" when discussing the white female franchise movement in the state. However, there were two feuding white suffrage groups in Louisiana, although it was a matter of personalities and trivial political nuance that separated them rather than profound difference of opinion over which women ought to vote (decidedly not black women, they agreed). The Gordon sisters, Kate and Jean, of the Equal Rights Association (ERA) argued for the option of continued black disfranchisement by espousing states' rights and the use of white women's votes to sustain white supremacy. The breakaway group, the Women's Suffrage Party of Louisiana, argued for white female suffrage by either federal or state enactment, with traditional state property and educational qualification methods to prohibit black women from voting. It was plausibly argued that the Fifteenth Amendment had not prohibited the South from eventually procuring white predominance and the wholesale disfranchisement of black men.[22]

However, the underlying fear that the struggle over the Nineteenth Amendment would admit the question of black suffrage to the state and national debate was well founded and was to increase pressure on electoral registrars in the parishes over the next half century. Mrs. Wilton McHenry of Ouachita Parish exclaimed that "if the Federal amendment was ratified, white women would be placed on the same par with Negro women [and] that although white men had been willing to keep the Negro male from the polls, this would not be the case with Negro women." This view was reinforced by Governor John M. Parker's declaration that black women were "far more fearless than black men." Louisiana failed to support the Nineteenth Amendment, and all the race issue achieved in the state was to dissipate the suffragist agenda and mute any common political objectives.[23]

In 1903 the National American Woman Suffrage Association (NAWSA) held its largest conference to date in New Orleans. Sylvanie Williams, president of the Phyllis Wheatley Club in the city, tried to attend the event but was disappointed by the racial exclusion policy of NAWSA, of which the NACW was an associate member. It has been suggested that other black women who could pass as white attended the convention, such as Adella Hunt Logan from Tuskegee. However, in her home city Sylvanie Williams was unable to hide her racial identification, or probably did not desire to in this instance. Fannie Barrier Williams of Chicago, social reformer and NACW leader, would later speak of Sylvanie Williams as "a fine example of the resourcefulness and noble influence that a cultivated woman can and will give to her race." She was the epitome of an elite middle-class woman who saw herself as a leader for black women in the battle for political rights.[24]

Indeed, Williams did not view civil rights purely as a racial issue but as a class-based dilemma. She saw that white society's sweeping denunciation of all black women as sexually promiscuous was palpably wrong, and she desired that class differences within communities be recognized. Therefore, to condemn those of the lower ranks of society in the black population was perfectly acceptable; as Williams stated, "We could not, nor would not feel aggrieved, if in the immorality of the Negro, the accusation was limited to the pauperized and brutalized members of the race." Chastity was the "litmus test" of the clubwomen's agenda to persuade the wider social arena that black women were respectable citizens who could perform effectively in the sociopolitical setting. Middle-class status and manners were the primary weapons of the NACW and its descendants, like the NAACP, which began with "fending off the advances of white men [which] would . . . preserve race integrity." In this way, historian Deborah Gray White claims, "Unwittingly, NACW women placed the burden of sexual exploitation and social improvement on the shoulders of the victim."[25]

The franchise for all women in the United States would have empowered about three million black women, with a majority of those residing in the South. Although the victory of the passing of the Nineteenth Amendment in 1920 was a hollow one for black women, it did motivate them toward a greater race consciousness with increasing determination to use overt political methods to achieve civil equality. Yet it was fundamentally a symbolic victory at this stage—an aspiration to achieve full citizenship in the future. In this manner, the amendment signaled a branching out for black women to increase their potential influence in the purely political sphere. The right to vote was now enshrined in the U.S. constitution, and it was the next step for black women to protest and attain the privilege. Many women transferred their service to the NAACP and other such organizations as the issue shifted to achieving general racial uplift. The issue appeared to be the attainment of the franchise for the entire black community, male and female, and gender was generally subsumed under broader civil rights matters.[26]

The NAACP drew women to its cause because the organization appreciated the fact that undermining the black female franchise was an attempt to denigrate black people generally in America and to deny all of them their political rights. The NAACP journal, *The Crisis*, related to its national readership that black women were attempting to register to vote in the 1920 presidential election despite purposeful delays and insults: "They have shown themselves in states like Georgia and Louisiana to be more modern and sensible than their white sisters; and throughout the country they cast a large and influential vote."[27]

The vitality of the voting issue had not waned by 1921, when the state of Louisiana held a constitutional convention. Walter White, assistant executive secretary of the NAACP, sent out letters to all its branches in Louisiana informing them to put pressure on convention officials to recognize black women as voters, stating, "We understand that the Suffrage question is to come up during this convention. It is exceedingly essential that this question be very closely watched by the Louisiana branch. By all means, we should have representatives at the Convention and a permanent lobby should be organized to prevent the inclusion in the new Constitution of adverse legislation framed for the purpose of disfranchising the Negro."[28]

The right of women to vote in 1920 was, therefore, not a clear-cut victory for black women. The problem was the same for black men who, even with the support of the Fourteenth and Fifteenth Amendments, were persistently discouraged from attempting to register to vote. The suffrage resolution did not give black women unconstrained access to the ballot, and it was the self-perceived role of the NAACP to prevent this new constitutional right from being a meaningless abstraction for blacks.[29] In its Eleventh Annual Report in 1920 the NAACP stated:

> The Association realized that much necessary work must be done to instruct the new voters in the fundamentals of civics, and to show them how to qualify, register and vote. It was felt that this work was especially necessary in the South since, not only would no effort be made by the white women's organizations to train colored women voters but also efforts would be made to prevent colored women from voting . . . In all of the southern states, colored women experienced difficulty in their attempts to register, and in a large number of cases they were told plainly that colored women would not be registered. In order to keep colored women from registering, the most difficult tests such as have never been required by law, were given.[30]

The establishment of women's suffrage did change, to some extent, the debate of the civil rights struggle. Access to the ballot, even in theory, transformed the vote from a collective possession of the black community to that of an individual or personal right. When blacks achieved the vote, women would not have to rely exclusively on black men to cast their vote for the benefit of black women and children. The right, however theoretical, was important to women in asserting and defining themselves politically in the coming decades, particularly as they became the vanguard of NAACP voter registration campaigns.[31]

However, the potential enfranchisement of black women did reinforce certain aspects of the age's gender expectations. Women carried ideas of respectability and of being nurturing mothers into the political sphere in an effort to temper the masculinity of the public realm. The difference was, however, that women no longer had to rely on men to represent them politically. This meant that black women, if they wished, could use their own organizations and initiatives to further their agenda, both personal and collective, in the strictly political sphere. Yet at this early stage, black women maintained the notion that the primary battle was against racism, with sexism as a secondary issue. In this manner black women put themselves onto the front line of the civil rights battle on terms of inequality with men.[32]

Women joined the NAACP in Louisiana to continue to advance their own political rights and that of their communities. The membership records of the very earliest branches in the state demonstrate that women could make or break the local organizations. Two cases in point are the New Orleans and Baton Rouge branches. The New Orleans branch was organized in 1915, although it only began to flourish in 1917. On its executive committee there was one female, Miss Charlotte M. Richards, who was assistant secretary at Gayle & Dunn African-American Books, which was owned by James Gayle and E. M. Dunn, who were both prominent organizers and financial backers to the fledgling branch. Charlotte Richards represented the local NAACP at a teachers' convention held in the city in July 1917 and sat on the committees for mass meetings and for nominations in branch elections. In 1918 Richards was again elected to the executive committee and was joined by two other women on the membership committee, Mrs. O. B. Flowers and Mrs. R. J. Walls, who was a midwife and nurse. Mrs. A. M. Henly was represented on the meeting committee in 1918, and Mrs. L. B. Landry was chairperson of the meetings committee and on the executive committee in 1921. Meetings were social occasions, and therefore suitable to a woman's expertise of organizing and entertaining groups and managing a public environment. Similarly, at this stage, affiliation on the executive committee, and on the membership committee in particular, entailed much organizational responsibility, as well as duties of recording administrative formalities, including business meetings and the cataloguing of members and their dues. It was apparent that the New Orleans branch was flourishing with female members at its heart.[33]

In contrast, there were fifty-nine members on the Baton Rouge branch's application for charter in 1919. Secretary of the branch, Mr. O. P. Richardson, a decorator by profession, expressed the reasoning behind this as a male-appointed preserve of organizing and leading. "I am happy to state, we had assembled together a body of the most substantial citizens of this city; this was accomplished without any flare of trumpets or beating of drums, as we decided that the men who lead in local affairs should take the lead in this, and urge upon our people the necessity of organizing to face ourselves from Oppression and lending our moral material and financial to the Greatest Association ever Organized for human rights." While enthusiasm was undoubtedly apparent, a female presence was not. The branch became dormant, struggled through 1921, had a flurry of activity in 1924, and was lost to the national office briefly thereafter. Only in 1929 did a new organizing meeting contain women. After Mrs. D. J. Dupuy took office as vice-president that year, she virtually ran the branch with a great deal of success for the next fifteen years.[34]

During World War I, members of the New Orleans branch saw civil rights as inextricably linked to a staunch adherence to the general war effort and to supporting black soldiers' fight for democracy abroad and at home, which, in turn, reinforced prevalent gender roles. For example, Mrs. Louise J. Ross of New Orleans was a member of the NAACP during 1917 and was heavily involved in patriotic women's work associated with the war effort. Ross was secretary on the NAACP-filled ranks of the "colored work" committee for the War Camp Community Day to "express their honor for our soldiers and sailors and our appreciation of their patriotism." Furthermore, Ross led the Red Cross Chapter Branch no. 6, which proclaimed the duty of "every patriotic woman in New Orleans . . . [to] volunteer her service to this most needed cause . . . in making garments for the soldiers."[35]

Attitudes toward citizenship in New Orleans society during the last years of World War I can be examined by the brief life of *The Vindicator*, a local newspaper printed under the auspices of the city's NAACP branch. The paper attempted to be a local *Crisis*, with state and national civil rights and society news. However, it had only 563 subscribers and struggled on for only two months (August and September 1918). It was filled with the prejudices and concerns of the leaders of the local NAACP branch, particularly its editor and manager, Mr. E. M. Dunn, and major contributor, Dr. E. W. White. The paper was to identify morality and religion as the cornerstone of race advancement.

In supporting U.S. involvement in the European conflict, the NAACP's underlying belief was that this would demonstrate to white America that black men should enjoy the fullness of American citizenship, including, most vitally, the vote. Women, in turn, were to be protected by men's legal, political, and economic empowerment: "This is the race's greatest opportunity since the emancipation. The race is on trial, and it is up to us to prove ourselves equal to the task before us . . . The Kaiser and Kaiserdom must be crushed everywhere. The weak is rising up to say to the strong stop your oppression . . . The black man joins hand in the great fight against Autocracy. He prays for a Democracy that will give to every man his just deserts . . . [O]ur first duty is to help win the war."[36]

Branch president Dr. E. W. White made it clear that the local chapter aimed to "remove those barriers that would keep [the black man] from coming into his fullness as a man[,] to unhamper and unfetter him, and bid him rise from the wreckage of prejudice and race hatred." White tied the idea of manhood and citizenship to the concept of morality and family values, allying this with decent white men: "We call upon every Negro in N[ew] O[rleans] who loves his race{,} who loves his wife and children{,} to stand by this association. The sensible White man, the honest White man[,] can not blame you for standing up for your rights . . . But to be denied rights and privileges that make us men, 'I had rather be a dog and bay the moon' than such a citizen."[37]

Such moderate black leaders, whom historian Daniel C. Thompson saw as "racial diplomats," had a class-orientation that gave them a predisposition to work with white leaders to achieve certain group goals. It was not that local NAACP leaders accepted segregation—indeed, theirs was the one organization in New Orleans that fervently did not—but they were gradualists who saw themselves as having an understanding of southern customs and how they could achieve their mission within this framework. Such middle-class arbiters with the white community perceived civil rights issues not simply as a black problem but as a humanitarian crusade. Black racial diplomats represented all mankind, not just oppressed blacks.[38]

Dr. White argued that black men should be given their political rights and then their economic rights would naturally ensue, the reverse of Booker T. Washington's assumption. This, in turn, would halt the exodus of blacks to the North in search of jobs and would generally ease racial oppression in the South. Expressed in curiously backward and fanciful language in *The Vindicator:* "[The NAACP] says give us a square deal, make the South fit for the black man to live in and we can . . . honestly tell our people from the pulpit and from the platforms to remain in Dixie and make the cotton fields bloom and the cane fields wave [and] the factories roar and the gins and steamers whistle as the black man in contentment and sa[t]isfaction sings his cornfield songs and plantation melodies, in the balmy breezes of Dixie's Land and under Dixie's blue skies." This was more in keeping with Washington's theory of industrial education, albeit with men's political rights reinforcing economic concerns in the first instance. To be both "prosperous and happy," black people "must be intelligent, temperate, industrious, skillfull, and constantly employed," making for the right kind of "manhood and womanhood."[39]

The underlying theme of *The Vindicator* was the belief that a general increase in the probity of the race was an essential element in the uplift of black people as a whole, and a prerequisite to a full attainment of their civic privileges. Women were seen as the vital link in maintaining (or attaining) virtue in this period: "The message is . . . the necessity of saving girls and women and fighting the evil influences that are a menace to this Country particularly during this war. We have to keep the soldiers fit to fight and it is equally important to consider the girls and women . . . [A]ll races must assume the responsibility of fighting vice and thereby protecting men and women. It is a patriotic duty that desolves [sic] upon every well thinking citizen man or woman. Let us begin now to help eradicate vice and we will not only co-operate with our Government's demand but will help to place our people on the higher moral and physical bases."[40]

Essential to the debate was the prohibition of alcohol and the crusade against the city's brothels, even though the red light district, Storyville, had been officially closed in 1917. On September 7, 1918, a number of euphemistically entitled "Society ladies" were caught in "the net" and "carried before the judge" in the "War on Joints." Subsequently, a committee was formed by the Central Congregational Church "for the purpose of establishing a rescue home for fallen women and girls," and *The Vindicator* explained that "large numbers of women of both races have been arrested recently because of their failure to comply to our country's call for a higher standard of morality—a better way of living . . . This movement, if successfully carried out, is going to mean much to our whole city. The morals of our boys and girls will be safeguarded and a better standard of living will be assured . . . This work cannot be done by the civil authorities alone. There must be united effort on the part of those who live on a higher plane. Much can be accomplished if each one of us, considering ourselves a committee of one, seizes every opportunity to lift our fallen sisters out of the mire."[41]

This effort concentrated on the moral standing of women and children, which continued the nineteenth-century theme of an inherently feminine morality. The work and aspiration of the New Orleans branch of the NAACP reflected this focus: "The Committee appointed to protest against the use of Colored women prisoners on the streets and in the public markets will call on the mayor in a few-days to present a petition from various organizations representing 5000 colored citizens . . . A committee is also working on a plan to co-operate with the mother's club in instructing the children as to their conduct in public etc. . . . We are also watching developments in regards to the segregation of the women in the red light district."[42]

Also in New Orleans during 1918, black women sat on the Women's Committee (otherwise known as the Committee on Women's Defense Work of the Council of National Defense), which dealt with organizing women's war efforts in the state. Black women saw this committee as having a dual purpose: to organize for their part in the national war effort and possibly to push forward social reforms, such as the dietary needs of the black population, public health, and war jobs for women. As Sylvanie Williams of the Phyllis Wheatley Club was active on this committee, it is unsurprising that training and employment as nurses was high on the list of war jobs seen as desirable for black women.[43]

On August 15, 1918, Alice Dunbar Nelson, field representative for the Women's Committee in Washington, visited New Orleans and held a mass meeting to organize them for the war effort and in raising social standards. Dunbar Nelson seemed duly impressed by the work of black women in "registering the woman and registering and weighing the babies of New Orleans." However, it appears that not much else was undertaken once the mothers and children were inspected. Merely highlighting the issue did not change dietary habits.[44]

Only New Orleans had the historical background for white and black women to work together and mobilize their energies toward the war effort in Louisiana. Reasonably stable race relations were important to this, although being the major urban center in the state was also a factor. When Dunbar Nelson questioned the reason for the lack of organization of black women for the Women's Committee in the cities of Baton Rouge, Shreveport, and Alexandria, she was informed that the "difficulties of accommodation [and] hard travel precluded any 'delicate lady's' [sic] going into the hinterland." New Orleans was the focal point of any organizing in Louisiana due to its geographical placing and population size, and it showed the complexities of organizing statewide, due to rural isolation and inadequate communication and transportation infrastructure. This was even more the case with setting up a civil rights group in which membership alone, without any additional protest, could upset local racial accommodation and produce extreme racist reprisals. The NAACP outside New Orleans took time to establish and longer to stabilize due to these circumstances.[45]

The NAACP was a natural beneficiary of established social and political African American groups in Louisiana that transferred their knowledge and expertise of a community to the Association's branches. Indeed, it could very well be claimed that black women were critical to the setting up of NAACP branches in Louisiana. Despite social repression and economic hardships it was these mainly middle-class groupings that kept the NAACP in existence in the state and were responsible for the propagation of a modern civil rights message. Yet women's political concepts became subordinate to male-oriented civil rights claims, which was to subsequently affect their perceived roles within the NAACP.

THREE

DESTINED TO BRING SPLENDID RESULTS
NAACP Women's Auxiliaries and Networks, 1921–1945

> It is almost invariably true that wherever there is an active, efficient branch, a large part of the work is done by women. This is especially true in cities where there is a Woman's Auxiliary to the Branch.

THE first full decade of the NAACP in Louisiana saw its organizational arrangements established along the lines of generally accepted gender practices. Black women worked for the NAACP as generators of ideas for fundraising and attracting other members to the organization and also acted as social network operatives who mobilized existing social groupings around civil rights objectives and campaigns. While these were not the highest or most publicly visible hierarchical roles in the branches, women's work allowed the organization in a specific locality to acquire grassroots stability, generate NAACP publicity, and have the potential for growth.

While the 1920s saw the NAACP developing on a steady and solid basis, the Depression brought a decrease in membership. The early 1930s saw a struggle to recruit the people who nominally filled the local membership lists, and there was a continued reliance on those who made up the long-term and committed leadership of a branch. For instance, Monroe branch president Mr. C. H. Myers sustained the chapter through the years 1930 to 1947. Other branches went silent or collapsed and were revived in the late 1930s and the early war years. With the approach of war, membership numbers recovered, although rivalries in larger branches erupted and, in New Orleans, caused paralyzing factionalism into the early 1940s. Also, from 1942 the establishment of a statewide NAACP network saw a stronger and more professional organization emerge to tackle specific issues, such as black teachers' pay and the fight against segregation.[1]

Historian H. Viscount Nelson, in his examination of African American leadership in the twentieth century, identifies the 1930s as a pivotal moment in the civil rights struggle. Whereas the 1920s held much promise for black American leaders in getting their agenda of political and cultural pride into an organizational campaign, the Depression caused them to reflect more on class interests at the expense of race consciousness. In the same manner by which Nelson proclaims that class interests "would receive greater priority in response to crises caused by the Great Depression," the gender patterns of the 1920s were perpetuated and became ever more rigid. Men had visible leadership roles to fulfill within the black community, and the Depression gave less room for women to supplant them in this function. Gender traditions became more entrenched with the Depression and continued with the war, when the well-defined role of women became central to branch survival and expansion.[2]

In Louisiana, New Orleans sustained an NAACP branch over this entire period. Two other strong branches did emerge during the 1930s, Baton Rouge and Monroe, despite the economic downturn, with a discernibly smaller membership base than in the Crescent City. By the time the United States entered World War II, Louisiana was a beneficiary of wartime production, military training, and increasing African American radicalization, and NAACP branches proliferated across the state. World War II saw unprecedented growth for the NAACP in Louisiana and across the United States generally, both in membership numbers in established branches and in the chartering of new chapters. Daniel E. Byrd, president of the NAACP Louisiana state conference in 1945, explained this increase in support due to "tolerance and patience . . . [being] at an end . . . [w]e must not wait another 80 years for the white man to give us justice." The NAACP in Louisiana, utilizing its experience of grassroots support, was able to capitalize on this rise in militancy to increase its membership numbers to an unprecedented high.[3]

New Orleans, Baton Rouge, and Monroe were to have the most viable branches in Louisiana throughout the 1920s and 1930s. Yet when they were first established, the chapters in Baton Rouge (1919) and Monroe (1928) had no female members; they only flourished when they were revived with women as integral members (Baton Rouge was rechartered in 1929 and Monroe in 1930). New Orleans, by contrast, had female members from as early as 1916. Between 1920 and 1945 women were to make up 25 to 50 percent of the membership of each flourishing branch. In the smaller branches this could make or break the organization, as fifty members were required to maintain a national charter. It was often difficult to get even that number during the early years of the Depression;

for example, New Orleans fell from a high of 505 members in 1928 to a mere 74 in 1930. Women, therefore, made up the margin of viability for most branches.[4]

The NAACP was explicit, however, about the inclusive nature of its membership in fighting for political rights for African Americans. In 1927 the NAACP national director of branches, Robert Bagnall, writing to Mr. S. B. Smith of Monroe with regards to setting up a branch, advised that "active" members "may be male or female, white or colored," the only requirement being "that they believe in the principles of the Association" in the fight to procure "the full citizenship and manhood rights of the colored people."[5]

Indeed, it was unambiguously acknowledged that women were the backbone of the local organization. As early as 1918 Mr. E. M. Dunn, secretary of the New Orleans branch, declared that "we expect great things from the South, when we get our fair sex behind such a great cause with principles such as the N.A.A.C.P. stands for." During 1936 the president of the Baton Rouge branch, Benjamin Stanley, highlighted the importance of such a dedicated core of members to the local branches: "The fact that we have always responded liberally to calls from the home office and other branches may have given the impression that we have a numerically strong branch. We have about 15 or 20 active members. We collected membership from several people who show no interest in our work but give the dollar because we are persistent. It's worth one dollar to get rid of us . . . Most people here are afraid to become identified with the N.A.A.C.P."[6]

The NAACP was built on a civil rights concept in which men and women were expected to play quite different parts in the body politic. While the right for women to vote was enshrined in the U.S. Constitution with the Nineteenth Amendment, it was vital for black women to actively protest and attain the privilege. In this process, civil rights organizing, such as membership in the NAACP, became a political act in itself and an overt undertaking on the road to general racial uplift. Women who were members of the NAACP directed their energies and resources into a battle against segregation that would reinforce middle-class values and prevailing gender perceptions, such as the patriarch-led family. Local NAACP campaigns in Louisiana tended to reinforce this point.[7]

One of the more successful NAACP campaigns in the 1920s against racial injustice in the state was a case in which two white men murdered two black women in Eros, Louisiana. The case illustrated how black women could be subjected to the caprice of white men in the Deep South without hope of legal redress. Because the case highlighted gender issues clearly, the NAACP hoped to turn it into a national cause célèbre. Although the nearest active branch was the newly established Monroe chapter, the New Orleans branch took the initiative. Monroe was to play the junior partner in raising money and garnering information, while New Orleans supplied legal and campaigning expertise and the major funding.[8]

The Eros murder case, according to the NAACP Annual Report of 1929, occurred on Christmas Day 1928. Two white men, D. J. Sanderson and Jack Bagwell, arrived at a black man's house in Eros, Louisiana, to pass on a dog intended for his landlord. The man was not home, but "his wife, four daughters and his grand children were . . . The white men ordered the colored women to line up to be killed. The women, thinking the men were jesting, made no effort to escape. They were fired upon. A girl of 15 and another of 20 with a baby in her arms were killed. The mother and another of the daughters were wounded."[9]

Such a case represented the powerlessness of black men to protect their womenfolk, not just in matters of rape or sexual exploitation but also in their own homes and everyday domestic situations. The two white men in the case were convicted of murder and given life imprisonment, a victory of sorts in the context of the South. The NAACP report for that year succinctly noted that it "is a commentary upon conditions in certain southern states that the conviction and jailing of two white men for wantonly killing two colored women and wounding two others should be an event of outstanding significance."[10]

The response to lynching further highlights attitudes to civil rights campaigning specific to the NAACP in Louisiana. White segregationists tended to defend lynching by arguing that it was a means to protect white feminine purity from the savagery of black men. The antilynching campaign at the local level in Louisiana, as elsewhere in the nation, deliberately reversed this notion. The idea that black men were lynched simply for sexual transgression was a falsehood debunked early on by the national office, and local cases in Louisiana turned the antilynching issue into one of protecting black men, their wives, and the family unit from white aggression and persecution.[11]

Such a cause was the Wilson (or Franklinton) case of 1935, which became a battle to save a Louisiana African American family. Indeed, for a short while, it was seen by the national office of the NAACP as a possible rival to the Scottsboro Boys case, which was seen as being undermined by Communist support and funding. The initial incident had originated over denied access of a white stock inspector, Joe Magee, to the land of the Wilson family over the issue of whether a mule had been dipped under a tick elimination law. When the local deputy sheriff became involved a fracas ensued and the deputy was shot dead. Most of the Wilson family was arrested and Jerome Wilson was lynched in January 1935.[12]

The New Orleans branch was particularly well organized and motivated over the event, organizing a mass protest meeting and arranging a committee on the Rehabilitation of the Wilson Family. The aim of the committee was more than publicity and justice over a high-profile lynching. There was a far-reaching moral "obligation to attempt restitution to John Wilson, in an effort to avoid what may become even a greater tragedy—the disintegration of the Wilson family." The committee declared it necessary to raise $2,000 to relocate the Wilson family in a community of black landowners in a southwestern state "where life is reasonably secure, and where his children will have the opportunities of a good elementary and high school in the vicinity." The wider moral aspects of the case also caught the attention of the white organization, the Association of Southern Women for the Prevention of Lynching, which offered to pay the costs of an investigation through the New Orleans branch.[13]

Similar cases also emphasize how central the concepts of masculinity and gender were to the concept of civil rights ideology. In another incident a girl, Hattie McCrary, aged fourteen, was assaulted and shot by a policeman, Charles Guerand, while she was working at a restaurant on Tulane Avenue. An NAACP committee in New Orleans saw the fight for a legal prosecution of the police officer as insurance that "our women are no longer shot down by white brutes for fun." McCrary was an example for all black women as she "gave her life to save her honor." In a public meeting held at the First Mount Calvary Baptist Church on March 9, 1930, the committee set the challenge to see "What . . . the Colored Men [will] give to Safeguard the Honor of the Future Mothers." Men, in this context, were the great defenders of women and children, particularly against white abusive authorities such as the police.[14]

Within this framework of citizenship and society, black men had the absolute duty to protect black women. In early January 1939, a black newspaper, *Louisiana Weekly*, depicted the following scenario as courageous yet a chivalrous obligation upon men: "Dr. A.W. Brazier, president of the New Orleans National Association for the Advancement of Colored People, was arrested when he stopped to see why a policeman was beating a Negro woman. Dr. Brazier swore out an affidavit and his trial was set for a future date. Later the charge was dismissed."[15]

Indeed, every copy of the *Louisiana Weekly* throughout the 1920s and 1930s had at least one page dedicated to women's groups and activities, which reinforced accepted ideas of a woman's role in respectable society. Such articles as "Do Decent Girls Flirt?" and "Do You Want a Baby?" certainly pigeonholed women to a world of finding a husband, having children, and homemaking. At the same time, the newspaper reported racial slights to black women and their attempts at reparations. For instance, during March 1930 Mrs. Katie Hawkins, a "popular young matron," was insulted over an attempted purchase of a hat on Canal Street in New Orleans. In May 1930 a bus conductor assaulted Miss Maggie Judge, a schoolteacher, and under the legal guidance of A. P. Tureaud, New Orleans NAACP attorney, the local branch instigated an investigation into the case. While details of these cases are meager, their importance lies in the general attitude toward black women in the public arena. If respectable black women were not safe alone on the streets of the city in such mundane circumstances as shopping or traveling, it was implicit that black men did not have their full civil rights to be able to defend their women.[16]

The *Louisiana Weekly* also detailed regular social groups for women, many of whose members were also NAACP supporters. Such groups customarily involved traditional skills like sewing, art, and literature appreciation, all of which invariably had nominal educational and charitable ends. The Primrose Art Sewing Circle, involving Mrs. A. Smith, NAACP member in 1926, was an organization set up to develop "ideas along the lines of needlecraft." The Bells of Joy Club, which was probably a card-playing social group, had a Mrs. M. Bell on its lists, and she was an NAACP member in the 1930s. Similarly, the Rose Bud Art Club involved NAACP members "Madames" F. Williams, B. Mason, and E. Williams. The group met at members' houses and involved "sewing for an hour" and listening to guests talk on charitable or noteworthy issues. In December 1929 the group listened to Mrs. Bessie Jennings "talk on charity," and the branch sent out several Thanksgiving baskets and donated to the city's Community Chest. Furthermore, the group was interested in improving their own domestic skills as a Mrs. Edinburgh "gave some helpful household hints." Louisiana's cities and towns were replete with such clubs.[17]

Consequently, women's roles in civil rights organizing were defined by a prevailing middle-class sense of propriety. In the 1930s these gender roles were more firmly fixed as men fought for the role of main provider and civil rights activity was a way of *normalizing* black family relations to white middle-class ideals. A woman's role within the family was seen as being innately different from a man's, and during the Great Depression, this concept of being a supportive wife and dutiful mother took on an increased importance. If work was a necessity, jobs with a particular female character were acceptable, such as teaching and youth work. However, the family unit was always expected to remain a strong nucleus of a woman's life.[18]

World War II continued to reinforce middle-class moral aspects of civil rights activity. The Young Women's Christian Association [YWCA], in which many NAACP members had direct experience, exemplified women's personal probity. The New Orleans YWCA in 1945 stated that it was for "Negro girls and women . . . a community investment in healthy, happy, efficient womanhood." This meant keeping young women away from corrupting influences that could destroy the virtues of the aspiring classes and their march toward full citizenship. The YWCA proclaimed: "BUT WHAT OF THE HOME FRONT? . . . Where shall our Negro girls and women live? . . . What about their health? . . . their minds? . . . their outlook? . . . their leisure-time? . . . do they have wholesome group contacts? . . . the *right kind* of social relaxation? The answers to these searching questions throw a revealing sidelight on New Orleans as a community."[19]

Black establishment figures, such as Fannie C. Williams, a teacher, YWCA worker, and NAACP member, provided guidance to young women. Through encouraging sport and craft skills, they hoped to keep young people away from sinful influences of wartime and keep them within a "Christian home influence." Apparently ping-pong was the ideal sport for young women, as it was "often more effective than a class-room lecture in teaching fair play, team work, and physical and mental coordination." African American groups were continually concerned with young women's moral and social behavior, doubly so during wartime, as they were seen as the future of black progress.

A collective role for women, along the lines of these gender expectations, could be suitably expressed via the organizing of women's auxiliaries to local NAACP branches. The NAACP constitution did not require such groups, although they were an expected accessory. The exact nature of the auxiliaries was often seen as problematic in the organizational sense. The national director of branches, Robert Bagnall, highlighted this in 1926: "We wish to have a Constitution which will enable the Auxiliary to work in harmony with the branch and the women at the same time to be able to be free to do the most efficient work for the association . . . We are trying to define carefully the relationship of the Woman's Auxiliary to the branch."[20]

Indeed, policy initiative was driven by the strong centralizing tendency of the New York office, which dictated to local branches and their various committees what they were to do. At a local level, the question was who had control over details of policy and how it was to be enacted. Therefore, the auxiliary was inevitably a subordinate to the broader functioning of a branch, as New Orleans branch secretary, Miss A. V. Dunn, admitted: "The Women's Auxiliary has grown in numbers and seems destined to bring splendid results. It meets regularly and is cooperating with the Branch in every respect. A dance was given on November 6 [1924] at the Temple Roof Garden . . . for the benefit of the segregation fight." There existed clear expectations of feminine propriety that included what was considered suitable for women to undertake in organizational work, and their job was to provide financial support and general encouragement to the local branch toward NAACP goals. For example, entertainment undertaken by the women's auxiliary for membership drives and fundraising was in traditional social areas, such as dances, refreshments, and competitions.[21]

In 1925 the national office suggested that the New Orleans branch hold a popular baby contest, a tried and tested method of raising money. The magical component, apparently, was to get three women interested in organizing the contest; thereafter the snowball effect would inevitably take over. William Pickens, NAACP field secretary, explained, "If you get as many as three really interested women the matter can be put through there. Of course they would get more friends to help but as many as three would insure success." Six months elapsed, and New York suggested the idea again. This time it was with an exacting and clinical eye to the untapped resources of the city: "The Baby Contest which deals in nickels rather than in dollars, would call on the great untouched resources of the common masses and even the poorest people. In spite of the fact that you have raised $10,000.00, there are perhaps twenty-five or thirty thousand colored people in New Orleans, who have not given a cent to you yet. The Baby Contest gives the very smallest givers a chance, and gets more money in a given time than any regular method."[22]

By such missives it was apparent that women's social networks were able, and expected, to coordinate an extensive plan to take into account various social strata to raise money for the NAACP. Yet such a plan came up against the particular social order of New Orleans and patriarchal blinkers of the branch president, who proclaimed, "I don't think a baby contest in New Orleans will work very well and especially during this season . . . And it is thought by many of those who have helped in this great fight that our people have been trained to give largely directly to a cause and a baby contest would likely break into this line of teaching. Secondly, peculiarly to New Orleans, babies are not very much in evidence and it would be a difficult problem to secure enough mothers who would enter their babies in a contest."[23]

However, the branch president, George Lucas, did suggest that the branch executive committee take the idea under consideration, although he thought it likely that they would concur with his assessment. It seems that no baby contest was undertaken, and there was probably an element of social snobbery behind the rejection of the idea in New Orleans. Baby competitions were seen as being perfectly adequate for lower social classes, particularly if a certain social matter was at issue, such as child health. However, it was not deemed proper that ladies of social standing parade their children in a display of vulgar pageantry alongside other social classes. Indeed, according to Lucas, children were neither seen nor heard in polite society. A civilized and socially appropriate dance attended by adults at one of the Masonic lodges was seen as much more befitting the city's cultured elite.[24]

In campaigns for funding in specific appeals women were invariably expected to entertain the NAACP membership and general public. During the fight to prosecute the police officer who shot a black woman, Lily Johnson, it was observed at a New Orleans meeting that "refreshments were served by a committee of ladies." Women's auxiliaries of the NAACP and other groups also cooperated throughout the United States. Following the 1927 flood, various organizations across the country sent donations of clothes and money to the New Orleans NAACP branch. The Lima, Ohio, NAACP branch sent clothes for distribution throughout Louisiana, as did the Women's League of St. Harford, Connecticut. A financial donation of $1,910 also came from the national office to the New Orleans branch. Secretary Mrs. D. J. Guidry documented the reports of peonage that had transpired in Louisiana after the flooding, as had occurred in Mississippi and Arkansas, where landowners were using police officers to keep black laborers on the plantations in virtual slavery. Documentation of these gifts linked a communications network that informed the New York office of detailed problems in the Deep South, which, in turn, could be used for national propaganda purposes. Nevertheless, it was the women who recorded events, distributed aid, and arranged entertainment committees, and who formed the hub of local activity on NAACP campaigns.[25]

The necessity of women in campaigning became ever more apparent during the Depression, which left the national office in such financial difficulty that it pressured its local branches to raise a minimum of twenty-five dollars each during 1935 for its central funds via local emergency committees. The committee in Monroe, according to the branch president, was made up of "the most influential and popular women." This led to repeated entreaties and further proposals from New York: "Some time ago you [Mrs. H. W. Johnson of Monroe] very graciously agreed to accept the chairmanship of a Special Women's Committee to raise $25.00 to help meet the emergency need of the National Office . . . The National Office needs your help desperately at this time . . . If your committee is not organized, will you not get together a committee of women to give some form of entertainment—a card tournament, dance, baby contest, popularity contest, whatever you think best—and endeavor to raise $25.00 for the National Office before the end of November."[26]

The New York office propounded the usual ideas for fundraising, yet its insistence on a women's committee emphasized that such activity was valued more than ever with the economic decline. William Pickens, field director, affirmed the litany of presumed female duties in 1934 by advising the Baton Rouge chapter to "give some popular form of entertainment for the benefit of the Branch and try to raise . . . $43.00 at once . . . Perhaps the women of the Branch could get up a popularity contest, or a dance, or a card party." In 1938 Mrs. D. J. Dupuy, Baton Rouge branch secretary, emphasized the success of the social aspect of Baton Rouge NAACP fundraising by stating to the national office that they were "planning to give some form of entertainment to try and make another donation as soon as possible." Having a hat-checking service staffed by women could raise further money. At a Temple Roof Garden at the Odd Fellows Lodge, Baton Rouge, in November 1935, this raised the total of fifteen dollars.[27]

Continual pressure to get women to undertake certain operations in raising money met with additional seasonal dictates from the central office. During the summer of 1932 entertainment especially in keeping with the season were "boat rides, lawn parties, [and] teas . . . [and also] station bridge or whist." The national office saw this information as invaluable in directing its local branches to maximum resource productiveness. Such social occasions would "induce both men and women to make a contribution to the work of the Association while they enjoy themselves at the same time."[28]

There could, however, be a negative aspect to the general popularity of fundraising through social events. The thirtieth anniversary of the NAACP in 1939 was intended as a major focal point in which to raise capital. However, the New Orleans branch held its celebratory Birthday Ball at the Autocrat Club during the "precarnival" period, when there was a glut of free dances in the city renowned for its social life. Only $1.47 was made at the ball and five dollars in total by the branch for the anniversary.[29]

An increasingly popular seasonal method of raising money for the NAACP by local branches was selling Christmas seals (adhesive stamps to stick to envelopes). These seals were described by the NAACP as "a sharp black silhouette on a bright Christmas green background depicting a virile figure of a man who has broken chains which held him captive. The seals bear the simple inscription, 'For Justice.'" The chairpersons for the inevitable committees for organizing the selling of Christmas seals in Louisiana were always women. This was a highly effective way in which to raise money in a short time period, while also propagating the NAACP message. In December 1932 Monroe raised thirteen dollars by selling seals through "workers in the various churches and other organizations throughout the town." By 1935 this was such a popular selling point at Christmas that Mrs. H. L. McClanahan of Monroe ordered an additional twenty dollars' worth of seals from the national office after her first batch sold out.[30]

Women were prominent on various other special working committees beyond fund raising and not always in the expected female positions that they undertook in the main organization. In 1928 the New

Orleans branch launched a competition to motivate and encourage its members to recruit new people to the NAACP by setting up a committee entitled "On to California, or Get an Education Contest." While the branch president, James E. Gayle, was the chairman of this committee, the secretary was Mrs. D. J. Guidry, and, unusually, Mrs. V. B. Thompson was its treasurer. By contrast, the position of treasurer to a main branch in Louisiana over the period was entirely a male preserve and was usually a role undertaken by certain individuals over a substantial time.[31]

The treasurer of the special committee was a teacher, Virginia Barnes Thompson, a native of the Crescent City who had been educated at New Orleans University. She was president of the Co-operative Workers of Negro Juveniles and a supervisor of the State Institution for Delinquent Colored Youths. Her assignment as treasurer for a special membership drive contest was not simply attributable to her general work in the community, although this undoubtedly gave her the necessary expertise. It was due to the fact that the emphasis of the committee was on education and, therefore, would encourage younger people to undertake the drive for membership to help them with their college funding. The option to go to the next NAACP National Conference in California was, it seems, a broader inducement for all ages. Women were overrepresented in the competition compared with male applicants, which reflected their role in membership drives more generally.[32]

The need to take the message beyond the annual membership drive and occasional campaign work was vital for local NAACP chapters. This was a difficult task, as acknowledged by the national office when it was observed by William Pickens, field secretary, that most members "do not feel inspired to take part in managing the Branch. It is good to get as many as possible out to the business meetings." Yet it was difficult to encourage participation even of those registered as NAACP members, and public meetings did not always motivate an audience to join. For example, 600 people, including a white judge of twenty-five years standing, attended the public meeting addressed by Pickens in Monroe in May 1932, but the membership levels went below fifty for the first time since the branch was chartered.[33]

Similarly, the New Orleans branch had difficulties in attaining membership during the 1930s. By 1930 its membership had collapsed to a mere seventy-four, from a high in 1928 of 505, and only recovered by the mid-1930s with dramatic help from national field director, Daisy Lampkin. In contrast the smaller and newer branches in Louisiana, notably Baton Rouge and Monroe, maintained their focus and avoided damaging disunity by sustaining a small and committed membership core, as New Orleans had done in the 1920s. Although Baton Rouge had its highest number of members in 1931 (101), it consistently maintained a dedicated cadre until 1940, when its membership rose dramatically. Monroe, likewise, saw a high of 104 members in 1931 and maintained some consistency throughout the decade, although by 1939 its register had dropped below the officially recognized number of fifty to a mere twenty-four. Membership drives needed considerable local energy and commitment and high-level organizational ability. The national office admitted that it invariably left the branches to conduct their own membership campaigns, as there was a lack of national field workers to commit to all of its local chapters. Women overwhelmingly assumed, in the definition of the Annual Report of 1936, this "local leadership."[34]

New Orleans was the most ambitious chapter in the state. In 1934 it sought to procure 10,000 members, although eventually only managed 750, which was still quite a feat given the economic climate. In 1935 the national office sent Daisy Lampkin to help organize the membership drives in New Orleans and Baton Rouge. Lampkin was a popular figure with the local branches and was constantly in demand with those who had contact with her in her official capacity. Three years after her visit to New Orleans, the branch president, Dr. A. W. Brazier, was imploring for Lampkin's return to sort out the chapter's membership campaign. Brazier emphasized that no one else would suffice hence underscoring the respect Lampkin had in the localities, and that such a unifying figure was needed due to discord in the New Orleans branch. Lethargy had been widespread in the branch since her last visit in 1935, Brazier explained, although the formidable task of getting a 20,000-strong membership was still an aspiration despite such obstacles.[35]

The national office had to carefully manage two field workers across the entire nation and gently rebuffed the constant appeals for Daisy Lampkin to revisit New Orleans. However, Lampkin sent letters to those she felt had helped her organize the drive when she had previously been in New Orleans. This was a useful way to maintain solid support from those people who had been active in previous membership drives and had been inspired and instructed by Lampkin on effective canvassing methods. Lampkin's "special thanks" went to sixteen people, ten of whom were women. Membership rose to over 700, a stark contrast to the forsaken days of the early 1930s.[36]

In 1937 the national office singled out Miss Fannie C. Williams as being a leader to entrust with organizing that year's membership drive. Apologies were sent that Daisy Lampkin could not be sent to run the campaign, but it was noted that she had praised "the splendid cooperation you [Williams] gave her [during 1935]. I do hope you will give us the same fine support this year." From the national office a list was sent of "New Orleans Friends" who had helped run the campaign of 1935; twenty-four of the forty-six were women. These were divided into Division "A" (women) and "B" (men). It is not made clear whether the division implied "A" being superior to "B," but unquestionably the division of labor was along gender lines even when the job was in a comparable area, such as recruitment of members. Indeed dividing men and women on recruitment drives was commonplace. Similarly, in Monroe in 1936, the spring membership campaign had a chair of the men's division, Mr. H. M. Carroll, and a chair of the women's division, Mrs. H. W. Johnson. There was also a chair of the youth's division in the drive, Mrs. H. L. McClanahan. An element of competition between groups as well as individuals was also a factor in generating even greater membership numbers. In Monroe during the 1935 campaign 10 percent of contributions raised by an individual went to the fundraiser, and prizes were further supplied for the top three proselytizers.[37]

Baton Rouge, by contrast, appears not to have solicited Daisy Lampkin's specific visitation after 1935. This was probably due to the fact that the branch was well organized and on a smaller scale than that of New Orleans. Even with the influx of new members in 1939 the state capital branch did not descend into acrimony and division, as its undisputed authority remained with its president, Benjamin Stanley. Conversely, New Orleans was on the eve of a sudden membership explosion that made the branch even more unwieldy. Baton Rouge, meanwhile, steadily increased its membership and retained a secure leadership group that was not challenged in its authority or capabilities. Monroe, on the other hand, consistently had a membership of fewer than 100, was never visited by Daisy Lampkin, and did not acquire any substantial strength until 1944. Yet it was an undoubted group of enthusiastic middle-class supporters in each of these cities that were to be commended for keeping their branches alive and active throughout this period.[38]

By the end of the 1930s and into the early 1940s, membership was on the rise and women were seen as ever more essential to sustain group enthusiasm and commitment to the NAACP. In late 1945 the New Orleans NAACP branch—described by Roy Wilkins, NAACP assistant executive secretary, as "one of the most energetic in the country, and also among the largest"—requested the national office to help organize a visit from a woman with a national reputation for their forthcoming membership drive. Their preference was for Judge Jane Bolin, the only black female judge in the United States, who sat on the Domestic Relations Court of New York and was also on the NAACP board of directors. The itinerary envisaged by Daniel Byrd, New Orleans branch executive secretary, included lectures at Louisiana's universities and a banquet:[39]

> Your [Roy Wilkins] most sacred and solemn promise was given that you would make every attempt to secure her honor [Judge Bolin]. And in addition to this you personally promised to do the publicity. I am sure you didn't forget . . . I would appreciate an immediate reply as to the availability of her Honor. If possible, I would appreciate her spending a week in New Orleans so that I will be able to arrange a $5.00 [per head] Banquet for women in her honor . . . In the event her Honor is not available, how about doing us a great big favor in getting Mrs. Eleanor Roosevelt [the First Lady] . . . I am very anxious, however, to turn this kick-off Meeting over to the ladies . . . Roy, I realize that sometimes we ask you to do the impossible but I have the utmost confidence of your ability to sometimes do the impossible.[40]

While Judge Bolin at the last minute could not meet the request, it was an admission that women were at the forefront of the most essential aspects of the NAACP in the Deep South: the internal momentum of the branches and the energy behind its local campaign drives.[41]

By 1945 the New Orleans NAACP branch was showing a great increase of membership, and Daniel Byrd reported to the national office that a "Woman's Group composed of twenty teams has been set up. Special letterheads will be printed. The women will go to work as of Friday, September 21, 1945 on their quota of $30,000.00." That there were twenty such women's teams indicated that the increase of membership corresponded with the traditional and amplified role of women in the movement. Yet despite growing numbers, it was still the legwork on the ground that remained vital. In Baton Rouge women went "house to house canvassing" during the membership campaigns. It was quintessentially a localized event reliant almost entirely on women and their relationship with their community. Women were, in the words of the Baton Rouge branch annual report for 1943, unambiguously "carrying the N.A.A.C.P. to the people."[42]

As was traditional in all the branches of the NAACP in Louisiana, women exclusively chaired entertainment committees and therefore kept the organizations alive by their publicity and fundraising work. In Lake Charles during 1944 Mrs. E. L. Thompson "conducted a prize contest for membership," and the chair of the entertainment committee organized something called a "Vanishing Party" on the March 3 which brought in six dollars. The chair of the entertainment committee in Alexandria in 1944, Mrs. Liley Jones, organized a show at the Ritz Theatre in the city and raised eighty-five dollars. Other popular fundraising events in the smaller branches included radio raffles, turkey raffles, dances, singing contests, parties, suppers, bus rides, and the selling of Christmas seals.[43]

The women who were joining and were active in the NAACP in Louisiana throughout this time had striking similarities between their occupations. Women who joined the NAACP throughout Louisiana tended to be educated professionals who asserted their rights through the gender conventions of the age via careers in three main areas of employment: business, the arts, and education. Family connections interwove with these positions and may have had a direct relevance for a wife and husband, as well as siblings and children, joining the NAACP.[44]

The arts were a minor area for recruitment by the Association, although this tended to be mainly in New Orleans, where a major flourishing musical scene existed. Maude C. Armstrong was a pianist in the city and an NAACP member in 1927 and 1935. Camille Nickerson, recruited in 1924, was also a distinguished pianist, a member of the board of directors of the National Association of Negro Musicians, and was musical directress at Howard University in Washington, D.C. It must be noted that this was the reputable division of the musical scene, namely, classical music, which reflected middle- and upper-class sensibilities, rather than the growing jazz or blues scene.[45]

Businesswomen were particularly well represented in the Louisiana

NAACP branches. The profession of beautician and hairdresser was a position of strength for black women as they were not served by white establishments and catered for a market of reasonably well-off women. Indeed the renowned Madame C. J. Walker, a native of Louisiana and on the executive committee of the New York NAACP branch, had pioneered the selling of beauty products to black women. Such a woman joining the NAACP was Mrs. Annette G. Hart, a "beauty culturalist," who was born in New Orleans, educated at Fisk University, and had taught in Louisiana's public school system. Similarly, Mrs. Eva White, "beauty culturalist," was a native of Texas, a teacher, and was the founder and proprietress of the Mme. White School of Beauty. White operated a large manufacturing plant of beauty products that exported to Central and South America. Her husband was Rev. E. W. White, who was NAACP branch president in 1918 and a member of the executive committee in the early 1920s.[46]

Other businesswomen represented in the NAACP included insurance executives, real estate agents, and undertakers. Ella Dejoie, Association member in 1926, was educated at Straight University, and was the wife of Dr. P. H. Dejoie, Sr., who ran the Unity Industrial Life Insurance Company of New Orleans. She was proclaimed by the Louisiana's black *Who's Who* as being a "prominent business executive" and "social and civic leader" of the city. Similarly, Mrs. L. M. Johnson of Baton Rouge dealt in real estate and was a member of the branch regularly from 1929. Embalmer Mrs. L. E. Lamothe of Monroe was an NAACP member from the branch's inception in 1928 up to 1936, and her husband, S. C. Lamothe, was an undertaker and sat on the chapter's executive committee in 1932.[47]

One of the most prominent businesswomen in the state who joined the NAACP was Mrs. G. G. Willis. Gertrude Geddes Willis, known locally as Miss Gert, was a prosperous undertaker and insurance executive who was personally valued at $70,000 in 1930. Born in St. Bernard Parish in March 1878, she was a Catholic, involved in the Ladies Auxiliary of the Knights of Peter Claver and later active in the National Urban League. She was involved with the New Orleans NAACP chapter sporadically in 1927, 1929, and 1935, although this would seem to be as a nominal recruit rather than as an active member. Willis was a financial contributor but was not involved in the decision-making or operational processes of the branch. Indeed her role would have been as a prominent and successful African American endorsing a national and local civil rights organization, thus giving it respectability and status within the New Orleans black social and business elite.[48]

The connection between family, usually marriage, and NAACP membership was a close one for many women in the local branches. In many ways families acted as units of shared socialization that led to group social and political consciousness raising. While this occurred across the board in Louisiana it was more pronounced in the smaller branches where family units produced longevity of membership. In New Orleans the turnover of membership did not engender extensive and prolonged group devotion, although certain families did have enduring allegiance to the NAACP. Women were often seen as co-equal partners to their husbands and this status was important to their own role in a social and organizational context.[49]

The Green family is a case in point of committed family loyalty to the NAACP. Mr. S. W. Green made his fortune as a grocer in New Orleans and became president of the Liberty Independent Life Insurance business. He was Supreme Chancellor of the Colored Knights of Pythias of the United States from 1908. Green organized and built the Pythian Temple in New Orleans at a cost of $225,000, and the state had eighty-one lodges with 9,000 members. He was assistant secretary of the New Orleans NAACP in 1920, and on its executive committee during 1921, 1925, 1934, and 1936. Mrs. S. W. Green, born in Alexandria, Louisiana, was seen in this social and business context by Louisiana's black *Who's Who* as being "of invaluable service in her husband's work and promotion." She was general manager and private secretary of her husband's office at the Pythian Temple, and assisted in her husband's businesses, as bookkeeper, cashier and purchasing agent. Paralleling her husband's fraternal affiliations, Mrs. Green organized the women's auxiliary of the Knights of Pythias, the Star of Calanthe, no. 27, and was the first Worthy Counselor of the Court. She was a member of the New Orleans NAACP branch during the years 1926, 1928, 1934, and 1935. Additional members of the Green family appeared on membership registers throughout the 1920s and 1930s.[50]

Monroe and Baton Rouge membership lists offer a direct correlation between husbands' status in the NAACP chapters and wives' position in the organization during the 1920s and 1930s. At the inception of the chapter in 1927, all four female members of the NAACP in Monroe joined alongside their husbands. There was one full-time "housewife," Mrs. M. G. Miller, whose husband, John, was a physician and on the branch executive committee in 1928, while only Mrs. L. E. Lamothe shared in her husband's work of undertaking. Mrs. A. L. Brunner was a retired teacher whose husband, a merchant, was secretary of the branch in 1928. Mrs. C. H. Myers, hairdresser, was wife to the long-term branch president from 1930; he was a mechanic and owned two movie theatres in Shreveport.[51]

At the organizing meeting of the Baton Rouge branch in 1929, of the eleven women present eight were designated as housewives, indicating that wives were seen as complementary adjuncts to their husbands rather than as having occupations of their own. Therefore, the gender difference between men and women was strictly defined between those who held power in the local chapters and those who assisted in the work of the Association. More generally, while women raised essential funds and organized social events and recruitment drives, this was seen as subordinate to the main task of leading. The junior partner role of many women in the local branches of the NAACP is shown by the death of New Orleans president George Lucas in January 1931. Up to this point Lucas's wife had not appeared on the membership lists yet thereafter appeared regularly. The new president's wife, Mrs. L. J. Labat, did not appear on the register of members until her husband's elevation. In both cases the wives were important connecting symbols for the local NAACP organization. Mrs. Lucas's involvement was the continuation of her husband's devotion to the NAACP that he had spent a decade working for, although she held no further position than that of nominal member. Likewise, Mrs. Labat became a member in June 1931 and was seen as supporting her husband upon his election to the presidency of the branch. Wives were seen as representing an assurance of faith in their husbands, dead or promoted, and their individual NAACP leadership.[52]

Similarly, in the 1930s the presidents of the smaller branches were expected to have their partners on the membership lists, even if no further activity on the NAACP's behalf was exhibited by them. This denoted a family commitment to the organization as well as bolstering membership numbers through a difficult decade. For example, the Baton Rouge president, Mr. B. J. Stanley, was joined on the membership lists by his wife, Mrs. A. R. Stanley, throughout the 1930s, and by his daughter, Sophronia, in 1939. This was indispensable to the membership count as Baton Rouge at times in the 1930s could only muster fifty members, the minimum number of an official chapter.[53]

The importance of family commitment to the NAACP is given further illustration by the Baton Rouge membership lists. In a typical example, Hazel S. King, a teacher, was on the membership roster with her husband, Cornelius. Yet such commitment could also extend beyond a husband-and-wife partnership and reach to their children and other relatives. Ida Nance-Givens's daughter, Miss M. A. Givens, joined the Baton Rouge NAACP in 1935. Likewise, throughout the 1930s Irma Curry was joined by her sister, Miss Olga Curry, and mother, Mrs. M. L. Curry. Furthermore, in New Orleans, Miss Althea Hart recruited her two brothers, James and Marcel, to the NAACP lists after having procured the assistance of the city's branch.[54]

Many of the women described here appear as middle-class professionals or as partners in marriage and business to successful career men. Women, however, were also involved in broader social and philanthropic gatherings that complemented their commitment to racial uplift groups like the NAACP. For example, the Young Men's Christian Association and Young Women's Christian Association (YWCA) were organizations that covered a multitude of social, religious, and physical welfare issues. That the YMCA was a prominent national organization probably attracted many women to it alongside membership with the NAACP. Mrs. M. V. Riley was a member of the YMCA in New Orleans during the 1920s, participating in its fundraising activities. In 1935 Riley joined the NAACP, although she does not appear to have been a prominent figure in either association. Nevertheless, such people were vital for the general raising of money, for the recruitment of new members, and for propagating the NAACP message.[55]

Other women in the New Orleans branch who also joined the YMCA and YWCA and reinforce this notion of a wider leadership role in the community include Mrs. E. O. Lyons-Taylor, head nurse at the Flint-Goodridge Hospital. Lyons-Taylor was chair of health education on the YWCA committee of management in the 1940s. Similarly, Mrs. Wylene Sazon was secretary of the Standard Industrial Life Insurance Company, an executive of the YMCA in the late 1930s, and also a coordinator in NAACP membership drives in New Orleans. In this manner women tended to have a broad view of how they could contribute and assist their communities, rather than a narrow political affiliation to just one organization, and they invariably joined many associations in order to play an active role. Women, therefore, fashioned extensive social networks by which to apply their various talents in multifaceted ways to meet civil rights and general race uplift objectives.[56]

Likewise, Masonic lodges were an essential element to the NAACP and to middle-class women's social lives. The crossover from such influential groups with the NAACP was important for the financial and organizational contributions they offered. The Catholic Knights of Peter Claver was especially important for the NAACP during the 1920s and 1930s, with such women as Mrs. G. G. Willis and Mrs. Oneida Brown being integral members of the group, as well as of the NAACP. However, the NAACP in New Orleans was not exclusively or predominantly Catholic, and there were many Protestant lodges within the African American community. Other NAACP members frequented the Mt. Olive Grand Chapter of the Order of the Eastern Star, which met at the Mt. Zion Baptist Church. Mrs. Lillie R. Thompson was a Royal Grand Matron of the Lodge and often officiated as Mistress of Ceremonies at their "Literary Feast" and other social affairs. Thompson, an NAACP member in the 1930s and fervent advocate and fundraiser for black juvenile charities in New Orleans, was described by *Louisiana Weekly* as "one of America's leading women in all religious, fraternal, civic and charity work; a friend of everybody."[57]

Black women's familiarity with fundraising and their extensive networking allowed them to lend their expertise to a variety of projects that complemented their NAACP work. The Community Chest campaigns held widespread importance to the black population in New Orleans during the 1930s as investment for local interests became ever more difficult to locate. The various Community Chest Campaigns (Colored Division) were generally explained to local people as ways to donate money to important black charity causes in the city, such as the Flint-Goodridge Hospital, black schools, and the Colored YMCA. Yet to read the various executive committees and lists of assistants of the campaigns is to recognize the extensive crossover of personnel with the NAACP.[58]

General campaign workers for the Community Chest in the 1930s who were also NAACP members included Mrs. George W. Lucas, Mrs. James E. Gayle, and prominent businesswoman Mrs. G. G. Willis. Women were also represented on the Community Chest's executive committees that implemented fundraising initiatives. Campaign director for the 1933 campaign was Mrs. E. C. Thornhill, who was also on the board for 1932, along with Mrs. Ida T. King. District chairperson for 1933 was Miss Oralee Baranco, while Mrs. Samuel Sazon and Fannie C. Williams were public speakers for the Chest at the New Orleans Masonic Pythian Temple in 1934. Williams was also on the publicity committee in 1933 and was the chair of the speakers committee.[59]

Women found that their differing roles could be carefully compartmentalized to take into account their wide-ranging expertise, particular concerns and ideals, and an appreciation of the social setting in which they worked. In 1929 Fannie C. Williams, an NAACP stalwart, started a health program in New Orleans distinct from the Association and its long-term professed aims. Williams was the principal at the Valena C. Jones elementary school, which was situated in a particularly deprived area of the city, and so her focus was necessarily on children's state of health. Under Williams's charge the health program raised funds to provide two dental chairs and two dentists to give free care to children. The central theme of Williams's agenda was a Children's Health Day that was observed on May 1. Dedicated and educated women saw it as their duty to hand down their knowledge and expertise to those less fortunate and therefore improve their lot in life. On May 1, children were to be encouraged to drink milk, while soft drinks were forbidden, and were to eat hot lunches, while on a wider social note they were encouraged to take flowers to local sick people and the aged.[60]

Fannie C. Williams's Health Day is an example of how ideological characteristics and practical deliberations operate together. Williams was a member of the NAACP, which was outspokenly integrationist, yet she was also forced to work within the constraints of Jim Crow segregation. Such black women felt the injustices of the apartheid system in the Deep South acutely. Yet they also appreciated that black people could improve the quality of their lives within the framework of segregation. Indeed, certain programs could be specifically targeted at black communities with little or no input from interfering white benefactors or racists. Black children could have the best dental care under Williams's health care program without having to put up with the indignity of enforced segregation and fund-starved facilities. It was a perfect self-help project by which the African American community conceived the project, raised funds, and implemented it without external assistance. Such undertakings were an example of community self-sufficiency and a way of fostering local black pride.

While Fannie C. Williams obviously appreciated the long-term objectives of the NAACP to integrate American society, she did not see it as incongruous to pursue other goals, such as the improvement of black schools and equalization with those of white institutions, through individual efforts and other organizations. Indeed it was the customary method of African Americans to organize and coordinate their groups and agendas to reflect differing states of affairs. Moreover, black women were adept at finding their audience and tapping their resources to finance particular projects. The NAACP was entirely the wrong sort of organization to appropriate for the health day exercise that Williams initiated. On top of its bureaucratic structures, it was simply not equipped to focus on the details of a project that a black educated female leader in a specific location could perform. While personnel did overlap with such a project, it was more an assignment for an individual to manage in the heart of a community than to leave to a broad civil rights organization.[61]

Indeed while the NAACP could argue the need for better or integrated medical services for African Americans, a local branch was not in a position to pursue a course of action that would implement a detailed welfare plan. The members of the NAACP invariably regrouped as a new organization to bring new amenities to black people in segregated conditions, as they had done when the Phyllis Wheatley Club had formed the Flint-Goodridge Hospital in 1896. During 1926, when the New Orleans NAACP had attempted to organize and find $300,000 of funds for a hospital for black people in their city, it was forcefully dissuaded by the national office, who argued it was impractical for a local branch to undertake such a monumental task. Philosophically, the Association was intended to confront racism and its consequence of segregation rather than building a hospital, which was seen as a distraction from its main work in the local community and may have misdirected its energies from fighting racism more directly.[62]

The National Urban League is the perfect example of this integrated concept of fighting a pragmatic battle for social, political, and economic rights for African Americans by an individual holding membership in a variety of organizations with wide-ranging purposes. The Urban League was an attempt "to improve the living, working, and housing conditions of Negroes in all parts of the nation" and allowed "prominent local white and colored citizens" of New Orleans to work together without the taint of political radicalism associated with the NAACP. There was much crossover of important NAACP leaders of the city with the Urban League, including NAACP presidents James Gayle (1934–1937) and Dr. A. W. Brazier (1938–1939). The Louisiana Industrial Insurance Company, the largest black business in the state, donated $300 to the city's Urban League in 1939. The Dejoie family, founders of the black newspaper *Louisiana Weekly*, had prominent executives in the insurance company, as did a host of other NAACP members. Of its seventeen directors, two women, Mrs. P. P. Creuzot and Mrs. J. J. Dejoie, were also associated with their husbands in the NAACP.[63]

Another group that NAACP members supported in the late 1920s and early 1930s was the Federation of Civic Leagues, a New Orleans voter registration group that also sought to assert black political leadership in the Republican Party in Louisiana. Although such aims were also NAACP objectives, purportedly without party political associations, members of this breakaway group sought to show their frustration at the slowness of change in the city and their desire to gain access to the ballot, and also elucidated their Republication connections. Crossover membership with the NAACP included prominent women such as Miss Fannie C. Williams, Mrs. D. J. Guidry, and Mrs. A. M. Trudeau.[64]

Women's organizational and social skills were transferable to a wide variety of community projects. Indeed many of the membership lists for charitable and political organizations within middle-class black communities replicated the names on NAACP rosters. During the early 1940s the focus was on the national war effort in which African Americans undertook their patriotic duty to support the fight against fascism in Europe within the confines of the American segregated system. As with World War I, this included financial contributions as well as issues of safeguarding the general morality of the black community.

The War Loans drives within the black community were organized and headed by many members of the NAACP. This was a direct consequence of the Association's customary and vocal patriotism during times of national emergency. African Americans in Louisiana involved in integrationist civil rights work instinctively supported the U.S. government at such times. In part this was with the usual hope that overt identification with the war effort would lead to an easier passage to their political rights and social integration into mainstream American society. This included the hope that African American workers would have access to defense industry jobs.[65]

NAACP members were active in the War Loans drives, which sought to raise funds for the federal government for the general war effort. Chairman and vice-chairman of the Fourth War Loan Orleans Parish drive (Negro Division) of 1944 were NAACP stalwarts George Longe, educator, and A. P. Tureaud. The secretary was Mrs. Naomi Borikins, who was public relations representative for Jackson Brewery Co.; assistant secretary, Miss Myra U. Hayward, McDonogh #37 schoolteacher; with office manager being Mrs. Julia B. Dejoie. On the executive committee sat Mrs. Corinne Azamore, a juvenile probation officer; Miss M. D. Coghill; and Mrs. Mada P. Kennedy, beautician. Many of these women had also been involved in the 1930s Community Chest campaigns. The New Orleans black community successfully raised $585,000 from war bonds in 1944. The transferal of this grassroots activism from the black community to a national patriotic cause was virtually seamless, merely requiring the setting up of a new committee to undertake a differing aspect of their integrationist vision of the future.[66]

Joining the NAACP was seen as a social responsibility for many of its female members. However, while membership was often of a nominal involvement, merely paying dues and then having little further engagement with the branch, this did show that race consciousness existed at some level. It was a duty to join the civil rights organization and support NAACP ideals, though this was at a dollar a year and was often sporadic. Women who were active in the organization at the local level, however, often had an elitist orientation, similar to the days of the women's club movement of the late nineteenth century. Yet the concern that segregation was inherently wrong and that black people must organize for social and political change was genuine. Affiliating with the NAACP was a defiant and brave act in itself and gave a distinct indication that many women hoped for a more equitable future and were prepared, at various levels of involvement, to push for this agenda.[67]

The NAACP in Louisiana was an organization sustained by a dedicated core of activists and their constant recruitment drives to keep the membership numbers stable and growing. Without such commitment the Association would never have built itself as a credible force in the state. By the early 1940s the beginning of mass NAACP membership across the United States had begun, and this was primarily built upon the long-term work of NAACP women who had kept the name of the organization alive through the difficult interwar years.[68]

FOUR

GOD'S VALIANT MINORITY
Teachers and Civil Rights

The great fight of the N.A.A.C.P. to equalize educational opportunities should inspire the colored people in the South, because there is where we are worst treated... But all of the old fight is still with us, against lynching, jim crowism, segregation, and legal injustice. The fight will go on for generations.

TEACHERS were the most natural constituency of the NAACP. Educators had stable jobs, earned a reasonable wage, lived and worked at the center of civic life, and were seen as being central to the general advancement of the entire black community. In 1940 there were over 4,000 black teachers in Louisiana, with women making up approximately three-quarters of their ranks. Of the twenty-eight teachers of Danneel School in New Orleans who joined the city's NAACP in 1935, only four were men. Most teachers were well educated and could respond positively to NAACP calls for educational improvement and greater social militancy. Many contributed their professional networks to the organization's campaigns, and there was a concerted attempt by the NAACP to attract mass teacher involvement in the civil rights struggle. It specifically promoted legal cases that sought to equalize black teachers' salaries with that of their white counterparts, which instigated one of the more successful NAACP campaigns in Louisiana. Yet teachers, in the main, contributed to the middle-class predominance of the NAACP and perpetuated the belief that a morally virtuous and educated community was the road to freedom.[1]

Education was one of the key campaigning areas of the NAACP national office, in equalizing facilities and standards with white establishments and, later, by seeking to desegregate institutions. However, the goal in the late 1930s was to have the "separate but equal" rule strictly applied, which would either force the educational system to be integrated due to the high costs of maintaining a dual system, or at least allow more evenly proportioned availability of schooling. Integration was increasingly the strategy during the 1940s, however, although local and state NAACP organizations generally preferred to concentrate on equality through separation of teachers' salaries and, consequently, in educational standards. The problem that beset the NAACP in attracting teachers to its ranks was the possibility of direct threats from their employers, the local educational boards. This was particularly challenging when it came to encouraging teachers to put themselves forward as plaintiffs in their parishes to fight an equalization case and to be so publicly affiliated to the NAACP. But in order to establish legal precedence, the NAACP needed to be prepared to challenge each separate parish education authority on equal salary until the whole state of Louisiana achieved teacher salary equality.[2]

Local branches of the Louisiana NAACP for the most part followed their own agenda for education as they saw befitting their communities. Mainly they attempted to force local authorities to equalize black education with white rather than actually advocating full-scale integration. In Baton Rouge during 1944 the branch secretary attempted to get the school board of East Baton Rouge Parish to provide transportation for the children of Istrouma, Louisiana, to school and back from remote rural locations. The Scotlandville branch in 1943 reported to the national office that it had secured "elementary and high school facilities for Negro children and authorization to select [the] location for [a] new high school building," as well as a "promise" for a senior high school. Meanwhile, the Iberville branch membership was looking forward to an equalization of educational facilities campaign and had the parish teachers "up for a fight," including the "older teachers too." In New Orleans the branch was persistently petitioning the Orleans Parish School Board (OPSB) for more teachers and high schools, playground space, trade schools, and a music supervisor. The NAACP and the Parent Teacher Association (PTA) at Macarty School, New Orleans (under the name of a parents' "Cooperative Club") raised money for a kitchen, a school radio, and a 16mm sound projector. The objective was to get the best education for black children in a district and make schools accessible for remote communities. Integration was not necessarily the priority; indeed, the Scotlandville example shows an issue of establishing black schools beyond the elementary and high school levels so that black children could simply continue their education beyond elementary level.[3]

Teachers may have been particularly drawn to campaigns to equalize educational facilities with those of whites, as conditions were so poor in their own schools that the prospects of immediate gains would have appeared attractive. This focus could have been to the disadvantage of the longer-term NAACP objective of integration, in which equalization was a mere staging post. Yet equal facilities were an incentive for teachers to join the NAACP education campaign. Schools in rural areas, where overt identification with an integrationist cause may have upset the white power structures, were badly in need of financial strengthening. School buildings were old and made of wood, such as the dilapidated two-room structure in St. Charles Parish. In East Carroll Parish there were no libraries in the black schools and no buses for students to get to classes. Furthermore, students did not have access to many of the essentials for proper teaching, such as blackboards, tables, and schoolbooks, which if available were often second-hand from white schools. Progression onto higher school grades was often only possible in the cities and larger towns. Indeed in twelve Louisiana parishes, even as late as 1956, there were no high schools for black students at all. In addition rural areas had their school terms limited by the harvest season and, for similar reasons, were primarily taught an industrial syllabus. However, Louisiana's cities suffered from comparable problems. In Shreveport some schools had no electricity and could not accommodate all their students, so church buildings were used to house them. With such pressing and immediate problems, improving local segregated conditions of blacks was a priority for teachers and communities.[4]

The NAACP purposely sought to attract teachers to its membership by its education campaigns and, in turn, hoped to gain from their leadership status within a community by utilizing their professional networks to further the Association's agenda. Of pivotal importance in this picture were the PTAs, which brought a community together to invest in black schools. Parents and teachers saw education as a mission for the general uplift of the entire race and personal advancement of their children. Many educators made sure that they personally knew the families and homes of their students, as well as the churches they attended and their employment situation. PTAs were organized to obtain vital school supplies, heating fuel, transport, and essential educational resources, and they often financed construction of school buildings. Their influence extended beyond the immediate educational environment for children: schools were also nondenominational community centers and offered adult classes on health and literacy programs. Indeed PTAs sometimes took out group membership of the NAACP, reflecting the strength of feeling within communities that the organization shared their broad values on education and were seeking rectification of inequalities. In New Orleans in 1938 the Wicker High School PTA affiliated with the city's NAACP at the price of five dollars, which included subscription to *The Crisis*.[5]

In this manner teachers had vital and extensive professional networks that the NAACP could draw on for its campaign work. An excellent case in point of this practice was Miss Florence A. Lewis, vice-president of the New Orleans branch in 1921. Lewis was an elementary teacher at the Macarty School and went on to become its principal in the early 1940s. Macarty School had all of its teachers paying the poll tax regularly in New Orleans under a local scheme, which was led by the city's NAACP, to encourage active political participation. Teachers throughout the city were encouraged to make a collective and organized effort to pay the tax as it was a prerequisite to be able to register to vote. Overwhelmingly women, teachers managed an impressive 94.3 percent poll tax compliance in New Orleans in 1932.[6]

However, not all black schoolteachers paid the poll tax in New Orleans, as it was not deducted from their salaries by the state. Under the teacher voter registration campaign, Danneel School had only 34 percent of its educational staff paying the poll tax, while Fisk School was 55 percent paid up and Marigny School had 90 percent. However, out of the twenty-five schools in the plan twenty-two of them had all of their teachers paying the tax. Moreover, out of the twenty-five schools in the scheme there was a potential of 390 teachers who could have participated, out of which a total of 368 had paid their poll tax in full for 1932. Many of these teachers, of course, were NAACP members, such as Miss Fannie C. Williams of the Thomy Lafon School and Miss Anna Mae Berhol of Wicker School, to name but two.[7]

The NAACP encouraged teachers to enroll and to become active in civil rights campaign work because it believed that educational institutions were environments of "collective liberation" that acted as a community resource for the entire African American community. An example of this broad social appeal of local schools was the Sylvania F. Williams Community Center, which was connected to the Thomy Lafon School and was situated in one of the rougher neighborhoods of New Orleans. The center was organized in March 1926 by NAACP members Professor S. J. Green, principal of the Thomy Lafon School, and Mrs. Eva Jones, president of the school's PTA. On the central council for the center were NAACP women Miss V. C. Cornelius, Miss Edna Richards, and Miss Ella Washington. They planned community projects for adults and children to the benefit of the whole community, yet such projects were often restricted within the confines of dominant middle-class gender expectations. For example, activities for girls included "handicraft clubs, calisthenics [sic], girls service groups, games, confidential talks and special projects." Boys were given the opportunity to join the Boy Scouts and attend manual training and athletic clubs.[8]

A part of this community approach through the educational institutions can be seen by the Williams Community Center's celebration of "Better Home Week," which became an annual event from 1932. The center saw that the "object of the project is to show how a home can be made attractive for a small amount of money . . . [This involves] some of the mothers and young people from the community center clean[ing] it thoroughly, [and] painting the walls and woodwork if necessary." During 1932 the project attracted 2,500 visitors. The center also funded the only organized children's playground for the black community in New Orleans and built a swimming pool. Additionally, it campaigned for safety, cleanliness, and beatification projects in poorer districts, such as having the local streets paved and refuse collected.[9]

The main focus of the Williams Center, however, was the general educational and moral instruction of the adult and child population, and for this purpose the volunteer teaching staff were mainly professional educators and college graduates. There were two full-time and one part-time paid staff and forty-nine female volunteers with, naturally, much crossover with NAACP membership and ideals. Mrs. Naomi K. Evans, executive secretary of the center, was a graduate of sociology from Fisk University, a qualified social worker, and was responsible for health and delinquency problems at the school. There were fifteen students of sociology from the University of New Orleans who volunteered in the center under a course credit scheme. These volunteers, entirely female, specialized in areas like "handwriting and story hour, . . . games, . . . band practice . . . [and] work with small boys." A further thirty-four volunteers were mainly college graduates, or were still at college, although there were also some housewives "assisting with sewing circles and bridge clubs." For example, Mrs. W. R. Adams, a housewife, organized "Young Peoples Bridge Clubs"; Miss Eunice Daniels, a student at New Orleans University, "instructs the toy band"; and Miss Helen Priestly, teacher at Lafon School, "drills the children's dramatic club." For adults there were a "Sewing and Mothers Club," prenatal clinics, home nursing supervision for pregnant women, and a "Better Baby Contest," which encouraged women to take their children regularly to health clinics. Miss Viola Dominique, a graduate of the Flint-Goodridge Hospital in New Orleans, was part of the scheme, although her work was cut out for her as she was the only nurse in New Orleans appointed to look after children in twenty-two black schools. She was an NAACP member throughout the 1920s.[10]

In a similar manner, the local PTAs' priority was to pursue a middle-class agenda of improving the lot of those in the community less fortunate than themselves. These groups defined education broadly, emphasizing virtue as well as knowledge. The East Baton Rouge Parish PTA during March 1933 held a large meeting in which its members, who were teachers and also NAACP members, dispensed domestic education to black women. Such topics taught to poorer women focused on homes, the family, and progressive ideas of the effects of environmental conditions on children. Mrs. Hazel S. King gave a group demonstration on better housing conditions, especially the kitchen, while Miss Irma Curry emphasized "correct furniture & furnishings for the home." Mrs. E. S. Burke gave the main talk on "How Homes Conditions May Affect the Child." The president of the PTA, Mrs. O. A. Powell, described the perfect domicile as not a "matter [of] how humble or pretentious the house, this counts for naught as a home unless love and understanding reign supreme."[11]

In the 1930s, domestic and moral education as a source of racial uplift began to include developing notions of black history. Teachers were enthusiastic to clearly define what black history was in the United States, with particular reference to Louisiana's cultural heritage. However, the concept of black history and its meaning for racial unity was not a straightforward matter. NAACP members and teachers in Louisiana during the 1930s saw social respectability as convergent with prevailing class and gender disparities. Educators saw this as part of their professional commitment for instilling racial pride and nurturing positive black images for their students. A knowledge of black history prepared students for life in segregated America, albeit with aspirations to equality and with a certain conception of their past. For example, the president of the New Orleans Negro Teachers' Association, Miss Myrtle Banks, declared during the annual celebration of the Emancipation Proclamation at St. Marks Baptist Church that the "True Emancipation of the Negro must come by his efforts through carefulness in rearing his children and remembering that his true friends are his own people."[12]

Clubs emerged in the 1930s to promote middle-class notions of interpreting black history and society. By the late 1930s New Orleans had a branch of the Association for the Study of Negro Life and History, with Miss Gertrude Green, a teacher at J. W. Hoffman High School, as its president. The Local History Association in the city instigated a National Negro History Week, February 5–12, 1939. The group enlisted the support of schools, churches, PTAs, and the Young Women's Christian Association (YWCA), and Gertrude Green again presided. Also teachers attended a forum at the Sylvania F. Williams Community Center on February 5, 1939, that posed the question: "Why Study the Negro in American History"?[13]

Similarly, the Texas Centennial Exposition of 1937 had "Exhibits of Negro Progress" in which displays were chosen by a committee at Dillard University in New Orleans composed mainly of women, many belonging to the NAACP. In the city Mrs. Mayme Osby Brown was on the Federal Commission on Negro Participation in the Texas Centennial, with Miss Maude Armstrong, principal of Dunbar Public School, and Miss Inez Labat, teacher at Albert Wicker High School, as advisers on what should be exhibited in the name of local black history. Exhibits chosen were a "fine hand embroidered quilt," a "collection of fine needlework," and a "Thesis from the graduate department" of Xavier University. However, the bulk of the exhibits were on the uplifting of black women's social standards by "showing progress of the Negroes in Handicraft . . . [especially the] work of Negro women who attend the home making classes at night in the public school buildings. Many unique pieces of knitting, embroidery, and crocheting." Black history in this context was firmly focused on the progress of the race and its middle-class acceptance of American social and moral values.[14]

During 1936 the New Orleans Colored Public Schools published a pamphlet on "A Tentative Approach to Negro History," by which it hoped to organize "a plan whereby facts of Negro life and history would be correlated with the regular history course throughout the Negro Public Schools." The committees for school grades one through four included many teachers who were NAACP members. On the first grade committee were members Miss Frances Lawless and Miss Maude Armstrong; second grade, Miss Alberta Burrell, Miss F. Lewis, and Miss A. L. Bauduit, who was the elementary principal at McDonogh School no. 6;

third grade, Miss Mildred Adderly, chair of the committee, Miss Naomi Jones, and Miss Fannie C. Williams. The fourth grade committee had many male teachers, showing the level where female educators were expected to plateau, although one woman, Miss Agnes Beauchamp, was a member. Of the twenty-one positions on the four committees NAACP members occupied twelve of them. Of the seventeen women on the committees, nine were NAACP members.[15]

The pamphlet proclaimed that if "we knew more about ourselves and our forefathers, there would be more pride, more respect for the race and for each other." The conclusions of the committees were vague on the specifics of what exactly black history was, especially in Louisiana, but they offered numerous examples of what ought not to be encouraged. The results showed a particular regard for *higher* European culture and language than for the poorer black experience. Firstly, there was to be no "dialect or slum materials. Be sure to omit dialect." While there was an expectation to "develop a love and respect for Negro Music" this was probably more for classical and religious music than contemporary jazz sounds. Indeed the address of the president of the Louisiana Congress of Parents and Teachers in 1939 specifically directed its colleagues to "foster proper music appreciation by purchase of classical records and sheet music. Establish bands in every school."[16]

"A Tentative Approach to Negro History" warned that "First Grade teachers should use their discretion in teaching the Negro National Anthem. In some situations it might be taught easily and in others it might be difficult." Why it was a difficult song to teach was not specified and can only be speculated upon. The committee could have been trying to avoid problems with the white school boards in a parish that may have seen black politics and racial pride infiltrating the schools and storing up trouble at some future event. However, the report does show that the school curriculum was controlled day to day by black teachers and that they were questioning and challenging the syllabus to provide more positive African American identities for their pupils. This was exactly what white authorities feared, and they may have asserted their influence if they were confronted with what they saw as militant instructors.[17]

Teachers' focus on fostering young people and children into a positive black identity also fit in with the general sphere of influence of women in a social reform capacity. A convention of the Louisiana Congress of Colored Parents and Teachers (LCCPT) during November 1939 in Alexandria saw its major focus of discussion being juvenile delinquency, particularly "broken homes, poor school facilities, [and an] absence of community planning." Furthermore, delegates also discussed eradicating adult illiteracy and plans for improved education that would lead to proper "citizenship." Mrs. Ida Nance Givens, teacher at Jeanes School in Baton Rouge, was "highly rated as progressive, active, alive and alert. Her Health Programs, Field Days, Seasonal Programs are interesting and educational." Mrs. Maggie D. Ringgold, also of Baton Rouge, was on the executive council of the Louisiana Colored Teachers' Association and president of the LCCPT; she advocated that each PTA unit in the state should "Investigate and publish the real status of the Negro child in Louisiana . . . Subject to each unit the idea of helping in a concret [sic] way some delinquent child in your town at once as well as beautifying grounds and school buildings . . . Foster a character building organization such as Boy Scouts, Girl Reserves, etc."[18]

Similarly, the New Orleans "Joseph A Hardin Playground Committee," an organization of NAACP members and teachers, also fought for a broad appreciation of educational issues facing the African American community, namely the moral and physical well-being of children. They helped finance free nurseries in the city, as "Hundreds of these little tots are presently roving the streets, making contacts that fit them for future delinquency and you . . . know [what] this means for their future and that of the community."[19]

One member of the Hardin committee and the New Orleans NAACP was Miss Fannie C. Williams, principal of the Valena C. Jones Jr. High School from 1921 until her retirement in 1954 and president of the American Teachers Association in 1930. Her full and varied career as a teacher and charity worker led to her appointment by President Herbert Hoover in 1930 to a White House Conference on the National Child Welfare Committee as assistant chairman on the subcommittee of the "Negro school child." In 1933 she was described by a teachers' journal as being a leader for her "Christian activities . . . Her personality inspires confidence. Soft spoken and quiet in manner, her influence is all the more effective because of the unobtrusive way in which it is exercised." Williams also opened the first black unit of the Girl Scouts in New Orleans at the Jones School, known as "Troup 99," and she was on the board of directors of the Girls Scouts of America.[20]

In 1946 *Louisiana Weekly* described Williams as an "educator, lover of children, builder of character, who by the quality of her personality, breathe [sic] of mind, in height of ideals, inspired thousands of New Orleans youth to useful lives and achievements." During the early 1940s Williams was to initiate a Parents Study Group, which addressed individual children's social and educational problems in the community and involved students' families in finding satisfactory resolutions to educational or behavioral problems. From 1921, in conjunction with the franchise pressure group, the 7th Ward Civic League, Williams petitioned the OPSB for a three-story brick building for her school and a playground as the original school had been blown down and flooded in 1915. By early 1928 the OPSB finally voted a quarter of a million dollars to the project. Furthermore, during World War II, Andrew Young, the 1960s civil rights leader, 1970s Congressman, and U.S. Ambassador to the United Nations from 1977 to 1979, remembered Williams bringing famous African American individuals, such as the singer Marian Anderson and boxer Joe Lewis, to the school to act as inspirational figures to her pupils.[21]

Like Williams, other teachers forged social networks and political alliances for causes close to their hearts and also joined organizations such as the NAACP to further opportunities for the entire black community. Of central importance to such networks were teachers' organizations and unions on a parish and statewide level. Virtually all of the teachers in the East Baton Rouge Teachers Association during the 1930s belonged to the NAACP and were active members. Miss Tracey E. Baker, on the Baton Rouge NAACP executive committee in 1939 and the early 1940s, was a teacher and financial secretary for the Teachers Association. The president of the Teachers Association was Miss Irma Curry, a regular NAACP member in the 1930s. Other members were Mrs. Hazel S. King, secretary, and Miss Hattie D. Scott, assistant secretary, who were also NAACP activists. Furthermore NAACP members Mrs. H. H. Huggins and Mrs. Ida Nance-Givens were on the Baton Rouge Parent Teacher Council. Huggins was president of the state PTA in 1939, while Nance-Givens chaired the executive committee. Also, NAACP member Helen Andrews Nelson was a school principal, and served two years as secretary of the State Teachers Association.[22]

While teachers were adept at using such professional networks to the advantage of the NAACP and other charitable organizations, they were expected to use their influence with their students to the benefit of race uplift. The NAACP saw teachers as leaders that could instill black youth with racial pride and an integrationist vision of U.S. society, or at least argue for equality within the current segregated system. Within the NAACP teachers could recruit students to the youth councils and organize and manage the groups. As early as 1921 the NAACP saw that for its own long-term future and for the political and social success of their aims, it was crucial for local branches to establish a "comprehensive system of work for juniors" to train "children in ideals of the Association." Association leaders believed that women had an almost exclusive appreciation of how young people should be organized alongside "the wisdom of the more experienced members of the [senior] branch." Those teachers who organized youth councils were given much latitude in the setting-up and running of such auxiliaries. But the onus was on these women to educate young black people into the program of the NAACP and encourage them to join the organization to battle for better prospects for the entire group.[23]

In June 1938 Mrs. D. J. Dupuy of Baton Rouge, a teacher, achieved some momentum in creating a youth council with the additional input of two schoolteachers, Mrs. R. Stanley Wilson and Mr. Freddye A. Pipe. Wilson and Pipe encouraged their pupils to join the NAACP, and the educators were counted as integral members of the youth chapter. It was common that teachers who were NAACP members advocated to their classes that they too join. So successful were some of them in recruiting youths that a local teacher in Lake Charles, Miss Lillian B. Carline, continued to supervise a junior branch in 1942 even when the town ceased to have a functioning adult chapter. In 1945 schoolteacher Mrs. Mildred C. Byrd was the senior adviser to a newly organized youth council in New Orleans. Byrd sat on the executive committee of the senior branch and was also the wife of the city's NAACP president in 1944, Daniel E. Byrd. Other aspects of an adviser's activities included wider social and charitable experiences. Miss Hazel A. Augustine, who was adviser to the New Orleans youth division from 1937 to 1939, was also "group work secretary" for the city's YWCA. There was much crossover with NAACP women teachers and the YWCA's membership, such as Mrs. C. C. Dejoie, YWCA treasurer, and Miss Myrtle Banks, who was also the president of the New Orleans Negro Teachers' Association.[24]

In most branches youth councils took until the mid-1930s to emerge as identifiable and practical entities, and their success was largely due to the persistence of individual women. Monroe's youth branch was the work of Mrs. H. L. McClanahan, who was also chair of the youth division in the annual membership drives, thus capitalizing on the supposed divisions of both gender and youth and the subsequent competition between various groups. The role of youth adviser was a prominent one, one that both the local and national organizations saw as pivotal. At the proposed first national youth conference of the NAACP in 1936 the national office implored Mrs. McClanahan to attend: "We simply must have Monroe at the Conference; as their advisor you must be there." McClanahan was instructed to head a youth division to the conference, while propagating the NAACP message along the way: "You might plan a motor caravan bringing a carload of youth delegates from Monroe. You could make a tour of the churches taking after offerings to help secure funds; you might sell tags; and also ask for a loan from the senior branch, payable in the fall." It is unlikely, however, that the Monroe youth council undertook the journey to the Baltimore conference, considering the various obstacles along the way.[25]

Similar demands fell on other youth council advisers in the region, although traveling long distances across the United States was not convenient or financially practical for many of them. In 1938 the president of the Lake Charles youth council, Miss Maude Kane, informed Juanita Jackson that they would not be sending delegates to the California Youth Conference, as they were unable to raise enough money for the trip. The onus fell on the female youth advisers to secure funds and inspire enthusiasm for such excursions. An adviser had multiple roles: organizer, educator, treasurer, motivator, and mediator with the adult branch. So although the youth leader was expected to conform to gender norms, the various tasks allowed her to escape some stereotypes.[26]

Some teachers did pursue a more radical agenda for education in Louisiana, which opened them up to accusations of communism, and not just because of their civil rights affiliation. During World War II the Federal Bureau of Investigation (FBI) had two suspected subversives in the New Orleans NAACP branch under surveillance. One was Mrs. Noelie Cunningham, who was on the branch executive committee in 1944 and 1945. The other suspect was unnamed. Cunningham was "the only known member" of the Louisiana Progressive Educational Association (LPEA), which was considered radical at the time for having unorthodox views on the education of children.[27]

Formed officially in 1919, the Progressive Educational Association existed before this date as a broadly liberal concept advocated by the Columbia University philosopher John Dewey. The group promoted ideas of child-centered learning, racial understanding, democracy, citizenship, and social justice. These concerns were a response to school curricula driven by principles of efficiency management and rote memorization. A progressive education would, PEA members believed, instill human values and good moral habits into children that would equip them for a rapidly changing industrial society. However, so radical did these views seem to the establishment, especially the advocating of national economic planning, that the group was attacked for being wholly collectivist and undermining beliefs in private enterprise.[28]

Most Louisiana teachers remained within the boundaries of mainstream ideas of education, albeit advocating greater focus on black history. However, those who were active in the NAACP were, in fact, striking directly at the heart of white power. They aimed to achieve equality between the races not just in education but also within the American political and economic system. Better education, they believed, would inevitably lead to equal opportunities in the work place and greater social status and income for African Americans generally. However, dual membership in the LPEA and NAACP proved too much for the FBI, and Noelie Cunningham was branded a suspected communist sympathizer.

As mentioned above, the NAACP worked to equalize black and white teachers' salaries in order to attract orthodox teachers to the organization, and in Louisiana the campaign was a major impetus for the group's state conference. The Association hired Miss Edith Jones, a "discharged Plaquemine Louisiana School Teacher," on a full-time basis "to do organizational work throughout the State" on the issues recorded in the "N.A.A.C.P. Citizens' Committee" manifesto of 1945, "The Right to Vote." On education the document was unequivocal. The ballot would bring "adequate schooling" by enforcing equal "educational facilities and opportunities." It did not advocate integrated schools, primarily because black schools were seen as an area of pride and social cohesion within communities, as well as a source of employment for black professionals. Some blacks perceived integration as a threat to the world they had built up to shield their children, for a time, from racism. The Citizens' Committee manifesto, however, appealed to black teachers' professional interests by arguing for black scholars to have a "chance to attend medical & law schools at home" (meaning within Louisiana state borders along the rules of the "separate but equal" provision rather than having to study outside the state), to "serve internships at state hospitals, . . . a full curriculum, . . . decent school boards . . . [and a] full nine month [academic year.]" This was plainly a battle for equality of separate institutions rather than integration. Orleans Parish at this time spent only $30.84 on its black pupils, compared with $62.50 for its white schoolchildren. However, there was far greater funding deprivation in other parishes. Between 1936 and 1937 St. Martin Parish spent a mere $2.16 for each of its black students. Equality of teachers' salaries was seen as a step toward greater equality of black educational funding and status.[29]

The immediate issue concerning the equalization case, beyond organizational and financial constraints, was to find a suitable and willing teacher who would put his or her name forward for a court case against the local school board. Most, of course, feared losing their jobs and suffering other social reprisals. The progress made on such cases was invariably slow, one of the reasons being that a number of NAACP branches were having contentious elections over the pace of racial change in their respective cities, particularly in New Orleans. The equalization suits across the parishes in Louisiana were directed by A. P. Tureaud, New Orleans NAACP attorney, the Louisiana Colored Teachers Association (LCTA), Donald Jones, prominent NAACP member and later a field secretary for the organization, and the NAACP Legal Defense and Education Fund under Thurgood Marshall, special counsel.[30]

The major case for the equalization of teachers' salaries in Louisiana brought against the OPSB in 1941 was *McKelpin v. Orleans Parish School Board*. Federal judge Wayne G. Borah's decision in June 1942 to support the plaintiff set in motion a whole set of cases across Louisiana. However, it also brought continued NAACP politicking with the authorities as the OPSB attempted to mitigate the decision, or at least delay it. Furthermore, teachers had to confront the problems of having merit tests imposed on them to deflect the equalization decision, which would have found a way around the legal case by pseudoscientific methods. The next seven years saw the NAACP filing cases in other parishes and attempting to challenge the obfuscation of the school boards throughout Louisiana.[31]

Before the *McKelpin* decision, black teachers across the South made 61 percent of a white teacher's salary. In Louisiana the situation was much below this baleful average. In 1940 white teachers in the state were annually paid an average of $1,331.88, whereas black teachers received $558.81, under 42 percent that paid to whites. An Iberville Parish white teacher earned $1,749 for a nine-month term, $194.33 per month, while black teachers only received $637 for a seven- or eight-month term, or $91 per month for the seven-month term. In Natchitoches Parish a white teacher during 1941 was paid a mere $1,080.78 a year, but their black counterparts received a paltry $367.09. By far the worst was St. John the Baptist Parish, where blacks were paid only $288.75 compared with $1,145.11 for white teachers. By 1944, due to the *McKelpin* case, black teachers' salaries increased by 50 percent over their 1940 levels, although this was mainly due to Orleans Parish, home to 12 percent of the state's black teachers. It took legal pressure from teachers in every parish to force local education boards to eventually accept the ruling.[32]

One of the most publicized teacher cases in the state concerned Eula Mae Lee during 1944. Lee volunteered under the NAACP scheme to attempt to equalize her salary in Kenner Colored School in Jefferson Parish. A. P. Tureaud duly represented Lee and was immediately confronted with the school board protesting that they were not against higher salaries for black teachers, though not necessarily equalization with white teachers, but that the budget for the academic year 1942 to 1943 did not allow for such expenditure. Indeed it was due to such attitudes that the president of the LCTA, J. K. Haynes declared, "Many of our teachers are leaving the profession [and] going to defense areas and other high salaried positions due to the inability to make a living wage teaching. This tremendous migration will render an effective school program impossible next session."[33]

Such attitudes struck at the core of the education issue for black people, especially teachers and NAACP members. While the ballot was necessary to secure full citizenship, it was education that would uplift the entire group. Indeed, it was civilization itself that would suffer in Louisiana, as Haynes described it, if black teachers were not valued both in financial recompense and professional equality. At the same time, civil rights leaders had to try and reassure teachers that equal wages for black educators would not mean the lowering of white incomes by showing that it had not been so in other states.[34]

A Citizens' Committee for Improving Educational Opportunities in Jefferson Parish was organized, under the auspices of the statewide NAACP, to garner greater teacher support and financial backing for the Eula Mae Lee case. The committee contained members of the New Orleans NAACP branch, of course, including Mrs. Noelie Cunningham as its secretary. From 1943 the LCTA announced that it would finance all the NAACP's education cases in the state. However, the attempt to encourage teachers to start lawsuits in their own parishes met with a further obstacle when Eula Mae Lee was dismissed from her teaching post in August 1944 for "wilful neglect of duty." The exact charge was that Lee had been "tardy 12 times," though on what occasions and in what manner was not specified. While this may have deterred some teachers from filing suit against their employers, Lee's case continued through the court process.[35]

Other teachers continued to protest the inequality in their wages, such as in Ouachita and Rapides Parishes. Mrs. Ozenia Secrease, elementary teacher at Tim Tippit School, Monroe; Clementine Peevy, elementary teacher at Richwood School, Monroe; and H. P. Williams of Alexandria all signed equality of salary petitions to their local education boards. Since its inception in 1941 the Alexandria NAACP branch had been sending contributions to New Orleans specifically for the teachers' salary case. In Iberville Parish, eleven probationary teachers were discharged when they undertook an equalization of salaries case under the guidance of the NAACP, but fortunately were all rehired in other parishes.[36]

Meanwhile, Eula Mae Lee moved to Washington, DC, obtained a war job, and became patriotically engaged in the Seventh War Bond Drive in the city. She was also a captain in the American Red Cross Drive of 1945. She kept a correspondence going with A. P. Tureaud as to how her case in Louisiana was going but was otherwise not deeply involved in the legal process. By July 1948 Lee's case was settled by "consent decree" by Judge Herbert Christenberry. Tureaud informed Mrs. Eula Mae Lee Brown (she had married in the interim) that the Louisiana courts had ordered the state to discontinue discrimination in teachers' salaries, and she was offered her old teaching job back from September 1948. Furthermore, she was awarded back pay from the 1947 to 1948 academic year equaling $1,791.[37]

By 1948 teachers' salaries across the state were finally equalized at the political instigation of Governor Earl K. Long. Between 1943 and 1948 there had been a dozen lawsuits against local parish school boards in attempt to enforce the *McKelpin* decision, and it had become an obvious losing battle for the education authorities to continue resisting.[38]

The success of the teachers' salaries case highlights the practical and ideological agenda that was at work in the NAACP at both national and local levels. These issues appealed to a professional and well-structured body of teachers that desired to raise educational standards in the black community. In getting black teachers to join and support the NAACP, and by inculcating black youth into a civil rights tradition, it was believed that most black people would eventually support a vision of integration. As a result, the NAACP saw an empowered community, being suitably educated and politically motivated, that could eventually defeat segregation in the United States.

By appealing to teachers the NAACP was attempting to converse with a wider localized constituency, one with which educators had intimate contact. Meanwhile, the black community could tangibly appreciate education as a vital resource in achieving greater group benefits and specifically for their own children's economic and civic prospects. Female teachers, according to the gender and class concepts of the time, could communicate with young people and children and transform black society into a morally healthy and intellectually enlightened group, which would eventually win them social and political acceptance and equality in mainstream white America. In this way, black female teachers were the epitome of the NAACP's "local leaders" that shared their core organizational values and could utilize their education and parochial knowledge for the Association to the advancement of a civil rights agenda.[39]

However, not all African Americans wished to pursue wholesale integration with the white community. Many saw benefits in maintaining facilities separate from white people. Indeed, for many black teachers, separate schools meant an obvious career path and a high level of status within a community, whereas integration of facilities suggested an uncertain professional future. The two-pronged attack by the NAACP on education, of equal salaries and facilities, would ultimately progress to an attack on segregation, yet such a plan did not resonate wholly with all teachers and parents. Either integration *or* equalization could motivate black teachers to join the NAACP and its campaigns, and it was more likely to be the latter for most in the profession.

The NAACP's complex use of education as an attack on racist America was a way of drawing teachers and educators into the civil rights movement, as well as being a committed philosophical stance of social equality and, later, for integration. As Daniel E. Byrd, NAACP assistant field secretary, observed in 1948, "Only a handful of our people want integration. And it is God's valiant minority who must war on the insidious evil."[40]

FIVE

LEADERS WHO PERSEVERE
Elected Officials

Select a campaign committee and select for chairman (if possible) a prominent person, who has a following and who will take the responsibility seriously. Preferably a woman—for they have a deeper sense of something-or-other than men.

N the years up to 1945, women were elected to very few positions in Louisiana's NAACP branches, certainly not proportional to their membership numbers, and none became presidents or treasurers. Women served mainly as vice-presidents, secretaries, and assistant-secretaries. New Orleans, as the cosmopolitan center of Louisiana, had the most stable branch over this period and had marginally wider avenues for women to enter the elected hierarchy of the organization, although within the parameters of traditional female roles. Baton Rouge and Monroe had only one female elective officer each throughout the 1930s and early 1940s. In Baton Rouge this was the redoubtable Mrs. D. J. Dupuy, who served as vice-president from 1929 to 1934; as secretary, 1935 to 1939 and 1942 to 1944; and briefly as assistant-secretary during 1941. Because of their administrative skills and social and professional links, women played vital leadership roles in the Louisiana NAACP branches, well beyond what their elected titles suggested.[1]

In the Monroe branch, the only woman to be elected as an officer was longtime NAACP member Mrs. H. W. Johnson, who served as vice-president from 1936 to 1938. Johnson's social and familial networks gave her access to this elected position. Her other official activities included being on the branch executive committee and chairing a special emergency committee in 1932 that raised funds for the NAACP central office. She was also an active Christmas seals seller, and was one of the managers of the membership drive of November 1935, chairing the women's division in that campaign. Johnson's role as vice-president, therefore, reflected her high-profile activism in the chapter and branch members' estimation of her work. Furthermore, the Johnson family was central to the city's NAACP organization when membership numbers were restrained by the Depression. The branch's 1939 membership roster includes Mrs. H. W. Johnson's entire household: herself; her husband, Dr. F. W.; a daughter, Miss H. C.; and, in all likelihood, a son and daughter-in-law, Henry and Mary. Additionally, at a time when membership was generally low certain families and individuals became fundamental to branch strength and coherence as officers and committee members.[2]

Several women were also vice-presidents of the New Orleans branch, albeit occupying the post for short terms. Like Mrs. Johnson, their backgrounds suggest that they were central to the NAACP as individuals who held broad community and social interests during times of fluctuating membership numbers. For instance, Miss F. A. Lewis was vice-president for just one year, 1921, although she was to hold regular membership of the NAACP throughout the 1920s and 1930s. Lewis was an elementary teacher at Macarty School in New Orleans during this period and was, as expected, involved in other professional organizations and philanthropic causes in the city. In particular, she served on the city's Parent Teacher Association (PTA), helped with voter registration drives, and participated in a collective effort by teachers to promote a form of black history via a New Orleans Colored Public School committee. Also she was heavily involved in working groups that sought to raise money for the W. E. & Frances Roberson Memorial Home for Colored Juvenile Delinquents under the auspices of the Tulane Avenue Baptist Church and other church denominations, which were mainly made up of NAACP members concerned for child welfare. The other two female vice-presidents of the New Orleans NAACP branch were also committed educators; Miss Thelma S. Shelby, who held the post in 1939, was a research assistant at Dillard University, and Miss Katie Wickham, 1941, was a teacher.[3]

The reasons branches elected women to serve as vice-presidents varied in the cities. The question remains, however, how far could it be said that such a role was a decision-making office, rather than just a symbol of status or respect? According to official descriptions, the vice-president served as a deputy of a branch president; in essence, a substitute in case the president was incapacitated or needed to delegate certain responsibilities. It would appear that women could be elected to such a post without necessarily infringing on the male prerogative of authority, and certainly not to be independent of it. However, to be elected to the post was also an acknowledgement of the importance of women to branch operations and achievements. Their activities took place essentially on two levels: the personal and the collective. For example, Florence Lewis was an important link with New Orleans' black schools and its teachers, and with students and their families whom she could recruit to NAACP campaigns. Yet it could be said that the office of vice-president was never a position of central authority as it was virtually always superseded by other posts, such as the president and secretary. It primarily appears to have been an office that reflected and acknowledged community esteem in an individual. Women became vice-president based on their established position in the community rather than for any new agenda they took up when fleetingly in the post.[4]

In New Orleans only three women held the office of vice-president during a twenty-five-year period, but for only one year each. Elsewhere in the state, however, women served longer terms. Besides Mrs. H. W. Johnson in Monroe, Mrs. D. J. Dupuy held the position for five years in Baton Rouge. The difference with New Orleans was specifically due to the types of branches in the other two cities. Smaller chapters, such as Monroe and Baton Rouge, gave women opportunities to establish themselves in selected roles, usually within the gender norms of the times and invariably without allowing them to dominate or direct the branch. Women's indispensability in bureaucratic roles was partly due to the generally low membership count, yet it also corresponded to their individual commitment and activism, often through their ability to utilize community and teaching connections. In New Orleans membership numbers fluctuated but were substantially higher than any other branch in the region, and the branch experienced a rapid turnover of members year to year during the 1920s and 1930s in particular. At the same time, elected posts in the Crescent City also underwent a quicker turnover of personnel than elsewhere in the minor elected positions.

However, when women wielded some responsibilities as vice-presidents these were not wholly different from the duties of secretaries in the local NAACP organizations: being branch coordinators and campaign workers in traditional female areas, such as membership drives and fundraising, and running the local office on a day-to-day basis. Indeed it would appear that the office of secretary had greater organizational importance than that of vice-president. The deputy role appeared to be only what its occupant could make of it and was, in the main, a minor post. For Johnson of Monroe it did become a significant bureaucratic role but for others, namely, in New Orleans, it was a brief placement of status and symbolic acknowledgment for community activity and networking. This also seems to be the case for male vice-presidents; indeed, the status associated with the post seemed a broad incentive for both sexes.

The office of secretary was the most vital post that women filled in NAACP branches. While it may have seemed at face value a stereotypical role, it was nevertheless an effective position from which to organize and view branch affairs. New Orleans was to have four female secretaries and four assistant secretaries between 1921 and 1944. A number of the smaller branches that arose throughout Louisiana in the 1940s also followed this pattern by having female secretaries, such as the Lake Charles, Independence, and St. Jackson chapters.[5]

Women's intricate networking between a multitude of charitable, political, and business organizations was to relate to their elected positions in the NAACP hierarchy. A good example of business links and the New Orleans NAACP is Camille Harrison, who was assistant secretary of the city's branch from 1936 to 1939 and a stenographer and saleslady at the James E. Gayle & Sons Publishing Company. James Gayle was a longtime supporter of the New Orleans NAACP, sitting on its executive committee (1918) and serving as the branch secretary (1920–1921), treasurer (1932), and president (1934–1937). Gayle always utilized his female assistants from his publishing company, such as Harrison, as either secretaries or assistant secretaries during his long tenure with the branch. During World War I, Charlotte Richards, who worked as assistant secretary at Gayle & Dunn's African-American Books, was to be closely involved in the branch, serving on the executive committee. Both Richards and Harrison were enacting a practice of a professional personal secretary, which came with the expectant role of charitable organizer.[6]

Likewise, James Gayle's business partner's daughter, Miss A. V. Dunn, was assistant secretary at the chapter in the early 1920s, during Gayle's own term as secretary, which suggests that family connections were, unsurprisingly, a contributing factor to elective involvement in a local branch. Alberta Dunn held the secretarial post in 1924 and 1925 while her father and Gayle were key financial sponsors and social contributors to the branch. Dunn's own career path was comparable to that of other women in the Louisiana NAACP. She had been a student at the University of Chicago, had returned to New Orleans to become an educator in 1918, and was principal at the Macarty School between 1925 and 1928.[7]

Another secretary of the New Orleans branch, Mrs. D. J. Guidry, who held the post from 1925 to 1932, gave credibility to her position by being a relatively high-profile activist and by undertaking various other roles in the branch. Guidry's secretarial responsibilities were necessarily bureaucratic and conventional: keeping membership rolls and organizing the branch into a manageable and workable group. However, Guidry was also a visible speaker at public meetings, listed on NAACP flyers along with the president, George Lucas, and other high-ranking officials. She attended national conferences and undertook some bookkeeping assignments for the branch. In early 1926 Mrs. Guidry reported to the national office that the New Orleans branch had collected an impressive $4,192.48 for the national segregation fight. While women generally did not serve as branch treasurers, there was latitude for a secretary to exercise some control over finances and its reporting to the national office. Indeed from 1937 the NAACP branch constitution required a secretary's signature to validate expenditure alongside the branch president's approval.[8]

Like other high-profile members of the branch, Guidry was active in both charity and reform work. The New Orleans branch often reconstituted itself under the guise of other organizational epithets in order to enact diverse benevolent works. For instance, Guidry's name was printed on a list of contributors on a brochure of the popular charity, W. E. & Frances Roberson Memorial Home for Colored Juvenile Delinquents, in November 1930, alongside her husband, George, who was also a member of the NAACP. In fact the list reads as a comprehensive register of NAACP members both male and female in the city. The upbringing of black children, of course, was a familiar subject for middle-class civil rights activists in their pursuit of uplifting the entire African American community into being reputable Americans worthy of their citizenship.[9]

Similarly, Mrs. Oneida Brown, secretary of the New Orleans branch for two years from 1934, was highly influential in African American society due to her affiliation with the fraternal order the Catholic Knights of Peter Claver. Masonic lodges were an essential element to the NAACP and to middle-class women's social lives. The Catholic

Knights of Peter Claver, which organized the same year as the NAACP, was highly influential in the New Orleans branch during the 1920s and 1930s, in particular due to its crossover membership and financial donations. This was a traditional fraternal and benevolent society that provided welfare for members' families in hardship and undertook charity and diocesan work. In 1922 the Ladies' Auxiliary of the Knights of Peter Claver was organized. It became an important aspect of daily life for Catholics in the South, particularly as the national headquarters of the group was in New Orleans.[10]

The first national meeting of the Ladies' Auxiliary of the Knights of Peter Claver was in Galveston, Texas, in August 1926, with Mrs. A. R. Aubry of Lake Charles elected as the first Supreme Lady. Its charter proclaimed that the organization was to promote "such social and intellectual intercourse among its members as shall be desirable and proper." The purpose of the "Auxiliary is to promote Friendship, Unity and Christian Charity." The links with such groups as the NAACP was important, not just for its financial contribution to the new civil rights group in Louisiana but also for its important organizational contribution. For example, Mrs. Oneida Brown was a long-time member of the Knights of Peter Claver, where she was to learn much of her practical organizational skills, and she later became the national secretary of the Ladies' Auxiliary. Brown first appeared on the NAACP membership rolls in 1928, and besides being the branch secretary was also elected to its executive committee in 1938. She was also involved in the local NAACP antilynching campaigns by giving public lectures and, in 1934, Brown was part of a line-up with fellow Association members, and national field officer William Pickens, advocating federal antilynching legislation at the New Orleans' Masonic Pythian Temple.[11]

As women had become trained in society work through the professionalized networks of the National Association of Colored Women (NACW) and Masonic orders, the NAACP itself was to become a valuable training ground for the middle classes. Women such as Mrs. Oneida Brown and Charlotte Richards were vital assets in establishing a civil rights tradition in the South from their own organizational experiences. Subsequently, other women benefited from such instruction and utilized NAACP work as a preparation for their future involvement in social and professional networks. Young women, such as Alberta Dunn, could join the NAACP and become fully trained in organizational techniques that they could use in their teaching careers and in further charity work. Consequently, the early civil rights movement became an important social and organizational lynchpin for a new generation of African Americans. In so being the NAACP was important to the continuity of an African American organizing tradition of racial uplift and became an integral part of New Orleans' social network system during the 1920s, one through which many middle-class women would pass at some time in their social and administrative education.[12]

While branch officers performed the everyday work of the local NAACP, the executive committee was the official decision-making body of a chapter. The Federal Bureau of Investigation (FBI) in 1944 recognized that the New Orleans NAACP was controlled by a small cadre of its members, specifically those on the executive committee: "[The NAACP] is a large negro group in New Orleans . . . [and] is an old-time negro organization in Louisiana. It enjoys greater respect than any other group among the negroes and also has a larger membership. The membership at the present time is claimed to be about 5,000. Naturally this is not a closely knit organization and the policies are controlled and dominated by one [of] a few people namely, the officers and the Executive Committee which is composed of twenty-five members." Such an elitist command structure was illustrated by the November meeting of the executive committee at the Autocrat Club, which the FBI described as "a social and pleasure club house owned by a member of the better class negroes in New Orleans."[13]

In other cities of Louisiana a small number of loyal and active members likely coordinated and pushed official NAACP policy, rather than it being a broad democratic assembly of all local members. It is difficult to precisely detail the mechanics of the executive committee and the role of individual members during its meetings, although membership was decidedly male dominated. Committee chairs (as well as branch officers) sat on the main executive committee, but women who were in these positions were associated, for the most part, with traditional female occupations and roles. For example, during 1925 in New Orleans, Mrs. F. A. Lewis chaired the schools committee, Miss A. V. Dunn headed the teachers committee, Mrs. M. T. Wells organized nursing work, and Mrs. Ida Tropaz and Mrs. Nancy Johnson were responsible for branch links with women's organizations. It would seem that these committees were associated with so-called female traits—education, healing, and social organizing.[14]

In New Orleans during the early 1940s there were increased numbers of women on the executive committees. This reflected women's high standing in the membership generally and within the broader community, as well the importance of their networks. In particular, teachers were well represented in the committees due to the NAACP focus on obtaining equal wages for black and white teachers. Local branch officers, especially from New Orleans, of course played important roles in the emerging statewide organization. Edna St. Cyr was on the New Orleans branch executive committee from 1941 to 1943, and was also secretary of the state conference in 1944. Educator Mrs. Mildred C. Byrd, wife of Daniel Byrd, executive secretary of the New Orleans branch, was on the branch executive committee and on the state board of directors from 1943 to 1944. Also on the state conference executive committee were several other women: Mrs. Naomi Parnell (1943–1944) and Mrs. J. Garner (1944), both from New Orleans, and Mrs. Atholia Ladd Lute from Lake Charles, who served as secretary from 1943 to 1946. In this respect women continued in their characteristic female roles as secretaries and organizers, reinforced by the attention on teachers' salary cases, which put women's professional and ideological world at the heart of the civil rights struggle.[15]

However, elsewhere in the state, women were not significantly represented on executive committees. Baton Rouge had no women elected directly to its executive committee until 1936. In Monroe only three women sat on the committee prior to 1945. During 1936, Mrs. H. L. McClanahan was an honorary member only, and it took until 1939 for her to get elected to the executive committee. This was due to her influence with the branch youth council, which was recognized as being essential work for the chapter. She was accepted on the executive committee in a purely honorary position, however, probably both because her work with young people was seen as a female role and because it was felt that this junior division ought to be conjoined, albeit subserviently, to the main body of the chapter.[16]

Existing records of branch executive committee meetings clearly show that they were not always held regularly. Branch meetings tended, on average, to be held every month, as expected, but executive committee meetings were far less regular. Only in New Orleans were NAACP branch guidelines practiced faithfully, probably due to its large membership numbers. In other parts of Louisiana decision-making concentrated in the hands of the small numbers of regular members who attended branch meetings and undertook civil rights work.

For example, in Alexandria during 1944 there were only five executive committee meetings, compared to fifteen branch meetings, and the general decisions seem to have fallen to regular and committed officers. Indeed, decision-making was so concentrated in the Alexandria branch that a protest committee was set up to inform the national office of its problems: "We have no real Executive Committee, it is true a group meet[s] at various times[, and] in the meeting some are members of the executive committee, and some are not (Just a few persons are called)." In the absence of a functioning or regular executive committee it became the responsibility of branch officers and committee chairpersons to undertake the bulk of administrative and managerial work in a chapter, and in Alexandria it fell to Miss Georgia M. Johnson to lead the branch through her chairmanship of the legal and redress committee (see Chapter 6).[17]

Likewise, in Baton Rouge during 1938 the branch held twelve branch meetings and four executive committee meetings. Although these were regular throughout the year, the burden of evaluating the needs and direction of branch activities fell to dedicated members who attended the branch gatherings and the officers, such as president and secretary. Executive committees were meant for broad matters, such as deciding when to hold a membership drive or implement specific polices, whereas the officers and committee chairpersons had to react to specific conditions in their cities and cope with all the administrative decisions.[18]

In this decision-making structure, women were leaders because of their administrative skills and social and professional links, which their elected or official designations only hinted at. Mrs. D. J. Dupuy of Baton Rouge is one woman whose career typifies the experience of the majority of women elected to leadership positions in the Louisiana NAACP. They worked for the organization in its daily routines and campaigning even while they were, in sociologist Daniel C. Thompson's words, "unalterably resigned to let men get the headlines." Dupuy is the perfect illustration of what historian Belinda Robnett terms a female "community bridge leader" who was "able to cross the boundaries between the public life of a movement organization and the private spheres of adherents and potential constituents" and recruit "men as formal leaders" to the civil rights movement.[19]

The NAACP in Louisiana's state capital had a history dating back to 1919, although the branch did not become well established until a decade later, when it was kept alive by the work of Mrs. D. J. Dupuy. Along with the branch president, Benjamin J. Stanley, Dupuy gave the Association in Baton Rouge a secure foundation from which to confront racism and helped forge a modern tradition of civil rights in the city. It is difficult to envisage any stable branch in Baton Rouge without Dupuy's confident organizational leadership over fifteen years of service, first as vice-president (1929–1934), then as secretary (1935–1939; 1942–1944), and briefly as assistant secretary (1941).

Mrs. Dupuy was a music teacher and highly committed member of the NAACP. In fact, she was the only elected woman officer of the Baton Rouge branch between 1929 and 1944. She appears to have undertaken much of the chapter's organizational and motivational work, and she dominated the branch organization in whichever post she held. Throughout Dupuy's service, Benjamin Stanley, insurance agent and chancellor of Castle Hall Ajax Lodge of the Knights of Pythias, served as branch president (from 1929 until the 1950s), providing stability and authority to the chapter over these decades.[20]

Dupuy's role reveals how women were perceived within the NAACP branches in Louisiana. She managed the Baton Rouge branch extremely efficiently and, in the main, used the gender stereotypes of the time to her advantage, using these expectations to dominate the bureaucratic leadership. Dupuy, therefore, conformed to the prevailing standards expected of organizational women and generally assumed a background approach to her work, with wide influence within the Baton Rouge branch alongside full cooperation with its president, Benjamin Stanley. In working within the gender expectations of her time and place, Dupuy is representative of the early civil rights female activists.

Dupuy and Stanley undoubtedly worked together as a symbiotic team. The president displayed all the signs of outward leadership and had a strong public presence, and Dupuy coordinated branch minutiae and organized the rank-and-file membership. She often worked without the president's explicit knowledge. During September 1944 attorney A. P. Tureaud of the New Orleans NAACP branch was surprised by Benjamin Stanley's lack of knowledge of Dupuy's entreaty that he visit the state capital and deal with a certain legal case. The case in question involved the negligence of the school board of East Baton Rouge Parish to provide transportation for black children of Istrouma, Louisiana, to get to school. Tureaud stated that he "was surprised to learn that Stanley knew nothing about the request coming from Mrs. Dupuy." Stanley did not appear to have found this a usurpation of his long-standing position and was, it seems, happy that Dupuy undertook the bulk of the organizational work at her own initiative.[21]

Mrs. Dupuy's work for the Baton Rouge branch was central to its effective running. As William Pickens, NAACP field secretary, wrote to her in 1937, "Any such work that succeeds at all, does so because of a small number of leaders who persevere, like you, and, perhaps, the half dozen or so who help you."[22] Such an appreciation by the central office of a small number of local activists in the smaller branches in the Deep South further emphasizes Dupuy's vital role. Indeed, her official designation did not seem to practically change her day-to-day work, and there was much consistency in her activities during her fifteen years at the Baton Rouge NAACP. The move from vice-president to secretary in 1935 reflected the true role Dupuy undertook: manager of the branch. Officials at the central office gave credit for the development and strength of the chapter to Dupuy. The NAACP national director of branches, Robert Bagnall, whom Dupuy had entertained during his visit to the city in 1929, expressly regarded her role as a "leadership" position, alongside her "fellow-officers," which enabled the branch to "become one of the strong units of the Association."[23]

Dupuy's official relegation to assistant secretary in 1941 was a result of the political domination of men in the branch at the end of the 1930s, when branch membership was also rising. Horatio Thompson joined the Baton Rouge branch in 1939 and soon became its secretary. Thompson was a graduate of Louisiana's public black college, Southern University, and was a highly respected local businessman who owned several service stations; he also was a property developer in the city's black districts. Thompson proved himself immediately by undertaking the grueling task of chairing the May 1939 membership drive. Mrs. Dupuy was impressed with the campaign and praised Thompson to the national office as "a very wide awake chairman . . . who shows signs of a real campaign." The membership roster more than doubled from the previous year and was the largest for the branch to date, standing at 254 people.[24]

However, the leap in membership also heralded the start of internal maneuvering for leadership places, although it was not the protracted affair that plagued the New Orleans branch at this time. Certain long-time members declared their despair at the internal politicking at the Baton Rouge chapter, and Mr. H. Horne Huggins, chairman of the executive committee, left for New Orleans to do a postgraduate course. By Christmas 1939 many of the elective positions of the branch had changed hands. Stanley remained as president, and the thankless position of treasurer remained with long-time member, Mr. P. A. Washington. However, the newer entrepreneurial members had apparently taken over the running of the branch, and Horatio Thompson supplanted Mrs. Dupuy as secretary.[25]

Part of this contest over official posts may have been tied to the constitutional expansion of the role of secretary in 1937. This expansion was to "aid, coordinate and integrate the work of the several committees and divisions" and, significantly, in "conjunction with the President, to sign requisitions for disbursements from the branch treasury and to maintain a file of receipts." The new financial responsibilities made the post more appealing to men. In New Orleans, as in Baton Rouge, women lost the secretarial monopoly from 1935, becoming assistants to male secretaries; the same thing occurred in most small branches that emerged during the early 1940s, such as Alexandria.[26]

Many of the men who joined the NAACP during the late 1930s were of an activist, enterprising character. They sought to immediately dominate local political structures and to push forward their policies in an uncompromising manner. Such a figure in New Orleans was James B. LaFourche, editor of the *Louisiana Weekly*, who believed civil rights was moving too slowly and that the NAACP old-timers needed replacing. LaFourche took Mrs. Oneida Brown's post as secretary in 1936 and proceeded to cause havoc with the local branch hierarchy for the next few years. LaFourche complained of "the selfish influences which now control the . . . local branch," and he threatened to form a group to break away from the city's NAACP, which he called "ultra-conservative" and incompetent. However, an elite remained very much in charge of the organization, in particular James Gayle, branch president, and Camille Harrison, assistant secretary, who retained administrative control of the chapter.[27]

In Baton Rouge the displacement of Dupuy by Horatio Thompson in 1940 was not followed by such acrimony as had occurred in New Orleans. Although Dupuy's name was absent from the 1940 membership roll, it was not necessarily from pique at being replaced in her leadership role. In 1941 Dupuy became Thompson's assistant and seems to have picked up her perpetual role of running the organization despite the apparent demotion in rank. During that year Dupuy continued to *act* as branch secretary, organizing campaign work and writing the annual report to the national office. The following year Dupuy was back in her usual position as secretary and was reporting that the branch had secured skilled jobs for carpenters and painters at the local company "Harding Field" in 1943. Also in that year the branch investigated defense jobs in the city and reported that with "all these contracts not one of the 14 major industries manufacturing war products . . . will hire skilled negro labor[,] the standard oil Co. included, yet they run public adds [*sic*] daily, [and] radio programs begging for laborers, skilled . . . [and] semi-skilled." She also undertook work in teaching black people how to register to vote during 1945. This included ludicrous aspects of suffrage application, such as calculating one's age in days and memorizing specific answers for the very fastidious registration forms. Most volunteers who gave their services to registration lessons in Baton Rouge and New Orleans during this time were women. Dupuy's vigor as the administrator of the branch, and her prominent commitment to the civil rights cause, gave her longevity in her elective positions in the organizational hierarchy, despite obvious blips.[28]

Dupuy's recognition of Horatio Thompson as a potential front-line leader of the civil rights struggle in Baton Rouge was a shrewd one. Thompson, as one of the leading African American businessmen in the area, helped found the Negro Chamber of Commerce with the goal of encouraging black business development in the city. Furthermore, in the city bus boycott of 1953, a prelude to the Montgomery protest over a year later, Thompson supplied private taxis with fuel at wholesale prices from his service stations located throughout Baton Rouge, thus allowing African Americans to avoid using public transport during the week-long action, which contributed enormously to its success.[29]

The change in membership that occurred in New Orleans, and to a degree in Baton Rouge, in the late 1930s and early 1940s did not necessarily take place so extensively in other cities and towns in Louisiana. Sociologist Daniel Thompson called this first wave of civil rights activists "racial diplomats" who were moderate in their dealings with the white power structures of their districts. During the 1940s and 1950s, according to Thompson, more radical black leaders were emerging who would eventually replace the old guard. World War II saw unprecedented growth for the NAACP in Louisiana and across the United States, both in membership numbers in established branches and in the proliferation of new chapters. Daniel E. Byrd, president of the NAACP

Louisiana state conference in 1945 and executive secretary of the New Orleans branch, explained this increase in support due to "tolerance and patience" being "at an end . . . [w]e must not wait another 80 years for the white man to give us justice." The NAACP in Louisiana, utilized its previous three decades of grassroots support and was able to capitalize on this rise in militancy to increase its membership to unprecedented numbers. Yet the racial diplomats in the NAACP were not entirely overturned by a new cabal of militant African Americans in such places as Baton Rouge, Monroe, and Alexandria. There was an acute awareness of local racial conditions by NAACP members and officers, and while frustration with the slow pace of civil rights was evident, there was not necessarily the incentive to cause major social unrest in their home cities.[30]

In Baton Rouge the so-called old guard of the NAACP, such as Benjamin Stanley and Mrs. D. J. Dupuy, continued to run the branch in very much the same attitude as they had in the 1930s. General frustration showed among most African Americans, but it was not the apparent generational shift that was to occur in the 1960s. In particular, Dupuy and Stanley often fought the civil rights cause along the lines of the "separate and equal" idea between the races. An example of this approach was the branch's campaign to get more African Americans employed at Sears Roebuck department store during 1941, and to have a restroom installed there for black shoppers, which, according to Dupuy, achieved "slight favorable results." This practical approach to civil rights campaigning remained for the rest of the decade, and while the "racial diplomats" had not been displaced, the status of those people radicalized by World War II, such as Horatio Thompson in Baton Rouge, did increase.[31]

While Dupuy's experiences in the NAACP in Baton Rouge typifies that of many women in Louisiana, it is interesting to note that her position within the branch was not related to any strong familial connection, as female officers in other branches often were. Throughout the fifteen years Dupuy was on the NAACP rolls, only two other Dupuys appeared as members. A man, Lee, lived at the same address as Dupuy and was on the membership roster for only 1939. However, married couples during the 1939 roll call, as in other years, tended to be placed together on the same line of the list. Such was not the case with Mrs. D. J. Dupuy and Mr. Lee Dupuy. This may indicate that they were brother and sister, or possibly a parental relationship of some kind, or merely that Mrs. D. J. Dupuy warranted a line to herself separate from her husband due to her status in the local Association. Another possible relative appeared on the membership lists in 1936, Mr. Ernest Dupuy, but he did not share the same address with Mrs. Dupuy. Of course, it is entirely likely that Ernest was from the same branch of the Dupuy family. He was a prominent member of the African American business community and an executive member of the city's Colored Business & Civic League, which could indicate a financial resource beneficial to the local NAACP. However, it is intriguing that neither Lee Dupuy nor Ernest Dupuy were regular members of the city's NAACP branch, which lends to the conclusion that they were not instrumental to Mrs. Dupuy's status as a leader within the branch itself, despite any kinship they might have had with her.[32]

As vice-president, secretary, or assistant-secretary, Dupuy should be recognized, for all practical purposes, as the deputy leader of the Baton Rouge branch. In all of her roles she undertook the bulk of the bureaucratic work of her local NAACP. This included writing the required annual report to the national office, maintaining communication with central office leaders in New York and field workers about local and national campaigns, and actually organizing such activities in the community. Such documentary evidence highlights the intellectual and emotional underpinnings that Dupuy, and other women, had in joining and being active in the Association.

A case that highlights Dupuy's conception of civil rights, as elsewhere in Louisiana, was in the antilynching campaigns. It was a passionate cause for many of those who had joined the NAACP, for moral and religious reasons. As Dupuy expressed in 1935, "We are planning and praying for the continued success of this organisation. On behalf of the entire Baton Rouge Branch we congratulate you [Walter White, NAACP executive secretary] for the efforts made in the recent (lynching) in our state . . . May *God* forever give you the *strength* and *courage* to plead for an almost helpless *group*."[33]

An actual Louisiana antilynching case that was hugely popular in Baton Rouge was that of Walter Ferguson, who it was assumed was likely to be executed for the murder of a white man. Curiously it was a project that met with disapproval from the national office for both reasons of cost and propriety. Ferguson had been charged with the murder of a white student, Dowell Briton, in the red-light district of Baton Rouge. The student had provoked a scene with a black prostitute and had attacked her with a broken whisky bottle. Ferguson had defended the prostitute and had hit Briton on the head with either a "stick" or a "piece of step."[34]

The moral ambiguity of the case did not prevent the Baton Rouge branch from launching itself wholeheartedly into Ferguson's defense and they set about raising $1,000 for legal fees and publicity. Dupuy, at this time branch secretary, had the idea of turning established national NAACP policy on its head by demanding New York assistance in organizing the 400 or so NAACP branches across the United States to supply them with financial aid by sending $2 each.[35] In October 1936 she exclaimed that the campaign was "to help save the life of 'Walter Ferguson,' whose one fault was to protect negro womanhood . . . Should we lose this case it means that the likes of 19,000 negroes of this city is at stake, and the protection of all the negroes and especially negro women is lessened . . . We have made a desperate effort to raise funds in time but the giving has been so *small* we are desperately in need of funds and a short time to get them in . . . Please do what you can for this is a *most worthy case* . . . In the name of God: give this your serious consideration."[36]

The question of prostitution was deemed immaterial to the campaigners of the Baton Rouge branch. It was a matter of safeguarding all black women from the sexual and violent impulses of white men. That Ferguson was defending a prostitute was not of great concern to the branch, as many white men perceived black women generally as sexually vulnerable and beyond full legal protection. Ferguson was making a stand where the law and police would never seriously involve themselves. However, the branch did not have great success in drumming up financial support for the case, and Dupuy's frustration showed: "We do not have the cooperation of the most intelligent people of this community. We have striven to get their interest but its [sic] of a short duration. We are anxious that you [Walter White, NAACP executive secretary] send some one to our town who can push them into a race loving attitude."[37]

Such an emphasis on the "most intelligent people" exemplifies Dupuy's notion that NAACP civil rights activity was primarily a middle-class struggle. This should come of no surprise, as an overwhelming number of Association members in Baton Rouge, as in New Orleans, Monroe, and elsewhere in Louisiana's cities and large towns, were from the aspiring bourgeoisie. Such a group envisioned civil rights as a political and legal struggle for integration into the American mainstream (white) society. Middle-class women, like Dupuy, were the mainstay of the NAACP because they had resources to devote to the organization, such as commitment, skills, and, most importantly, money.

No NAACP dignitary visited Baton Rouge regarding the Ferguson case. Not until December 1937 did a national NAACP officer appear in the capital city, and then it was purely on organizational business. Indeed, the needs of the national office, characteristically, governed all other considerations. William Pickens's visit to Louisiana in 1937 was due to the fact that the NAACP was $8,000 in debt, and the national campaigns for a federal antilynching bill and the equalization of teachers' salaries took precedence over any parochial issues. While specific cases seemed to cause a flurry of activity, such as canvassing local people and soliciting funds, there seemed little sustained effort over time that might have created a long-term and popular cause for civil rights. In 1935 the Baton Rouge branch held no mass meetings at all. In January 1936 a public conference was held in the Mt. Zion Baptist Church in Baton Rouge with the chief speaker being James E. Gayle, president of the New Orleans branch. However, this talk was on new NAACP methods and appealed for the greater cooperation and support of the city's citizens. During the war years the Baton Rouge branch did continue to be concerned about the defense of black people from racist violence, particularly with the issue of police brutality. In 1941 Dupuy observed that "Police Brutality has been on the encrease [sic] in our city for the past three months," and the branch "joined the other civic organizations in a protest."[38]

The Ferguson campaign was all consuming for the branch throughout 1937. It eventually raised approximately $750, primarily through churches, which coincided with a membership drive and distribution of NAACP literature. The branch employed a full-time lawyer, and Walter Ferguson was eventually convicted of murder but without capital punishment. This was unusual for the Deep South, where the death of a white person at the hands of an African American invariably led to the death penalty, regardless of circumstances. However, the concentration on the case shows how NAACP branches with only a small active membership did not have the resources to implement all their plans.[39] Dupuy wrote about her disappointment at the reception of the Ferguson case in the city and the effect it had on the other duties of the branch: "This last case of Walter Ferguson has really worked us, and to collect membership on top of such an effort has put us in a rather awkward position . . . How ever [sic] we are mindful that the work of the organization must go on. We would realize that just a little willing cooperation on their part would mean so much for our future living we could succeed in a large way. But we have to run the people down and then beg them to pay at least . . . one dollar per year for justice and fairplay. We are not complaining, but we hate to fail at this particular time. You may expect a good financial report in the near future."[40]

With that said, however, the Baton Rouge branch seemed to be especially responsive to direct appeals from the New York office. It was on nearly every annual report honor roll for meeting the financial quotas of the national office between the years 1931 and 1943, with the only exception being 1936. In 1931 and 1932 it exceeded its apportionment. Assistant executive secretary of the NAACP, Roy Wilkins, praised the Baton Rouge chapter by claiming that he did "not recall a single instance in which we have made an appeal to our branches that Baton Rouge has not responded to the best of its ability." Indeed this could be put down to the relatively stable membership of the branch and, remarkably, in 1937 Dupuy was able to announce a unique success for an NAACP branch in Louisiana: "We are proud to get *two* white members . . . this is encouraging to us." Baton Rouge was the only branch in Louisiana to officially record white members on its rolls throughout this entire period. There is no indication who these new white members of the branch were, however, probably to protect their identity from political or physical retaliation.[41]

Like other prominent NAACP women in the state, Dupuy was proficient at encouraging younger people to join the organization. She was continually "urging the Youth to read 'Crisis,' and to feel the need of keeping in close touch with this organisation, their future may depend heavily [sic] on this gesture made now." Dupuy held meetings at her own home for NAACP youth, although she found the attempts to initiate and maintain their interest was a difficult task, and youth councils were often sporadic and short-lived affairs. Indeed in Baton Rouge a youth council existed for a time during 1935, then from 1937 through to 1939, and was revived briefly in 1942.[42]

One area where the Baton Rouge youth council departed from the adult branch was its early embrace of economic concerns. The council launched a "Buy Negro Campaign" in 1938, boasting that they had "launched a program in October and have seen great result[s]. That program was educating the Negro to trade with Negro."[43] Members issued a flyer to launch the campaign, expressing their hope to "create interest among Negroes towards patronizing racial enterprises":

> We must take advantage of the fact that we have Negroes engaged in every field of business—groceries, doctors, nurses, cafes, shoe shops, drug stores, filling stations, insurance companies, newspapers, magazines, and many others. An under-privileged race such as ours cannot ignore the appeal to patronize racial businesses . . . We believe that you love your race and would like to see it progress in business. You can do much toward bringing this about. Simply spend your money where it will do the most good for you and your race. Spend it where your boy or girl will be able to obtain jobs of trust and be paid decent wages. No matter what you buy . . . if you can get it at a Negro business place, we are appealing to you to buy it there . . . We assure you that if you will co-operate in this movement, you will be rendering a service that will enable us as a race to be better able to stand on our own feet and to secure the respect and consideration of other races.[44]

Such a campaign would, the youth council insisted, lead to larger black businesses with "more colored employees," engender "economic solidarity," and create "greater racial recognition" and "better living conditions among Negroes." Dupuy's role in directing young people toward economic goals cannot be wholly ascertained, although it must be assumed that she was involved and had intimate knowledge of their aspirations, as she was closely connected to the youth division and her own actions, as with Sears Roebuck, relate directly to this strategy. Strengthening the African American community in Baton Rouge was as much a part of the work of the local NAACP as was integrating it into the American political system. Black schools and philanthropic and social organizations represented a source of strength and dignity for the African American community, while excluding as far as possible white discriminatory influences. To enhance the local African American economic community was an additional way to promote black pride and unity, thus leading to greater resources to fulfill NAACP ideals. It was also an implicit acknowledgment that the African American community in Baton Rouge commanded significant financial resources, which could be of use in forcing civil rights change in the future.

Civil rights activity for an overwhelming number of black women in Louisiana reflected prevailing perceptions of American citizenship and gender distinctions. At the local level, the NAACP utilized certain women within the gender conventions of the time to advance the civil rights cause. One obvious example is Rosa Parks of Montgomery, Alabama. Parks, who initiated the Montgomery bus boycott by refusing to give up her seat, was the historical epitome of female respectability and acceptable militancy in the early civil rights movement. Being a black woman with an unimpeachable moral character gave the Montgomery movement a symbolic legitimacy that other people would not have been able to give it. Though Rosa Parks had been a longtime NAACP activist, the press and public overlooked her radical political stance and concentrated on her aspiring middle-class propriety and her desire to be treated with respect as any other U.S. citizen.[45]

The standard definitions of leader and follower seem inadequate when describing the work and level of activism undertaken by such women as Dupuy or Parks. Dupuy was the office secretary who fashioned the bureaucratic organization into a workable entity. But she was also a spokeswoman for the antilynching campaign, a fundraiser for the NAACP, a youth worker, and a voter registration activist. She also appreciated that civil rights work was based on hard work and long-term commitment. Moreover, Dupuy's role was to inspire and motivate membership and to discover new talent in the community for the NAACP cause. This was a mature and cohesive approach to organizational management and civil rights work. By using established gender practices, Dupuy came to command the Baton Rouge branch office. She did not achieve this position simply for egotistical leadership ambitions but to promote a community project that aspired to uplift the entire African American society.

Dupuy was integral to the NAACP in Baton Rouge, and it is difficult to envisage any stable branch in the city without her confident organizational leadership over fifteen years of service. Without her efforts, it is likely that by the 1950s there would have been little or no NAACP chapter or civil rights practice to generate the week-long bus boycott. Yet, unlike Parks, Dupuy is an unrecognized stalwart of the early civil rights struggle, as were a host of other women in local branches of the NAACP.

Conversely, when women did not adhere to the gender expectations of the age in the Louisiana NAACP it could have dramatic and revealing consequences. One such individual was Miss Georgia M. Johnson, the subject of the next chapter.

SIX

WE ARE BUT AMERICANS
Miss Georgia M. Johnson

When you are militant you are simply placing
a rope around your own neck.

In stark contrast to Mrs. D. J. Dupuy of Baton Rouge, Miss Georgia M. Johnson of Alexandria, Louisiana, helps to portray the expected role of NAACP women not because of her conformity to social and gender expectations but by many of the organizational taboos she breached. Johnson was a forceful individual in a racially conservative city in the Deep South who was extremely active in the early civil rights movement. She was highly conscious of the dual nature of discrimination, in particular of sexism and racism, within the community where she worked and among the white society she encountered during the first half of the 1940s. The record of Johnson's leadership reveals the interpersonal dynamics of a local NAACP branch and the conflicts and frustrations, as well as the occasional successes, of an individual female activist within a bureaucratic and male-led organization.[1]

Georgia Johnson was one of the few people in Louisiana during the 1940s to articulate an extensive and coherent ideological stance for her involvement in civil rights protest, through a blend of religious belief, political activism, and class-consciousness. Her prolific and lengthy correspondence with the New Orleans NAACP branch and the national office in New York shows the motivation and passions of an individual who found it restrictive to work within an organization that did not accept women other than in a traditional and subordinate role. Women could safely be secretaries and chairpersons of committees on entertainment or fundraising, as long as they were collectivist organizers in the background rather than individual leaders in the public gaze.

Johnson, however, was the only woman to chair a legal redress and legislation committee in an NAACP branch. This position, like president and treasurer, was a male preserve in Louisiana and other states, such as Alabama. The branch constitution stated broadly that the committee existed to "examine local ordinances for possibilities of discrimination, work for better equal enforcement of the laws . . . and work for the repeal of discriminatory laws." Its more significant and prominent role, however, was the investigation of "all cases reported to it for legal redress . . . and [the observation of] all litigation in which the Branch is interested." Such a high-profile position was to lead to intense personal politicking within the Alexandria branch between the militant Johnson and the city's gradualist male leadership, as well as direct threats from the white establishment to suppress her investigations into racism in the city.[2]

Alexandria in Rapides Parish, central Louisiana, had short-lived and struggling NAACP branches in 1921, 1927, and 1930, usually inspired by single issues that directly affected the city's black community. During 1921 the city's black elite organized a branch under the leadership of Rev. H. R. Norris in response to a constitutional convention being held in the state in which the franchise question was of prime interest, including the issue of female enfranchisement. The branch was reorganized in 1927 in response to the Mississippi floods and focused on welfare issues that affected African Americans in the disaster. At a national level the NAACP campaigned against labor peonage in levee camps in Mississippi and Louisiana and publicized discrimination in federal aid to blacks who had been displaced from their homes and workplaces. The chapter chartered in April 1930 proclaimed that it was "proud of the fact" that it had recruited 102 members in the depths of the economic depression, although it too was soon disbanded.[3]

The Alexandria branch did not establish itself again until May 1941, when it was inspired by the statewide NAACP campaign to equalize teacher salaries and to undertake vigorous voter registration drives. The economy was rapidly changing due to the war. There were five military bases within a five-mile radius of Alexandria, which acted as the center for all basic training of the U.S. armed forces, and the urban growth was to prove spectacular. Before 1941 the total population of the town stood at 26,000, of which 11,000 were black. By the latter part of that year the population had grown to 67,000, with 26,000 blacks. This included soldiers as well as civilians employed in the wartime industries. While the population explosion heightened racial tensions, the exaggerated military composition of Alexandria reflected general wartime stresses across the United States and with it the subsequent rise in civil rights militancy.[4]

Outside New Orleans and Baton Rouge, most of Louisiana was seen as a remote and dangerous "hinterland." Dr. George W. Lucas, New Orleans branch president from 1921 to 1930, stated, "When . . . investigating a criminal case . . . in New Orleans, I am as safe as I would be in New York. When [I] . . . go into the country, that is another matter. But . . . I go." Madison S. Jones, who made an official NAACP staff visit to the city in 1942, characterized Alexandria as "perhaps the roughest place, as far as race relations are concerned" in the state.[5]

Even in this atmosphere, Georgia Johnson kept the NAACP alive in Alexandria almost single-handedly as chair of the legal redress and legislation committee. No other woman had held this position in Louisiana, which signifies various issues at work within the Alexandria chapter. Johnson was a resolute woman, active in the community and with a high public profile on civil rights matters, and standing for chair of the legal redress committee was a direct consequence of her own personal enthusiasm in the civil rights battle. Yet the Alexandria NAACP had maintained a disappointingly low level of activism in the early 1940s, and bubbling beneath the surface were personal disputes between the leadership that would eventually render the branch ineffectual as an organization.[6]

Johnson had for a long time been the solitary beacon for the NAACP in Alexandria, having been a member-at-large since 1920, when there had been insufficient numbers to constitute a chapter. Johnson was a staunch believer in exercising her citizenship via the ballot, and as soon as the Nineteenth Amendment was passed she was attempting to register to vote. Indeed, she was the first black woman to eventually do so in Rapides Parish, although she admitted in her own correspondence that it was a struggle over the next forty years to re-register, and it is not clear whether she actually ever voted. Regardless, her voter registration struggle in 1920 sent a clear and unequivocal message to both the African American community (who should follow her example) and to the white authorities (who had no right to stop them). Such manifest dedication to the civil rights cause was to win her supporters in the African American community in Alexandria. In 1945 some NAACP branch members commended her as a staunch believer in the organization's ideals and "capable[,] agreeable, proud, independent, . . . [having] the facts in hand and ready to defend the branch."[7]

When Madison S. Jones, of the NAACP national staff, visited Alexandria in late December 1942 he noted that the "branch is rather small at the present time, and plodding, but doesn't know just what to do. However, there are some younger men on the Executive Committee who should be able to take over." His statement is blatant, yet predictable, in its omission to recognize Georgia Johnson's invaluable contributions. When he went to see the mayor of Alexandria to discuss the oppressive level of Jim Crowism in the city, Madison Jones reported that he "went . . . in the company of the Branch president and [was] joined later by a Miss Johnson, secretary of the Branch." Johnson was never the branch secretary, and it was only pure chauvinism that allowed Jones to suspect that she was. Men occupied the official secretarial positions during the early 1940s in Alexandria, namely, D. Bell from 1941 and Freddie J. Spear from 1944. However, Georgia Johnson typed all the annual reports and kept in regular contact with the New York office throughout the early 1940s, technically the responsibilities of the elected branch secretary. Johnson often complained of her multifarious roles in the branch and claimed a leadership position, as she saw it, almost by default, rather than a position that she had actively sought: "Not only did we [sic] ac[t] . . . as chairman of the Legal Committee but in a measure was an Executive Secretary and also wrote publicity to the various [news]papers. Not because I wanted to nor had the time but some one had to act or others would have suffered."[8]

Johnson apparently viewed her fight for the civil rights cause as a moral responsibility that was not being undertaken by those that should have accepted the call, in particular the city's black elite. Johnson's legal redress committee was often seen as the only operational aspect of the branch. In 1945 it was applauded by a group of NAACP members who were disillusioned with the running of the branch as being "the only committee working . . . through appalling handicaps. Oftimes [sic] going over the wishes of some of the views of some of the members of the branch [in] defending the rights of [black] soldiers [in Alexandria's segregated army camps]."[9]

Although very little can be ascertained about Georgia Johnson's childhood or general upbringing, her professional career from the 1920s through to the 1960s demonstrates an extremely busy entrepreneurial spirit that would also be evident in the work she undertook for the NAACP. Like so many women who joined the NAACP in Louisiana, Johnson had been a public school teacher and principal. In the 1930s she was to be the first black social worker in Rapides Parish and also worked selling insurance to supplement her income, considering herself to be a "business and a general civic worker for a number of years for my group." During her time working for the city's NAACP, Johnson edited and managed a small African American newspaper, the *Alexandria Observer*, of which no entire copies seem to have survived. She also owned a café, the Royal Garden, in which she employed two nieces and a nephew as managers. Later, in the 1950s and 1960s, she became an Independent Booking Representative of Southern States, "Booking bands, orchestras, spirituals and shows, [and] all types of theatrical musical presentations" and by the late 1960s she was also the owner of the Holly Oak Cemetery in the parish.[10]

Georgia Johnson was evidently an enterprising businesswoman, as well as a civic-minded and self-conscious race woman, all of which fed into her passion for the civil rights movement. Johnson remained unmarried throughout her life and was a firm and committed Methodist who was to use her understanding of the Christian message of Christ's martyrdom to relate directly to her role in the civil rights struggle. Suffering as a redemptive power has been popularly attributed to Martin Luther King Jr. during the 1950s and 1960s. Yet this belief was widespread among African Americans who had suffered under slavery and Jim Crow and was integral to the self-identity of many local leaders fighting their corner of the civil rights struggle on a day-to-day basis. Indeed, Johnson seemed to take great solace in the biblical connotations of Christ being "crushed and misrepresented," which alluded both to her own personal troubles being associated with the NAACP and to the black population as a whole suffering racial oppression.[11]

However, Johnson's underlying perception of the fight for constitutional rights was essentially an elitist one. She perceived that it was the job of "well thinking educated members of the branch," a self-selecting social elite, to work for the liberation of the entire black population. Well-informed, middle-class leaders would lead the fight for equality, while also guiding by personal example so that the lower classes could see the way forward. In 1941 Johnson stated that "Action is paramount. Thinking is in order. Classes should think for the masses, but help by pulling them along and helping them find themselves in this great civilization." However, this was not just a middle-class moral example to all African Americans, as was generally perceived to be a woman's role in black society, but was based on a commitment to practically confronting political repression in her community. So not only did Johnson regularly register to vote, but she expected others to be inspired by her actions to follow suit and to be brave enough to join the NAACP and suffer the reactions from white society that she did.[12]

This concept of leadership differed significantly from the democratic vision for the civil rights struggle espoused by Ella Baker, NAACP director of branches, although Johnson sympathized with the idea of leaders emerging from within a community rather than being imposed from without. Johnson and Baker corresponded in the mid-1940s, with Johnson venting her feelings that the Alexandria branch was too conservative and not moving radically enough on civil rights. Yet Johnson believed in a much more elite-based movement than did Baker, and she was more akin to W. E. B. Du Bois in his political phase at the start of the century with the Niagara movement. Johnson likely agreed with Du Bois's ideas of an African American Talented Tenth, an elite who could lead the black masses into their full political rights by their erudition and understanding of the race situation in the United States.[13]

Johnson's reliance on the idea of an elite NAACP led to occasional frustrations with the apparent inertia of the so-called masses, although it was invariably the black middle classes she blamed for the failure of civil rights progress in Louisiana. When A. P. Tureaud of the New Orleans NAACP branch and Thurgood Marshall, NAACP special counsel, both failed to respond to Johnson's request for legal help during a 1944 voter registration campaign, she wrote, "I do not understand colored people. No matter how great or how important their position is they are poor business people." Though she directed these private comments at high-profile NAACP officials, the real focus of her wrath was directed at the slow pace of change in race relations, exacerbated by the feeling that not every person had her passion and strength for the fight.[14]

Similarly, a protest committee set up in January 1945 by sixty Alexandria NAACP members, writing to the New York office, argued that their branch officers suffered from a "lack of vision as to the great work of the N.A.A.C.P."[15] Johnson, co-chair of the committee, accused the leadership of not acting when atrocities were perpetrated on black soldiers in the city: "[Seeing] incident after incident were [sic] happening among citizens and soldiers coming from other sections of this country and . . . [feelings] were growing more and more intense . . . no one [was] acting, no one in the "Branch" acting had committees . . . [A] soldier was killed in [the] upper part of the city [and] the elected chairman of [the] legal committee was ill. [I] went to him [the president of the branch and] stated [the] fact [that] every one [was] afraid [but] explained that this was the... duties of the Branch and not just to hold meetings... [S]ome have resorted to mud-slinging and have forgotten the real principle upon which the [NAACP] is built[,] that is to Advance and not to degrade."[16]

Johnson accused the branch leaders of continually trying to "appease the white people" for she had no patience with a gradualist approach to civil rights matters. She was uncompromising in her expectations of NAACP leaders and thought they should take a firm stance in confronting racism rather than just being an ineffectual elitist clique. Johnson claimed that she had resigned from being a school principal at the Rosenwald school in the area and a social worker in the parish as "I could not be an uncle tom." By 1946 she was reflecting on the alleged inadequacies of the Alexandria branch officers, whom she saw as merely interested in maintaining their own social status in the city, and their fainthearted approach to the white power structures: "Now what do the Negro leaders say[?] 'Miss Johnson should go to the North, East or West [if] she wants to be a politician.' We know she... had no business doing all she did in that N.A.A.C.P. The president and some of his cabinet [are] telling white people and colored this... I know Negroes and their organizations, they want only a little group of their friends to sop while the others stand and look on."[17]

Sexism was another element of discrimination that Johnson understood clearly. Black middle-class society perceived women to be morally virtuous people who needed protecting from male indecorousness and, in some cases, shielded from their own hypersensitivities to certain matters. For instance, after his meeting with the mayor of Alexandria in 1942, Madison S. Jones exclaim shock at the foul language the mayor used "in front of my two colleagues, including a lady [Georgia Johnson], and also his own secretary." Attorney A. P. Tureaud of the New Orleans NAACP branch during 1944 believed that Johnson was "too sensitive about things," which made her "too hasty" in her opinions, although he had been on the receiving end of her criticisms regarding the slow progress on a registration drive and had criticized her knowledge of state legal matters. Johnson also reported a cryptic warning from Alexandria's Rev. E. Charles Curtis "to be careful because I was a woman." Men within the NAACP were evidently conscious that Georgia Johnson ought to be treated in a particular manner and felt a need to safeguard her from possible violence and harassment.[18]

Similarly, the state district attorney informed Georgia Johnson upon one of her periodic arrests, "You are an agitator... We are going to do all we can to teach you a lesson. You dictated the policies . . . [and] used your influence in this organization [the NAACP] to get negro soldiers free accused of raping white women . . . [Y]ou had better leave that . . . Nigger Organization alone and that nigger paper [*Alexandria Observer*]." A state judge concurred with this assessment: "Well you are an agitator and we know you are a good educated nigger woman but you have these white people against you fooling with that Nigger organization N.A.A.C.P." Besides the physical intimidation these officials' statements implied, Johnson's commercial situation was also under threat, as she noted in 1945: "When a member of our race group displays his or her militancy they are denied many things from a financial point of view . . . When I think of the time I spent when I could . . . have been doing [other business] and I am not . . . rewarded but very much discouraged and see no hope for the race as a whole."[19]

The unifying theory behind Johnson's activism resounded in her claim, during a rare moment of optimism, that "the day will come that all men and women regardless of color will have their rightful place in this nation and that we will no longer be the FOOT MATS of this American Country and will not be Semi-slaves as we are but Americans." Her religious beliefs reinforced this idea of equality: "Of one Blood God [has] made all Nations to Dwell upon the face of the Earth . . . will be practice in reality." Although her haste to achieve these goals was often apparent, she was also aware that NAACP principles would be achieved only in the long term, when "I may be sleeping in my grave." This was, to Johnson's eyes, a battle that would endure for generations, although it did not make it any easier for her to endure the existing repression.[20]

This theory very naturally fit into the uncompromising rhetoric of the NAACP as a forthright integrationist organization. Johnson sought social and political equality for African Americans. However, inherent in Johnson's demands for integration was an understanding that women had to work, that African American women had to work more often than not due to financial factors, and that a freedom to have similar opportunities in the economic world was fundamental to any demands of social equality. After all, Johnson was herself a very successful businesswoman in her community. Her business office on Lee Street was in the heart of the area known as Little Harlem. In civil rights debates she balanced political and economic factors. Equality and integration, in this sense, meant a fair share of opportunities for African Americans, not necessarily actual social mixing with whites. Such opportunities included equal access to education, employment, military service, and participating and representing one's community in the body politic. Johnson accepted U.S. society based on the U.S. Constitution: equality before the law, entrepreneurialism, and opportunity alongside an implicit acceptance of social distinctions. Some people would be successful in their life pursuits, others would not, but it was unfair to impede an individual's progress simply because of racial stereotyping and discrimination. World War II was under way, a fight supposedly based on ideals of democracy and freedom, yet Alexandria, as a center for all U.S. military training, exemplified all the paradoxes of America's own rhetoric.[21]

The actual practicality of this civil rights philosophy was apparent in Georgia Johnson's grueling daily work as chair of the legal redress committee. The committee's daunting task was to mitigate racial discrimination and prejudice for Alexandria's black population. Johnson's activism forced the city authorities during 1944 to supply water to "sprinkle a dusty section of Alexandria" that had been neglected for seventeen years. Such activity made life more bearable in the heat of the Deep South in the city's black residential areas. However, Johnson spent a large amount of her time investigating judicial cases of the black civilian and military population. The task was made even more complex by the huge rise in the city's population due to the wartime industries. The NAACP saw an opportunity to showcase employment discrimination and to campaign for job opportunities for black people; however, this was a monumental task for the city's small NAACP membership, and, unfortunately, they received very little help from the New York office.[22]

During 1941, the first year of the new Alexandria NAACP branch, Georgia Johnson declared that the chapter was examining the defense industries, civil service, and other job opportunities in the city that were rapidly expanding. After a mass meeting at the Shiloh Baptist Church on the September 29, consisting of a hundred "outstanding citizens," Johnson, the meeting's chairperson, explained that "Alexandria [is] in the midst of one of the greatest National Defense Programs in the nation [and the NAACP has] . . . lots to do in the city." Nevertheless, the committee on labor and industry, which was technically responsible for "improving the status of colored people in labor, industry and agriculture," was inactive during the ensuing years. The failure to have a functional labor committee was partly due to the intense factionalism between the older race leaders who controlled the committee and a much more militant group, of which Johnson was the standard bearer. Meanwhile, the chair of the legal redress committee spent her time investigating criminal cases, observing that there was "much police brutality in this section" with "persons of color being beaten by officers nearly everyday." Sometimes Johnson was merely recording incidents of abuse and lodging complaints to city officials, but these complaints often led to major legal cases being undertaken by the branch to save black soldiers' lives.[23]

A case in point occurred during 1944 when Johnson investigated the case of Herbert Anderson, who was accused of murdering the chief of police, W. H. Bishop, after he had beaten Anderson's fiancé in Oakdale, Louisiana, and then attempted to kill Anderson. Within the Alexandria branch only Johnson had wanted to pursue the case, and she claimed, "Poor Anderson would no doubt [have] been electricuted [sic] were it not for my persistent effort." Johnson accused the branch hierarchy of misappropriating $184.50 that had been raised for Anderson's legal fees, and a check for $134.27 was turned down by a bank due to apparent lack of funds when the "Branch should have had several times this much." Johnson tried to get black men appointed to the jury to ensure a fair trial for Anderson. Despite such efforts and prolonged legal entanglements, Anderson was executed in June 1945. Johnson accused the local NAACP branch of not being active enough in the case, yet she also blamed "White Southern Lawyers" for "keeping our group financially . . . depressed while they grow fat."[24]

Much of Georgia Johnson's work concerned black soldiers at the training camps around Alexandria, particularly "soldier slaying" cases. The personal dangers an NAACP investigator, male or female, regularly faced were even more so within a military context. No case was more perilous, however, than researching the Alexandria riot of January 10, 1942. The race riot was caused by the arrest and treatment of a drunken black soldier in Lee Street in Little Harlem, though it expressed the general resentment felt by black soldiers at their experiences in the segregated army camps and city facilities. There were over 3,000 arrests, and at least twenty-eight African Americans were shot. Madison Jones reported that it was a constant source of fear among whites that a larger rebellion would take place, and it was thought that "a great deal of ammunition is missing from many of the army camps . . . [O]ne unit had been stood up in the sun last August, at attention for an hour, in order to make them break down and confess . . . At Camp Claibourne there are several Negro tank divisions and the boys are very vocal in saying that they expect to drive their tanks down the streets of Alexandria before they drive to the front."[25]

There was such anxiety from the white authorities that a machine gun was prominently situated on top of the city hall for some time after the riot in case of further social unrest. Johnson's determination to investigate the causes of the riot came up against hostility from the white population and authorities, as she explained in 1945: "Next came the 'Alexandria Soldiers Riot' due to my writing articles to the various 'Negro Papers' . . . I was called to report to the 'City Police Station' to account for . . . defend[ing] my group. [T]his I did to the best of my ability. Rev. E. Charles Curtis[,] President of the Inter Denom[inational] Ministerial Alliance[,] and Mr. Louis Berry of Howard Law School[,] who at that time was [sic] members of my [Legal Redress] committee and [had] assisted me in writing articles and making investigations concerning the appalling Alexandria Riot[,] when it was reported a number of our soldiers were killed . . . I was [also] called over the phone, and stopped in the streets by . . . many of the members of the 'White Group.'"[26]

In this atmosphere of fear and heightened racial tensions, Georgia Johnson was "carried down to the city courts for an interview twice concerning the Alexandria Riot" and her inquiries. However, the Japanese attack on Pearl Harbor had taken place a month previously and, in the spirit of wartime unity and patriotism, the federal government suppressed and censored the full story of the Alexandria riot, so successfully, in fact, most historical works that mention the event give it only a line or paragraph, despite its being the largest race riot in the United States during World War II. Consequently, Johnson's inquiry came up against the full weight of the federal government, as well as the local white establishment, and it made little headway or impact, even with the NAACP in New York.[27]

This veil of concealment, however, did not prevent Johnson from further investigations in Alexandria. One incident that became, for a short while, the focus of a national campaign was the "three soldiers' case." Three black soldiers—Richard F. Adams, John Bordenave, and Lawrence Mitchell—were accused of raping a white woman at Camp Claiborne. There was some confusion over jurisdiction: the alleged crime had taken place on military grounds so the men faced a court martial, but in the meanwhile the three men were convicted of rape on August 10, 1942, by the Federal District Court in New Orleans. The court martial did take place at Camp Maxey, Texas, and the soldiers were again convicted and sentenced to die, despite Johnson's attempts at raising money and getting proper legal representation. The three men later had their sentences commuted to life by President Roosevelt in 1944, and they were finally paroled in 1947. Not all such cases were lost at the outset by the Alexandria branch, however. In 1944 a private at Camp Livingstone, Eddie Anthoney, was accused of attacking and attempting to rape a white woman, but the Alexandria NAACP employed a local white attorney, John R. Hunter, to defend him and the soldier was acquitted at a court martial hearing.[28]

Another high-profile case involved the shooting of Private Edward Green. During 1944 Green had been killed by a bus driver, Odell Lackney, as the soldier had "been requested to change his seat on a [racially segregated] bus" and had refused. The white bus driver was arrested but quickly released on bond and was back at work in Alexandria within a few days of the murder. Johnson took the matter up with the War Department, which merely announced that there was "no justification, moral or legal, for the slaying." However, the Department of Justice, pressured by the NAACP New York national office, declared that they officially had "no jurisdiction over such crimes" and declined to act on the matter. While Georgia Johnson attempted to achieve fair trials and highlight racial oppression and discrimination in Alexandria, the military was uninterested in civil rights aims, whereas the civilian authorities simply upheld Jim Crow conventions. No formal restitution for Green's murder was ever achieved, although the NAACP highlighted the case to illustrate the problem of segregation and contradiction of black soldiers fighting for freedom and liberty abroad but being denied such rights at home.[29]

Because of her high public profile in Alexandria in the civil rights struggle, Georgia Johnson had to deal with systematic persecution from local authorities in 1945. As Johnson related, on July 29 two police officers "came to me stating that my nephew had taken some sugar from Cotton Brothers Baking Company." The police forced an entry into Johnson's café, the Royal Garden, but "found no sugar." Instead they claimed that "two cans of lard" worth ten dollars had been stolen, and the officers "carried me to Jail [and] kept me there a day . . . Monday they came with a warrant [which they] would not allow me to read . . . [I]nstead [they] called me a smart Negro agitator fooling with that Negro Organisation N.A.[A].C.P. and said lots of things. They were glad they had me [as] they were going to make an example out of me . . . Having references from various outstanding white[s] and Negroes I . . . [got] out on a Bond of $750."[30]

One of Johnson's nieces, the café manager, was also arrested on the charge of "Receiving Stolen Property." Johnson employed a white lawyer at a personal cost of $100 and was informed by him that it was well known that "you were never at the [Royal Garden] . . . [b]ut you spent your time with that nigger organisation." It was made clear that the harassment over the alleged theft was due to her public affiliation with the NAACP. However, Johnson was fully prepared to sue the city authorities over police procedural irregularities, and the case was eventually dropped.[31]

Johnson also suffered defamation from within the Alexandria NAACP, which eventually led to the branch's temporary demise. The central charge, as stated by the branch president, Spencer Bradley, was that Johnson was "not good with finance" and for this reason had lost her position as a committee chairperson in the chapter's election on November 13, 1944. Johnson did not accept that the election had been legitimate, and a lengthy and abusive campaign began between the winning and losing factions. The situation was inflamed when Johnson refused to turn over the financial books for her committee in an act that can only be characterized as stubbornness in the face of her persecutors.[32]

From the safe distance of New Orleans the NAACP attorney A. P. Tureaud reported to Ella Baker, NAACP director of branches, that the "Alexandria problem" was mostly due to a "clash of personalities" but also acknowledged that the real issue had erupted over "Election irregularities." A small cadre of officials had rescheduled the November 1944 branch elections from eight o'clock to a half-hour earlier, and it "was held without adherence to the rules and regulations of well regulated bodies," and no one was "elected by ballot." This was essentially a coup in order to reappoint the current leadership minus Georgia Johnson, whom the branch hierarchy resented for her militancy and for upsetting the city's white political establishment. A protest committee was formed on Johnson's behalf, with sixty signatories, which indicated substantial support from within the branch but also throughout the city church network, mostly Methodists but also some Baptists. The protesters, in turn, accused the branch leaders of being financially incompetent and lacking commitment to the equality cause. The committee stated that Johnson was "paying [her] own expenses, for example, postage, trips to prison[,] making interviews at Army Camps . . . and other duties too numerous to mention."[33]

One of the central accusations leveled at Georgia Johnson was that she had no head for the complex financial issues involved in running an important committee and for branch fundraising. This seems strange considering Johnson's involvement in her various businesses. The branch hierarchy maintained that Johnson had omitted from branch accounts twenty dollars that she had raised for NAACP funds. The Methodist minister Rev. J. M. Murphy, chair of the protest committee, explained that he had personally raised the twenty dollars from his congregation specifically in Johnson's name and not for the NAACP. Johnson's methods of circumventing the bureaucracy of the local branch to use money she raised for her own committee work was simply to not "even mention the Alexandria Branch to get money . . . I can go to any of these churches in the city any Sunday [to] speak and get a collection . . . I do not have to . . . mention the N.A.[A.]C.P. to get a little money." This was possible because she was an activist with longevity in the civil rights cause and her work for African American civil rights was well known in the city.[34]

In retaliation, Georgia Johnson had the city's NAACP leaders arrested during an attempted branch meeting in April 1945 and indicted for civil libel. This included the president, Spencer Bradley, vice-president Freddie Spears, and Earl Smith, the new chair of the legal redress committee. They were all subsequently released on $100 bonds. The trial was later dropped by Johnson due to pressure from the New York office, which did not want the bad publicity in Alexandria and foresaw factionalism leading to the collapse of the branch, and also because of certain technical legal points. However, Johnson was not attempting a personal vendetta; her goal with the arrests was to get NAACP national authorities interested in the irregularities of the election and to reinvigorate the branch into a more vibrant and effective body, rather than just being a personal vendetta. Her effort failed because the central office was uninterested in such a small branch, notwithstanding its potential to highlight racism in the armed forces training camps. Despite much correspondence between Georgia Johnson, A. P. Tureaud of New Orleans, and Ella Baker, NAACP director of branches, very little was done to investigate the claims of the protest committee. After the personal wrangling continued over 1945 and on into early 1946, Ella Baker finally declared that as the election problems of 1944 had gone on for well over a year, the issue was now redundant because new elections had taken place in November 1945.[35]

However, the issue was by no means concluded or irrelevant, and it continued to provoke personality differences in the civil rights movement in Alexandria. By mid-June 1945 Johnson and the protest committee had set up a rival NAACP branch in the city, which collected membership dues under the guise of being the official organization, which it was not. Yet with all the factionalism and the reluctance of the state or national organizations to investigate thoroughly, the NAACP in Alexandria dropped into nonexistence for most of 1946. When it resurfaced in 1947, the protesters were firmly in control. Georgia Johnson was back as the chair of the legal redress committee, with her primary defender, Reverend Murphy, as branch president. The group relaunched its civil rights activities, including a protest against a local registrar who had refused to let blacks register to vote, "as a result the books are now open to all citizens of the parish," declared Johnson. The branch also continued lobbying the mayor of Alexandria, J. A. Blackman, to improve black education, fight racial injustice, secure the vote for all American citizens, and to put a stop to lynching. Johnson also undertook wider duties as an NAACP state organizer. With the city's NAACP old guard gone, the branch seemed to work better as a cohesive unit for a while, rather than Johnson's legal committee existing as a sort of independent wing to the branch, which is how it seemed in the first half of the 1940s.[36]

Nonetheless, Georgia Johnson's individualistic methods continued to plague her NAACP career. By the end of 1947 she was suing a local black lawyer, Louis Berry, for "criminal libel," after he had accused her of "embezzlement without having receipts and affidavits to prove [whom] you collected the funds from." Johnson soon dropped the case due to national NAACP insistence that it would ruin the organization's citywide reputation and again prevent the chapter from being effective. Although she worked untiringly for NAACP policies, she did not adhere to rules that she considered inconveniently bureaucratic to her committee work. When Johnson's integrity was questioned she immediately went on the offensive and could be personally abusive to all those who disagreed with her. Although Johnson's participation in the Alexandria branch lapsed during the late 1940s and 1950s, she reemerged in the mid-1960s with renewed vigor for civil rights work as the chair of the labor committee of a revived NAACP chapter. Yet her approach to civil rights work got her into trouble again with the new branch hierarchy. During 1968 she accused the Alexandria NAACP branch president, "Old Houston Jackson" (or "old Ignorant Jackson" as Johnson preferred to call him) of "cow-towing" to white politicians in the city. Indeed in 1968 Johnson refused to attend a mass meeting of the branch as she was aware that white politicians were going to be there, "and I know I will get angry."[37]

Georgia Johnson's idiosyncratic methods of operating continued into the 1960s, as she continued to bypass the local branch hierarchy by sending money she raised to the central office in New York. Having personally solicited a twenty-five-dollar check from J. Hall LeBlance, a "liberal white man of Alexandria," she sent the donation directly to New York, thus depriving the local branch of its share. This was due to her perception that the branch was not being run as effectively or radically as she would have liked and, therefore, ought not to be trusted to spend funds appropriately that she had raised for particular purposes or to uphold certain principles. Like W. E. B. Du Bois, she found it difficult to engage with bureaucracies. Du Bois's own sense of independence and self-regard for intellectual autonomy led him to resign from the NAACP in 1934, and he was expelled in 1948 after a brief return as a researcher. Johnson also had a strong regard for her own autonomy and a belief in her own approach to confronting racism in her home city. Unfortunately, her breaches of expected gender protocols led to her unceremonious expulsion from the Alexandria NAACP.[38]

Georgia Johnson's style of fundraising and operating ought not to obscure her work as a genuine leader of the Alexandria NAACP branch. Despite her claim that her leadership of the legal committee was an unwanted position and hers only by default, the African American population in the city recognized that she was a dedicated and courageous advocate on their behalf. Her power base was located within the broader African American community rather than in a strictly political or organizational arena. Johnson's personal and religious value system, epitomized by extensive social relationships and church networks, exemplified the views of a black constituency frustrated by racial repression and the imperceptible movement toward change. Curiously, she never declared herself a leader and only stated that she was working for "my race," even though as a self-styled elitist she saw this as her class and Christian duty.[39]

Georgia Johnson's tactics stand in stark contrast to those of Mrs. D. J. Dupuy of Baton Rouge, but both assist in exploring issues of gender and race in the early modern civil rights struggle in Louisiana. The concluding chapter undertakes a direct assessment of these issues.

CONCLUSION

Black women's work in the NAACP was the foundation upon which the civil rights movement of the 1950s and 1960s was built. Women activists drew together broad social and professional networks under the auspices of a committed integrationist and politically minded association. Indeed, in Louisiana there would have been no NAACP at all if it had not been for this group.

Women's participation in the civil rights struggle created a stable NAACP presence in the South through the maintenance of local branches. Their efforts enabled the organization to take advantage of a growth in its membership during times of general black political mobilization, such as World War II. They adapted their social and political networks, such as the churches, to work for the NAACP, which could then channel community feeling toward specific civil rights aims, like voter registration and antilynching campaigns. The New York–based NAACP understood the influence of these women and made it an organizational policy to tap into community networks to establish branches, raise money, campaign, and spread its message across the United States. An example of this is the Masonic lodges' contribution to the early establishment of the NAACP in the Deep South. The women's auxiliaries to the Knights of Peter Claver and the Knights of Pythias gave crucial organizational experience to the NAACP, a tradition established during the clubwomen's era, and also offered membership numbers and financial sponsorship to the fledgling association. This focus on the community did not fundamentally change during the 1930s; indeed, the Great Depression did little to alter women's traditional roles, and women's roles in the NAACP, although pivotal, continued to circle around their traditional areas of expertise. Moreover, the NAACP tended to be a highly bureaucratic and centralized body that sent continual missives to its branches demanding financial contributions, which emphasized fundraising, another province dominated by women and their local networks.

Black women suited such a network-centered model of local leadership. They maintained community contacts on various levels, most notably as teachers, and had the advantage of a wide perspective on civil rights activity that influenced much of their organizational lives.

Their roles as educators alongside their professional associations, such as Parent Teacher Associations and their unions, gave them direct access to a local community, and their social status permitted certain financial latitude to speak on political matters. Charity and church work was an extension of their commitment to a better community existence both within and beyond segregation. Individual concerns could also interweave with local issues and have wider implications for civil rights causes and racial uplift. For instance, the New Orleans teacher Fannie C. Williams had interests in education, racial pride initiatives, health day programs for children, and the Republican Party, as well as the NAACP. This wide focus and integrated approach to career, philanthropy, and other personal commitments made her and other women's participation in civil rights a comprehensive ideological proposition.

While civil rights work combined individual and collective involvement, there was also a strong personal connection to the cause by families. The majority of NAACP branches in Louisiana survived because of the personal connections of its long-term membership, in which certain family names became virtually synonymous with civil rights organizing. The Baton Rouge and Monroe NAACPs were led by family groups that maintained membership levels through the 1920s and 1930s. The Johnsons of Monroe are a prime example of a family that persistently supported the NAACP through at least two decades. This could mean the difference between existence and nonexistence when national guidelines required more than fifty members to charter and maintain a branch.

Businesses, Masonic lodges, and family ties provided a firm foundation for the Louisiana NAACP. For instance, the Greens of New Orleans were not only members of the city's branch from the 1920s through to the 1940s but were also major financial contributors to the NAACP. Indeed, the Greens were one of the wealthiest black families in New Orleans, with their grocery business and involvement with the Liberty Independent Life Insurance Company. They were major figures in the Knights of Pythias Masonic lodge, and were involved in many racial uplift groups. Nevertheless, individual women also contributed to the NAACP without necessarily having family links to other members. Such a person was Mrs. G. G. Willis of New Orleans, who was twice married, was a successful businesswoman, and contributed her wealth and social standing to the city's NAACP. Willis was a Catholic, involved in the Ladies Auxiliary of the Knights of Peter Claver, and active in the

National Urban League, all of which added to the levels of intricate social networking in New Orleans between African American organizations. While her two marriages may have given Willis respectability as the widow of successful businessmen of status, her independent work in the community also stood as a testament to her own beliefs in civil rights and local affairs.

Yet families and individual women did not have to be associated with wealth to be major contributors to the NAACP. In the main, they had middle-class jobs and shared a concept of civil rights work as being intricately linked to personal and collective morality. Teachers are a prime example of this connection between occupation and middle-class assertiveness. Education was the key to racial uplift programs in the United States generally, but in the Deep South, where blacks had been deprived systematically of school funds and facilities, it was believed to be the salvation of the race. Teachers were leaders within African American communities not because of their income, although the work provided a reasonably steady wage, but due to their educational capital. They had close links to the community they lived in and personally appreciated the circumstances of their pupils and their families. Indeed the success and ambition of parent teacher associations rested on this intricate relationship.

Education was a comprehensive social concern in African American communities, the vital component to wholesale racial improvement. Intricately bound up with this appreciation of public education and racial uplift was a developing perception of teaching black history, which was left out of the white-dictated history syllabus, as a midwife for collective self-confidence. Teachers brought African Americans' unique history not just to students but to the entire community. Indeed, schoolhouses were community buildings and were also used to educate adults about cleanliness and health, as well as reading and writing. The push for education highlighted middle-class ideals of what racial uplift meant and propagated concepts of industriousness and respectability. The message seemed to be that the general black population ought to pursue middle-class status and conduct themselves in a suitably dignified manner. In short, all blacks ought to be like their teachers and their middle-class associates in the NAACP.

Such ideas were firmly entrenched in the gender conventions of the time. The social disparities between men and women were reinforced to demonstrate the progress of black people in conforming to white value systems. Men were supposed to be the major, or preferably the sole, wage earners for the family unit, with women acting in a supportive role. Wives were to have complete responsibility for the domestic environment and the rearing of children. The reality was somewhat different from the ideal, however. Black women often had to work, albeit at such jobs that indicated a feminine disposition, such as teaching or nursing. The NAACP bureaucracy emphasized these gender expectations as well. Women were to help behind the scenes while their protectors and providers would lead the race into the Promised Land of American liberty.

Despite such marginal expectations, women were ideologically central to the achievement of civil rights objectives. Because women were seen as the moral bastion of the family and community, they were able to bring virtue and morality to the civil rights arena, as well as to political debates. Thus, the focus of racial improvement often fell disproportionately on their shoulders. During both world wars, members of the NAACP concentrated their concerns for group probity upon women's conduct. As white society tended to label African Americans by the lowest common denominator, black middle-class women were tasked with improving the standards of those deemed lower than they in the social order. Therefore, protecting the virtue of single women in urban areas, castigating prostitution and low morals, propagating ideals of a domestic idyll, and encouraging notions of gender inequality were important facets of civil rights work. This notion of the *ideal woman* was at the very heart of racial uplift movements and dictated the role of women in its implementation.

Many historical studies have reinforced this image of women working in the background for male leaders of the civil rights struggle by avoiding all mention of them or offering only token acknowledgment of their efforts. Yet the achievements of the NAACP's women's auxiliaries in campaigning, membership drives, fundraising, and youth councils were an integral part of the work branches did. Women's success in these areas derived from an intricate series of social and professional networks in which they were involved. Many of these networks complied with the gender definitions of the age, but without this extended community support, the local branches would never have garnered their local knowledge to the advantage of growing and stable membership numbers, propagation of the NAACP's message, and, importantly for the national organization, raising funds that kept the organization in existence.

Christopher Reed has characterized the participation of women in the Chicago NAACP as "quiet leadership." Yet in the Deep South attempting to register to vote and even joining the NAACP were actions that were equally as dangerous for women as for men, which certainly denotes a not-so-quiet definition of civil rights work. The experience of Louisiana's NAACP activists shows clearly that women were open to reprisals for their activities. It also contests the idea that women were involved in civil rights due to some *differential-reprisal* explanation, that they suffered less retaliation from white society than black men by participating in the movement. Still, many firsthand accounts and documents failed to record their courageous acts in any detail. The work of women has been silenced through a selective reading of recorded history and, in essence, their roles have been accepted as being so integral to the movement that it was barely referred to by many contemporaries.[1]

Women, of course, occupied positions of power within local NAACP branch hierarchies. They were vice-presidents and secretaries, such as Mrs. D. J. Dupuy of Baton Rouge, who occupied both jobs, Mrs. D. J. Guidry of New Orleans, secretary, and Mrs. H. W. Johnson of Monroe, vice-president. Their letters and reports to the central office in New York reveal the extent of their organizational control over the local branches.

Without this internal management, NAACP branches would have been merely vehicles for sporadic protest with little or no ideological continuity between disparate localized campaigns. Sociologist Gunnar Myrdal in 1944 described this trend as the "irregular vitality cycle" of community activism, in which a local issue stirs a population into brief political activity and then the organization becomes defunct after the issue subsides. Black women in the Louisiana NAACP turned branches into long-term community investments. The NAACP gave a city or parish some organizational structure in which to protest racial discrimination, with the possibility of some success in obtaining remedial action. Because branches were part of a broad national effort for integrationist policies, they also had clear political objectives through which to execute local campaigns. Therefore, maintaining strong local branches served the NAACP as a coherent strategy by which to coordinate activities and to establish a strong, identifiable reputation in a local setting. Women's contributions to this practical and ideological unity should not be underestimated. While it may have been referred to as a faith in the progress of race and belief in the eventual attainment of full American citizenship, these were powerful and meaningful principles to those who held them.[2]

The black middle classes channeled their social status and traditions within this framework of activism into the civil rights movement. It is perhaps asking too much of a social group to disengage entirely from its class roots and traditions of protest and engage in either contrary or revolutionary behavior. NAACP members did not wish to become less middle-class because they did not see their social standing as a detrimental position. Indeed they wished African Americans to achieve such social and cultural aspirations and obtain equal citizenship under the promises of the Declaration of Independence and the Constitution.[3]

The contrast between Miss Georgia M. Johnson of Alexandria and Mrs. D. J. Dupuy of Baton Rouge reveals how women were perceived within the NAACP branches in Louisiana. Johnson and Dupuy both were committed members of the NAACP. Both focused on integration and equality and the fight against racial discrimination. Yet their organizational approaches were very different. Dupuy managed the Baton Rouge branch extremely efficiently and was generally representative of the gender norms of her time; in fact, she used these expectations to dominate the bureaucratic leadership. Dupuy maintained her wide influence within the Baton Rouge branch with full cooperation of its president, Benjamin J. Stanley. As vice-president and secretary, Dupuy had a certain influence throughout the chapter, yet she did not have an overtly public leadership position.

Georgia Johnson, on the other hand, went against the conventions of the time and the norms of branch hierarchy, leading the crucial legal redress and legislation committee. Moreover, she acted in a highly individual manner. She was rarely constrained by NAACP bureaucracy, and her frustrations at the slowness of change led her to circumvent many local branch conventions. She grew increasingly disaffected with the Alexandria branch, while its leaders opposed her strong personal characteristics. Her uncompromising leadership of the Alexandria branch went against gender expectations of female participation in the NAACP and led to her isolation within the branch. Eventually she was even usurped, unconstitutionally, from her chairmanship of the legal committee.

Dupuy and Johnson shared the radical aims of the NAACP and did not flinch from fighting for the ballot and against racism in Louisiana. Dupuy worked within the structures of the time while Johnson attempted to break them. Dupuy typified the gender expectations in

Louisiana and therefore represented the early civil rights female activists. Johnson's approach pushed beyond such boundaries and challenged black male leadership in Alexandria, and illustrates the constraints upon women in the organization and the sexism and racism they all had to confront.

Johnson and Dupuy shared many of the same ideological convictions that spurred them on to join and to be active in the NAACP, namely, social awareness and religious beliefs. Their personalities affected their approach to civil rights activity. Dupuy's role can be seen as more operational compared to Johnson, who was much more of a front-line leader. Yet both could be described as leaders in their branches of the NAACP. Indeed Johnson's leadership role caused disquiet for the male-dominated hierarchy of the Alexandria chapter due to her more typical behavior as a front-line leader. In this way her role seemed to be a challenge to the NAACP hierarchy as it crossed well-drawn gender lines to traverse into male definitions of public leadership and domination of civil rights debates. There were no female leaders comparable to Johnson's uncompromising style in Louisiana at this time. Much more typical and, perhaps, more vital to NAACP stability in Louisiana was Dupuy, the archetypal organization woman. Even though she did not serve as a public spokesman, her wide-ranging activities in the NAACP and extensive social networking indicates that she was a true leader for the organization. Indeed her success in the Baton Rouge NAACP was entirely due to her recognition and acceptance of gender precepts and her ability to mold them into a workable managerial role for herself.

Black women's civil rights activity in Louisiana during the first half of the twentieth century covered the personal and communal elements of their concerns and hopes, and it complemented their preexisting benevolent and social organizing. Their work was interdependent with prevailing perceptions of American citizenship and gender distinctions, which saw the NAACP bringing together women and men to confront discrimination. Black women understood the double binds of racism and sexism, yet they joined the civil rights fight with the belief that racial discrimination took precedence over sexism, if, indeed, the latter was an applicable political issue for many women in this period. Chauvinism was a problem for NAACP women if it manifested itself as a Victorian morality preventing women from voting or exercising their political and social will. Yet the NAACP nationally and locally entirely accepted the Nineteenth Amendment as a beneficial and progressive reform for all

American society. The political battle for racial equality became relevant for many African Americans in part because it incorporated the differences between the sexes into a unified platform. Indeed women were supposed to have the potential to uplift the black population because of their inherent moral superiority. In the civic and political arena, therefore, women were the bedrock of collective progress.

Black women fought the NAACP's battle against segregation and racial discrimination on the front lines. As active members they directed public campaigns, recruited new members to their organizations, and encouraged youth participation. Individual women also acted as managers of local branches, which allowed them to run smoothly and effectively through challenging times. Arguably, without such dedication there would have been no NAACP of any substance in Louisiana.

APPENDIX 1

NAACP Administrative Structure, 1939

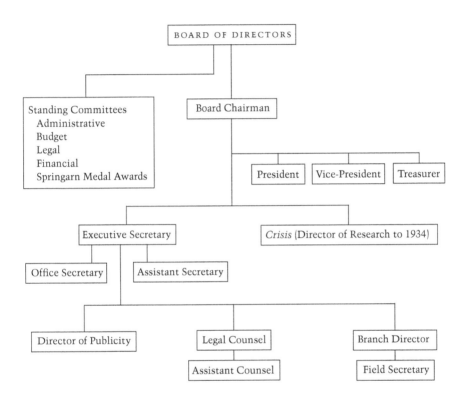

Source: Reproduced from the collections of the Manuscript Division, Library of Congress.

APPENDIX 2
NAACP Branch Organization

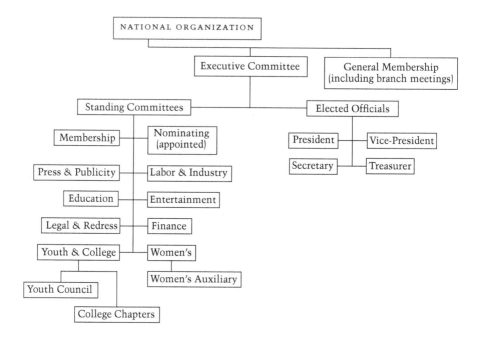

Source: Constitution and By-Laws for the Branches of the National Association for the Advancement of Colored People, 1917 (amended 1919, 1924, 1931). Papers of the NAACP, microfilm, Cambridge University Library.

APPENDIX 3

Selected NAACP Branch Membership Numbers, 1917–1945

	NEW ORLEANS	BATON ROUGE	MONROE	ALEXANDRIA
1917	56 (14)			
1918	100			
1919		59 (0)		
1920				
1924	206 (23)			
1925				
1926	267 (88)			
1927	415 (130)			
1928	505 (185)		63 (4)	
1929	109 (15)	67 (11)		
1930	74 (16)	74 (15)	52 (1)	102
1931	91 (42)	101 (21)	104 (11)	
1932		50 (10)	46 (8)	
1933		50 (15)		
1934	750*	75 (23)	77 (13)	
1935	714 (344)	90 (27)		
1936	907	70 (18)	77 (17)	
1937	359	133 (27)	51 (11)	
1938	348	123 (34)		
1939	1,154	254 (89)	24 (8)	
1940				
1941				
1942		21		
1943	3,019	1,433		152
1944	4,992		503	181
1945	8,077	1,671	1,059	212

Sources: Papers of the NAACP: Part 12: Selected Branch Files, 1913–1939, Series A: The South, Reels 13-15; Papers of the NAACP: Part 16: Selected Branch Files, 1940–55, Series B: The South, Louisiana, microfilm, Cambridge University Library.

Notes: Only membership numbers that could be confirmed from this source have been included. Figures in parentheses are the number of female members where known.

* An approximate number.

APPENDIX 4
*Women in Elected Office in Louisiana
NAACP Branches, 1917–1945*

NEW ORLEANS
Vice-President
  Miss F. A. Lewis, 1921
  Miss Thelma S. Shelby, 1939
  Miss Katie Wickham, 1941

Secretary
  Miss A. V. Dunn, 1925
  Mrs. D. J. Guidry, 1925–1932
  Mrs. Oneida Brown, 1934–1935
  Miss Edna St. Cyr, 1944

Secretary of Local Office
  Mrs. Gladys Greenwood, 1940

Assistant Secretary
  Miss A. V. Dunn, 1921
  Irene A. Williams, 1927–1930, 1932
  Mrs. O. M. Brown, 1935
  Miss Camille Harrison, 1936–1939

Executive Committee
  1917—Miss Charlotte Richards
  1918—Miss Charlotte Richards
  1921—Mrs. L. B. Landry
  1925—Miss F. A. Lewis (schools), Miss A. V. Dunn (teachers),
    Mrs. M. T. Wells (nurses), Mrs. Ida Tropaz (women's organizations)
  1931—Mrs. V. C. Thompson
  1936—Miss Elsie Lenoir, Miss Camille Harrison
  1938—Mrs. E. O. Lyons-Taylor, O. R. Brown
  1940—Mrs. Wylene Sazon, Miss N. Sanders, Miss A. Williams
  1941—Miss Edna St. Cyr
  1943—Mrs. Mildred C. Byrd, Mrs. Naomi Parnell, Miss Edna St. Cyr

1944—Mrs. Mildred C. Byrd, Mrs. Naomi Parnell, Mrs. M. P. Kennedy, Mrs. Noelie Cunningham, Mrs. G. G. Downey
1945 —Mrs. Noelie Cunningham, Mrs. G. G. Downey

BATON ROUGE
Vice-President
  Mrs. D. J. Dupuy, 1929–1934

Secretary
  Mrs. D. J. Dupuy, 1935–1939, 1942–1944

Assistant Secretary
  Mrs. D. J. Dupuy, 1941

Executive Committee
  1936—Mrs. Maggie Nance Ringgold
  1938—Miss Tracey E. Baker, Mrs. Maggie Nance Ringgold
  1939—Miss Tracey E. Baker
  1942—Miss Tracey E. Baker, Mrs. Jessie Ricard
  1944—Miss Tracey E. Baker, Mrs. Jessie Ricard

MONROE
Vice-President
  Mrs. H. W. Johnson, 1936–1938

Executive Committee
  1932—Mrs. H. W. Johnson, Mrs. Henrietta Lyles
  1936—Mrs. H. L. McClanahan (Honorary)
  1939—Mrs. H. L. McClanahan

ALEXANDRIA
Chair of Legal Redress and Legislation Committee
  Miss Georgia M. Johnson, 1941–1944

LAKE CHARLES
Secretary
  Miss Artholia Ladd, 1944

Executive Committee
  1944—Mrs. D. A. Combre, Mrs. A. Deboash

INDEPENDENCE
Secretary
    Myrtle Gordon, 1945

ST. JACKSON
Secretary
    Miss Leona F. Lasby, 1944

Sources: Papers of the NAACP: Part 12: Selected Branch Files, 1913–1939, Series A: The South, Reels 13-15; Papers of the NAACP: Part 16: Selected Branch Files, 1940–55, Series B: The South, Louisiana, microfilm, Cambridge University Library.

APPENDIX 5
NAACP Reported Lynchings in Louisiana, 1920–1945

YEAR-BY-YEAR

1921 (5)
    February 1, Port Allen—George Werner, black; shot and wounded rice planter; hanged by mob
    February 6, Monroe—Unidentified white man burnt to death
    April 15, Rodessa—Tony Williams, black; charged with rape; shot to death by posse
    September 13, Columbia—Gilman Holmes; alleged attack on a station agent; hanged, riddled with bullets, and burnt by mob of 500 men
    October 25, Winneboro—Sam Gordon, black; charged with murder of white farmer; hanged by mob

1922 (4)
    March 13, Holly Grove—Brown Culpepper, white; shot
    July 7, Benton—Joe Pemberton, black; shot two black women; hanged
    August 30, Bossier Parish—Thomas Rivers, black; said to have confessed to an assault on a white woman; hanged
    August, Mer Rouge—Watt Daniels, black, and Thomas F Richards, black; murdered by KKK*

1923 (1)
    January 3, Shreveport—Leslie Leggett, black; complaints that he was associating with white women; body found riddled with bullets

1924 (1)
    August 2, Athens—John Wilson, black; charged with murdering his wife

1925 (1)
    February 26, Benton—Joe Airy, black; alleged killer of a state highway officer; hanged by mob

---

*It turns out that Watt Daniel and Thomas Richards's racial identities were much more complicated. Jim Ruiz, *The Black Hood of the Ku Klux Klan* (London: Austin & Winfield, 1999), claims they were white.

1926 (2)
>August 4, Lachute—John Norris, black, twenty-four years old; allegedly attacked a ten-year-old girl; surrounded in cotton field and shot by a posse; reported to have died trying to escape
>October 7, Eunice—Louis Ledet, black; alleged attack on a six-year-old girl; taken from jail by masked men and lynched

1927 (1)
>April, DeQuincy—unnamed black man taken from jail, beaten and shot

1928 (1)
>June 2, Boyce—Lee and Dave Blackman, black; killed deputy sheriff; lynched by squad of officers

1931 (1)
>Pointe-A-La-Hache—Oscar Livingstone, black; alleged attack on a white woman; taken from jail and shot

1932 (1)
>November 19, Wisner—William House, black; two white women claimed he had insulted them; hanged by gang of men

1933 (4)
>January 12, Homer—Fell Jenkins, black; died of beating by three white men
>February 19, Ringgold—Nelson Nash, black; said to have confessed to beating to death of a cashier of Ringgold Bank
>September 26, Opelousas—John White, black; accused of an attempted attack on a white woman; shot to death by mob
>October 12, Labadieville—Freddy Moore, black; arrested for questioning over murder of a white girl; hanged

1934 (2)
>July 9, Bastrop—Andrew McLeod, black; said to have confessed to an attack on a nineteen-year-old white girl; hanged by mob at courthouse
>August 3, Caddo—Grafton Page, black; beaten to death by another black man after alleged insult to a black girl

1935 (2)
>January 11, Franklington—Jerome Wilson, black; convicted of killing Sheriff D. C. Wood; shot and beaten to death

February 24, Maringouin—Anderson Ward, black; fought with a white man; shot to death by a mob

1938 (1)
   October 13, Ruston—R. C. Williams, black; suspected of killing a white man and beating his female companion; hanged, shot, and burned

1939 (1)
   May, New Orleans—Robert Eggleston, black; drowned, body not identified

Total = 30 (28 black, 2 white)

BREAKDOWN OF JUSTIFICATIONS FOR BLACK LYNCHINGS
Murder = 8 (2 planters, 4 law officers, 1 girl, 1 unknown)
Assault on whites = 6
Rape/attempted rape = 5
Associating with white women = 1
Unknown = 4

Source: Annual Reports of the National Association for the Advancement of Colored People for the years 1920–1945, Spingarn Collection, Howard-Tilton Memorial Library, Tulane University, New Orleans.

APPENDIX 6

Honor Roll of NAACP Branches in Louisiana, 1927–1943

1927
Lake Providence*

1931
Baton Rouge*, Monroe*

1932
Baton Rouge*

1933
Baton Rouge

1934
Baton Rouge, Jennings, Monroe

1935
Baton Rouge, New Orleans, Plaquemine

1936
Monroe, New Orleans, Shreveport

1937
Baton Rouge, Lake Charles, Shreveport

1938
Baton Rouge, Lake Charles, Monroe, Transylvania*

1939
Baton Rouge, New Orleans

1940
Baton Rouge, Monroe

1941
Baton Rouge, Monroe

1942
Alexandria, Baton Rouge, Donaldsonville, Monroe, New Orleans, Plaquemine, Shreveport

1943
Alexandria, Baton Rouge, Lake Charles, New Orleans, Plaquemine, Shreveport

Sources: Annual Reports of the National Association for the Advancement of Colored People, 1927–1943, Spingarn Collection, Howard-Tilton Memorial Library, Tulane University, New Orleans

Note: Honor rolls appeared in the NAACP annual reports congratulating branches for reaching their calculated apportionment to national funds.

* Indicates that a branch contributed more than its apportionment in that year.

NOTES

INTRODUCTION

Epigraph: Gerda Lerner, ed., *Black Women in White America: A Documentary History* (New York: Pantheon, 1972), xvii.

1. John H. Scott with Cleo Scott Brown, *Witness to the Truth: My Struggle for Human Rights in Louisiana* (Columbia: University of South Carolina Press, 2003), 124–125.

2. Papers of the NAACP, microfilm, Cambridge University Library; NAACP Field Director Reports, Louisiana, Amistad Research Center, Tulane University, New Orleans, Louisiana.

3. Charles Payne, "Men Led, but Women Organized: Movement Participation of Women in the Mississippi Delta," in Vicki L. Crawford, J. A. Rouse, and Barbara Woods, eds., *Women in the Civil Rights Movement: Trailblazers and Torchbearers, 1941–1965* (Bloomington: Indiana University Press, 1990), 1–11.

4. Manning Marable, *How Capitalism Underdeveloped Black America* (Boston: South End Press, 1983), 70.

5. Ibid., 103; Paula Giddings, *When and Where I Enter: The Impact of Black Women on Race and Sex in America* (New York: William Morrow & Co., 1984), 5, 178, 183, 257.

6. Cheryl Townsend Gilkes, "Holding Back the Ocean with a Broom: Black Women and Community Work," in La Frances Rodgers-Rose, ed., *The Black Woman* (London: SAGE, 1980), 226–227; Jewel L. Prestage, "Political Behavior of American Black Women: An Overview," in ibid., 233–234.

7. Robin D. G. Kelley, "We Are Not What We Seem: Rethinking Black Working-Class Opposition in the Jim Crow South," *Journal of American History* 80 (June 1993); Peter J. Ling and Sharon Monteith, eds., *Gender in the Civil Rights Movement* (London: Garland Publishing, 1999); Lynne Olson, *Freedom's Daughters: The Unsung Heroines of the Civil Rights Movement from 1830 to 1970* (New York: Scribner, 2001); Mark Robert Schneider, *"We Return Fighting": The Civil Rights Movement in the Jazz Age* (Boston: Northeastern University Press, 2002).

8. Charles M. Payne, *I've Got the Light of Freedom: The Organizing Tradition and the Mississippi Freedom Struggle* (Berkeley: University of California Press, 1995), 267–271.

9. Payne, "Men Led, but Women Organized," 3–9; Payne, *I've Got the Light of Freedom*, 3–9, 274–276.

10. Bernice McNair Barnett, "Invisible Southern Black Women Leaders in the Civil Rights Movement: The Triple Constraints of Gender, Race, and Class," *Gender and Society* 7, no. 2 (June 1993): 176–177; Barbara Omolade, *The Rising Song of African American Women* (London: Routledge, 1994), 47; Darlene Clark Hine and Kathleen Thompson, *A Shining Thread of Hope: The History of Black Women in America* (New York: Broadway Books, 1998), 200.

11. Belinda Robnett, *How Long? How Long? African-American Women in the Struggle for Civil Rights* (Oxford: Oxford University Press, 1997), 19–21, 190–193.

12. Dorothy Autrey, "'Can These Bones Live?': The National Association for the Advancement of Colored People in Alabama, 1918–1930," *Journal of Negro History* 82, no. 1 (winter 1997): 2–9.

13. Christopher Robert Reed, *The Chicago NAACP and the Rise of the Black Professional Leadership, 1910–1966* (Bloomington: Indiana University Press, 1997), viii, 3–4, 69, 116; Kelley, "'We Are Not What We Seem,'" 112; Barnett, "Invisible Southern Black Women Leaders," 163; Belinda Robnett, "Women in the SNCC: Ideology, Organisational Structure, and Leadership," in Ling and Monteith, *Gender in the Civil Rights Movement*, 8.

14. Reed, *Chicago NAACP*, 116, 144.

15. Merline Pitre, *In Struggle Against Jim Crow: Lula B. White and the NAACP, 1900–1957* (College Station: Texas A&M University Press, 1999), 62.

16. Ibid., 25.

17. Ibid., 129, 133–134.

18. Barbara Ransby, *Ella Baker and the Black Freedom Movement: A Radical Democratic Vision* (Chapel Hill: University of North Carolina Press, 2003), 4, 9, 106, 136–139.

19. Quoted in Joanne Grant, *Ella Baker: Freedom Bound* (New York: John Wiley & Sons, 1998), 227–228.

20. Ransby, *Ella Baker*, 122–124.

21. Glenda Elizabeth Gilmore, *Gender and Jim Crow: Women and the Politics of White Supremacy in North Carolina, 1896–1920* (Chapel Hill: University of North Carolina Press, 1996), 63, 75, 101; Anne Standley, "The Role of Black Women in the Civil Rights Movement," in Crawford et al., *Women in the Civil Rights Movement*, 183; Deborah Gray White, *Too Heavy a Load: Black Women in Defense of Themselves, 1894–1994* (New York: W. W. Norton, 1999), 178–179; Olson, *Freedom's Daughters*, 16.

22. Rosa Parks, with Jim Haskins, *Rosa Parks: My Story* (London: Puffin Books, 1992), 69–77.

23. Ibid., 80–81; Rosa Parks, with Gregory J Reed, *Quiet Strength: The Faith, the Hope, and the Heart of a Woman Who Changed a Nation* (Grand Rapids, MI: Zondervan, 1994), 21, 84.

24. Douglas Brinkley, *Mine Eyes Have Seen the Glory: The Life of Rosa Parks* (London: Weidenfeld & Nicolson, 2000), 48; Parks, *Quiet Strength*, 21.

25. Adam Fairclough, "State of the Art: Historians and the Civil Rights Movement," *Journal of American Studies* 24, no. 3 (December 1990): 392; Brian Ward and Tony Badger, "Introduction," in *The Making of Martin Luther King and the Civil Rights Movement* (London: Macmillan, 1996), 3.

26. Adam Fairclough, "The Civil Rights Movement in Louisiana, 1939–54," in Ward and Badger, *The Making of Martin Luther King*, 17.

27. Adam Fairclough, *Race and Democracy: The Civil Rights Struggle in Louisiana 1915–1972* (Athens: University of Georgia Press, 1995), xv–xvi; Fairclough, *Teaching Equality: Black Schools in the Age of Jim Crow* (Athens: University of Georgia Press, 2001), 47; see also Fairclough, *Better Day Coming: Blacks and Equality, 1890–2000* (London: Penguin Books, 2001), 100–101.

28. Fairclough, *Race and Democracy*, 17–18, 48.

29. Schneider, *We Return Fighting*, 49.

ONE
WEAPONS OF THE UTMOST VALUE

Epigraph: Twentieth Annual Report of the National Association for the Advancement of Colored People for the year 1929, 43, Spingarn Collection, Howard-Tilton Memorial Library, Tulane University, New Orleans.

1. Mary White Ovington, *The Walls Come Tumbling Down* (New York: Arno Press, 1969), 104; Carolyn Wedin, *Inheritors of the Spirit: Mary White Ovington and the Founding of the NAACP* (New York: John Wiley & Sons, 1998), 106; Charles Flint Kellogg, *NAACP: A History of the National Association of Colored People, vol. 1, 1909–1920* (Baltimore: Johns Hopkins University Press, 1967), 15; Warren D. St. James, *NAACP: Triumphs of a Pressure Group, 1909–1980* (New York: Exposition Press, 1980), 242–248.

2. Constitution of the National Association for the Advancement of Colored People, February 1936, Article II, Article IV, Sections 1, 2, 4; Constitution and By-Laws of the NAACP, June 22, 1936, Article II, Article IV Sections 1, 3, 5. The 1946 Constitution and By-Laws for Branches of the NAACP is set out in Appendix E of Warren D. St. James, *The National Association for the Advancement of Colored People: A Case Study in Pressure Groups* (New York: Exposition Press, 1958), 182–200; see Article II, III, IV, Sections 3, 5 (172–175); Appendix 1.

3. Langston Hughes, *Fight for Freedom: The Story of the NAACP* (New York: W. W. Norton, 1962), 26; Wedin, *Inheritors of the Spirit*, 115–116.

4. W. E. B. Du Bois, Editorial Opinion, "Votes for Women," *The Crisis: A Record of the Darker Races*, September 1912, 234; Adella Hunt Logan, "Colored Woman as Voters," *Crisis*, September 1912, 242–243; Mary B. Talbert, "Women and Colored Women," *Crisis*, August 1915, 184; W. E. B. Du Bois, "Woman Suffrage," *Crisis*, November 1915, 29–30; "New Orleans Number," *Crisis*, February 1916.

5. Hughes, *Fight for Freedom*, 27; B. Joyce Ross, *J. E. Spingarn and the Rise of the NAACP, 1911–1939* (New York: Atheneum, 1972), 52, 55–59; William B. Hixson Jr., *Moorfield Storey and the Abolitionist Tradition* (New York: Oxford University Press, 1972), 123–124, 144.

6. Wedin, *Inheritors of the Spirit*, 123, 137–274; Lynne Olson, *Freedom's Daughters: The Unsung Heroines of the Civil Rights Movement from 1830 to 1970* (New York: Scribner, 2001), 71–73.

7. Mark Robert Schneider, *"We Return Fighting": The Civil Rights Movement in the Jazz Age* (Boston: Northeastern University Press, 2002), 45, 48; Kellogg, *NAACP*, 118; Elliott Rudwick and August Meier, "The Rise of the Black Secretariat in the NAACP, 1909–35," in Meier and Rudwick, *Along the Color Line: Explorations in the Black Experience* (Urbana: University of Illinois Press, 1976), 94, 114; Sandra Kathryn Wilson, *In Search of Democracy: The NAACP Writings of James Weldon Johnson, Walter White, and Roy Wilkins* (Oxford: Oxford University Press, 1999), 4; Ovington, *Walls Come Tumbling Down*, 111.

8. Rudwick and Meier, "Rise of the Black Secretariat in the NAACP," 94, 228; Kellogg, *NAACP*, 236, 291; Wilson, *In Search of Democracy*, 138; Mary Childs Nerney, cited in Rudwick and Meier, "Rise of the Black Secretariat in the NAACP," 102; Ross, *J. E. Spingarn*, 79–80.

9. Rudwick and Meier, "Rise of the Black Secretariat in the NAACP," 111.

10. David Levering Lewis, *W. E .B. Du Bois: The Fight for Equality and the American Century, 1919-1963* (New York: Henry Holt, 2000), 335-348; W. E. B. Du Bois, *Dusk of Dawn: An Essay Toward an Autobiography of a Race Concept* (London: Transaction Publishers, 1940), 309; St. James, *National Association for the Advancement of Colored People*, 212; Mark V. Tushnet, *The NAACP's Legal Strategy Against Segregated Education, 1925-50* (Chapel Hill: University of North Carolina Press, 1987), 160; August Meier and J. H. Bracey Jr., "The NAACP as a Reform Movement, 1909-1963: To Reach the Conscience of America," *Journal of Southern History* 59, no. 1 (February 1993): 17; Wedin, *Inheritors of the Spirit*, 269; W. E. B. Du Bois, editorial, *Crisis*, January 1934; Rudwick and Meier, "Rise of the Black Secretariat in the NAACP," 114-115.

11. Kellogg, *NAACP*, 143-144; Ross, *J. E. Spingarn*, 39.

12. St. James, *National Association for the Advancement of Colored People*, 44; Wedin, *Inheritors of the Spirit*, 161.

13. Wilson, *In Search of Democracy*, 16; Robert L. Zangrando, *The NAACP Crusade Against Lynching, 1909-1950* (Philadelphia: Temple University Press, 1980), 11, 19, 83; Charles M. Payne, *I've Got the Light of Freedom: The Organizing Tradition and the Mississippi Freedom Struggle* (Berkeley: University of California Press, 1995), 19; 25th Annual Report of the NAACP, 1934, 23; Appendix 5.

14. Kenneth W. Goings, *The NAACP Comes of Age: The Defeat of Judge J. Parker* (Bloomington: Indiana University Press, 1990), xi.

15. Ibid., 56, xii; Hughes, *Fight for Freedom*, 74; 21st Annual Report of the NAACP, 1930, 43.

16. 23rd Annual Report of the NAACP, 1932, 28; in *Smith v. Allwright* (1944) the Supreme Court declared white primaries to be racially discriminatory.

17. Walter White, *A Man Called White: The Autobiography of Walter White* (Athens: University of Georgia Press, 1948), 129, 133; Wedin, *Inheritors of the Spirit*, 247-250; Kenneth Robert Janken, *White: The Biography of Walter White, Mr. NAACP* (New York: New Press, 2003), 148-154; Robert L. Jack, *History of the National Association for the Advancement of Colored People* (Boston: Meador Press, 1943), 56; Meier and Bracey, "NAACP as a Reform Movement," 16; Ross, *J. E. Spingarn*, 152, 160; Lerone Bennett Jr., *The Shaping of Black America: The Struggle and Triumphs of African-Americans, 1619 to the 1990s* (London: Penguin Books, 1975), 270-271; St. James, *NAACP*, 71-72; 20th Annual Report of the NAACP, 1929, 23; Social Security Bill (Wagner-Lewis), 26th Annual Report of the NAACP, 1935, 5; Wages and Hours Bill (Sen. Hugo L. Black), 28th Annual Report of the NAACP, 1937, 12; Beth Tompkins Bates, "A New Crowd Challenges the Agenda of the Old Guard in the NAACP, 1933-1941," *American Historical Review* 102, no. 2 (April 1997): 340-341, 370-372.

18. John M. Barry, *Rising Tide: The Great Mississippi Flood of 1927 and How It Changed America* (New York: Simon & Schuster, 1997), 313, 315, 320, 322-323, 325, 328, 388; the Colored Advisory Committee was chaired by the conservative Robert Russa Moton, successor of Booker T. Washington as principal at the Tuskegee Institute.

19. Edna Lonigan, "Report of the Survey of the National Association for the Advancement of Colored People," March 22, 1932, Container 22, Folder: NAACP Crisis Magazine and NAACP Finances, 1932, Roy Wilkins Papers, Manuscript Division, Library of Congress,

Washington, D.C., 80–83 (hereafter Lonigan report); the report's radical conclusions were never officially implemented by the NAACP board of directors as it was a privately commissioned study.

20. Ibid.

21. Ross, *J. E. Spingarn*, 169–170; Sheldon Avery, *Up from Washington: William Pickens and the Negro Struggle for Equality, 1900–1954* (Newark: Associated University Press, 1989), 129–130; Andor Skotnes, "Narratives of Juanita Jackson Mitchell: The Making of a 1930s Freedom Movement Leader," *Maryland Historian* 1, no. 1 (fall/winter 2001): 48; Bates, "New Crowd Challenges the Agenda of the Old Guard," 352; Roy Wilkins and Tom Mathews, *Standing Fast: The Autobiography of Roy Wilkins* (New York: Da Capo Press, 1994), 150.

22. 23rd Annual Report of the NAACP, 1932, 7; Bettie E. Parham, "What of the Negro Bourgeoisie?" *Crisis*, July 1936, 215; White, *Man Called White*, 193; Zangrando, *NAACP Crusade Against Lynching*, 110; Mary Ellison, *The Black Experience: American Blacks Since 1865* (London: B. T. Batsford, 1974), 132.

23. Report by Bureau Agent Harry D. Gulley, January 16, 1923, New Orleans, in Roberts A. Hill, ed., *The Marcus Garvey and Universal Negro Improvement Association Papers* (Berkeley: University of California Press, 1990), 10 vols. (hereafter *Garvey Papers*), 5:178; Papers of the NAACP: Part 12: Selected Branch Files, 1913–1939, Series A, Reels 13–15: The South, Louisiana, microfilm, Cambridge University Library.

24. Report by UNIA secretary general Henrietta V. Davis in the *Negro World*, August 1929, *Garvey Papers*, 7:404; Report of Activities in UNIA Divisions and Garvey Clubs by Samuel A. Haynes, 7:671; Appendix 3.

25. Zangrando, *NAACP Crusade Against Lynching*, 167–169; Ernest Obadele-Starks, *Black Unionism in the Industrial South* (College Station: Texas A&M University Press, 2000), 112, 121–122, 127; Adam Fairclough, *Better Day Coming: Blacks and Equality, 1890–2000* (London: Penguin Books, 2001), 157, 186–188; Genna Rae McNeil, *Groundwork: Charles Hamilton Houston and the Struggle for Civil Rights* (Philadelphia: University of Pennsylvania Press, 1983), 164, 166.

26. Fairclough, *Better Day Coming*, 197.

27. White, *Man Called White*, 153; Kellogg, *NAACP*, 121; Ovington, *Walls Come Tumbling Down*, 111; McNeil, *Groundwork*, xvii–xix, 30, 71, 83; Tushnet, *NAACP's Legal Strategy Against Segregated Education*, xii.

28. McNeil, *Groundwork*, 117, 134–135; Kellogg, *NAACP*, 293; White, *Man Called White*, 142.

29. 11th Annual Report of the NAACP, 1920, 13.

30. McNeil, *Groundwork*, 152; Tushnet, *NAACP's Legal Strategy Against Segregated Education*, 100.

31. Kellogg, *NAACP*, 293; Wedin, *Inheritors of the Spirit*, 124, 194.

32. Tushnet, *NAACP's Legal Strategy Against Segregated Education*, 14.

33. Ibid., 34.

34. Ibid., 71–74, 85.

35. Ross, *J. E. Spingarn*, 35; Tushnet, *NAACP's Legal Strategy Against Segregated Education*, 99; Wilkins, *Standing Fast*, 147.

36. Constitution of the NAACP, 1936, Article VII; St. James, *National Association for*

the Advancement of Colored People, 73; 1st Annual Report of the NAACP, January 1911, 5; 20th Annual Report of the NAACP, 1929, 43; Jack, *History of the National Association,* 19; 32nd Annual Report of the NAACP, 1941, 37.

37. 20th Annual Report for the NAACP, 1929, 48–49; St. James, *National Association for the Advancement of Colored People,* 73–75.

38. St. James, *National Association for the Advancement of Colored People,* 77; Branch Constitution and By-Laws of the NAACP, 1917 (amended 1919, 1924, 1931), Article 1, Section 2, Article 2, Sections 2, 3, 1, 4; Appendix 2.

39. Branch Constitution, 1917, Article II, Section 4 (a, b, e, and f), 5; Constitution and By-Laws for the Branches of the NAACP, 1937, Article II, Section 4 (d), 5.

40. Branch Constitution, 1917, Article X, Section 1, 14; Branch Constitution, 1937, Article II, Section 4 (g) and Article IX, Section 1, 5, 17; see also Christopher Robert Reed, *The Chicago NAACP and the Rise of Black Professional Leadership, 1910–1966* (Bloomington: Indiana University Press, 1997), 55–57.

41. Branch Constitution, 1917, Article III, Section 1, 7; Branch Constitution, 1937, Article III, Section 1, 6; Constitution of the NAACP 1946, Article III, 186.

42. 16th Annual Report of the NAACP, 1925, 60; Branch Constitution, 1917, Article XIV, 16; Branch Constitution, 1937, Article XIV, 20; 20th Annual Report of the NAACP, 1929, 49.

43. 16th Annual Report of the NAACP, 1925, 33; Branch Constitution, 1917, Article XI, Section 2, Article XIV, 15, 16; the $50 minimum was omitted from the 1937 revision as the Great Depression made it a difficult task for smaller branches to achieve.

44. 12th Annual Report of the NAACP, 1921, 88–89; 19th Annual Report of the NAACP, 1928, 31; Branch Constitution, 1917, Article XIII, 16; St. James, *National Association for the Advancement of Colored People,* 80–82.

45. Skotnes, "Narratives of Juanita Jackson Mitchell," 47–49.

46. Program Book for NAACP Branches: Education for Negroes, 1935, 19–20, A. P. Tureaud Papers, Roll 10, Amistad Research Center, Tulane University, New Orleans.

47. *Crisis,* September 1938, 308; Program Book for NAACP Branches: *Education for Negroes,* 1935, 19–20.

48. Aaron Henry with Constance Curry, *The Fire Ever Burning* (Jackson: University Press of Mississippi, 2000), 40, 44; Daisy E. Lampkin, "On the N.A.A.C.P. Southern Front," *Crisis,* May 1935, 140, 153; New Orleans, Selected Branch Files, 1913–1939, Reel 15, Papers of NAACP.

49. Ibid.; Adam Fairclough, *Race and Democracy: The Civil Rights Struggle in Louisiana, 1915–1972* (Athens: University of Georgia Press, 1995), 272–273, 278.

50. Kellogg, *NAACP,* 61, 119; Jack, *History of the National Association,* 9; St. James, *National Association for the Advancement of Colored People,* 77; W. E. B. Du Bois, *The Autobiography of W. E. B. Du Bois: A Soliloquy on Viewing My Life from the Last Decade of Its First Century* (New York: International Publishers, 1991), 339; Lonigan report, 25.

51. Constitution of the NAACP, June 1936, Article II; Constitution of the NAACP, 1946, Articles II, IX, X, in St. James, *National Association for the Advancement of Colored People,* 177.

52. Lonigan report, 37–38; NAACP Branch Constitution, 1931, Article V, Section 4, 8, 17; NAACP Branch Constitution, 1937, Article V, Sections 4, 5, 13; the apportionment was 50 percent of all membership money that was sent to the New York office and $15 of every $25 raised by a branch.

53. Lonigan report, 39.

54. Ibid., 40–41.

55. Ibid., 46; the Lonigan report stated that "Mrs. Lampkin's salary certainly does not appear too high," especially in comparison with Pickens', 86–87: Lampkin earned $3,000 in 1931, $2,700 in 1932; Pickens $4,000 in 1931, $3,600 the year after, 27th Annual Report of the NAACP, 1936, 25. Lampkin was national field secretary for the NAACP from 1935 to 1947. Darlene Clark Hine, ed., *Black Women in America: An Historical Encyclopaedia* (New York: Carlson Publishing, 1993), 1:690–693.

56. Walter White, NAACP executive secretary, to William Pickens, director of branches, April 9, 1935, cited in Avery, *Up from Washington*, 163; Pickens to White, 12 April 1935, ibid.; Daisy Lampkin, national field secretary, to Pickens, 8 February 1935, ibid.

57. Payne, *I've Got the Light of Freedom*, 85–88; Olson, *Freedom's Daughters*, 132–133.

58. Evelyn Brooks Higginbotham, "Beyond the Sound of Silence: Afro-American Women in History," *Gender and History* 1, no. 1 (spring 1989): 54–55, 63.

59. Carol Mueller, "Ella Baker and the Origins of 'Participatory Democracy,'" in Vicki L. Crawford, J. A. Rouse, and Barbara Woods, eds., *Women in the Civil Rights Movement: Trailblazers and Torchbearers, 1941–1965* (Bloomington: Indiana University Press, 1990), 51–62; Hine, *Black Women in America*, 693; Joanne Grant, *Ella Baker: Freedom Bound* (New York: John Wiley & Sons, 1998), 54–55, 69, 73.

60. Skotnes, "Narratives of Juanita Jackson Mitchell," 44, 48–49, 47.

61. Fairclough, *Race and Democracy*, 19; "Economic Program for Branches," 22nd Annual Report of the NAACP, 1931, 33; Ross, *J. E. Spingarn*, 24.

62. 16th Annual Conference of the NAACP, 1925, 39.

63. Gunnar Myrdal, *An American Dilemma, vol. 2: The Negro Problem and Modern Democracy* (London: Transaction Publishers, 1944), 820; 15th Annual Conference of the NAACP, 1924, 2.

TWO

THE SYMPATHY OF WOMEN

Epigraph: Sylvanie Williams, suffragist and president of the Phyllis Wheatley Club of New Orleans, to National American Woman Suffrage Association board member Susan B. Anthony during the NAWSA New Orleans Convention in 1903, cited in Rosalyn Terborg-Penn, *African American Women in the Struggle for the Vote, 1850–1920* (Bloomington: Indiana University Press, 1998), 116.

1. Claude F. Jacobs, "Benevolent Societies of New Orleans Blacks During the Late Nineteenth and Early Twentieth Centuries," *Louisiana History* 29, no. 1 (winter 1988): 21.

2. Laura Foner, "The Free People of Color in Louisiana and St. Dominique: A Comparative Portrait of Two Three-Caste Slave Societies," *Journal of Southern History* 3 (1970): 406; Joseph G. Tregle, *Louisiana in the Age of Jackson: A Clash of Cultures and Personalities* (Baton Rouge: Louisiana State University Press, 1999), ix, 23.

3. Adam Fairclough, *Race and Democracy: The Civil Rights Struggle in Louisiana, 1915–1972* (Athens: University of Georgia Press, 1995), 2–5, 15–17; Mark Robert Schneider, *"We Return Fighting": The Civil Rights Movement in the Jazz Age* (Boston: Northeastern University Press, 2002), 295–296; A. P. Tureaud, New Orleans NAACP branch, to Rob-

ert Bagnall, NAACP director of branches, 24 October 1931, Papers of the NAACP: Part 12: Selected Branch Files, 1913–1939, Series A, Reel 14: The South, Louisiana, microfilm, Cambridge University Library; these racial identities were often seen as important in the emerging jazz scene in New Orleans, such as Creole of Color clarinetist Sidney Bechet and black American trumpeter Louis Armstrong; Louis Armstrong, *Satchmo: My Life in New Orleans* (New York: Da Capo Press, 1954), 22–25, 31, 181–186; Sidney Bechet, *Treat It Gentle* (London: Cassell & Co., 1960), 83–91; Louis Armstrong, *Louis Armstrong, in His Own Words: Selected Writings* (New York: Oxford University Press, 1999), 5, 24.

4. Willard B. Gatewood, *Aristocrats of Color: The Black Elite, 1880–1920* (Bloomington: Indiana University Press, 1993), 214.

5. Jacobs, "Benevolent Societies of New Orleans," 24, 32.

6. Nancy S. Dye, "Introduction," in Noralee Frankel and Nancy S. Dye, eds., *Gender, Class, Race, and Reform in the Progressive Era* (Lexington: University Press of Kentucky, 1991), 5; Anne Firor Scott, "Most Invisible of All: Black Women's Voluntary Associations," *Journal of Southern History* 51 (February 1990): 6, 11–12; Angela Davis, *Women, Race, and Class* (London: Women's Press, 1982), 5.

7. Shirley J. Carlson, "Black Ideals of Womanhood in the Late Victorian Era," *Journal of Negro History* 77, no. 2 (1992): 61–62; H. E. Sterx, *The Free Negro in Ante-Bellum Louisiana* (Madison, NJ: Fairleigh Dickinson University Press, 1972), 228–231; Robert C. Reinders, "The Free Negro in the New Orleans Economy, 1850–1860," *Louisiana History* 6 (1965): 281, 278; Joel Williamson, *New People: Miscegenation and Mulattoes in the United States* (New York: Free Press, 1980), 91; Mary Gehman, *Women and New Orleans: A History* (New Orleans: Margaret Media, 1988), 56.

8. Kim Lacy Rogers, *Righteous Lives: Narratives of the New Orleans Civil Rights Movement* (New York: New York University Press, 1993), 200–201.

9. Linda O. McMurray, *To Keep the Waters Troubled: The Life of Ida B. Wells* (Oxford: Oxford University Press, 1998), xiv; Patricia A. Schechter, *Ida B. Wells-Barnett and American Reform, 1880–1930* (Chapel Hill: University of North Carolina Press, 2001), 134–135, 137; Elsa Barkley Brown, "Negotiating and Transforming the Public Sphere: African American Political Life in the Transition from Slavery to Freedom," *Public Culture* 7 (1994): 139, 140, 144.

10. Linda Gordon, "Black and White Visions of Welfare: Women's Welfare Activism, 1890–1945," *Journal of American History* 78 (September 1991): 587; Stephanie J. Shaw, "Black Club Women and the Creation of the National Association of Colored Women," *Journal of Women's History* 3, no. 2 (fall 1991): 12; Paula Giddings, *When and Where I Enter: The Impact of Black Women on Race and Sex in America* (New York: William Morrow & Company, 1984), 5.

11. Gordon, "Black and White Visions of Welfare," 583, 587; Stephanie J. Shaw, *What a Woman Ought To Be and To Do: Black Professional Women Workers During the Jim Crow Era* (Chicago: University of Chicago Press, 1996), 81; Anna Julia Cooper, *A Voice from the South: By a Black Woman of the South* (Xenia, OH: Aldine Printing House, 1892), 22.

12. Gerda Lerner, "Early Community Work of Black Club Women," *Journal of Negro History*, 59 (1974): 160, 167.

13. Ibid., 162; Beverly W. Jones, "Mary Church Terrell and the National Association of Colored Women, 1896 to 1901," *Journal of Negro History* 46, no. 1 (spring 1916): 24; Debo-

rah Gray White, *Too Heavy a Load: Black Women in Defense of Themselves, 1894–1994* (New York: W. W. Norton, 1999), 54.

14. Jones, "Mary Church Terrell," 24–25, 28.

15. Ibid., 26.

16. Giddings, *When and Where I Enter*, 105, 108.

17. Anne Meis Knupfer, "'If You Can't Push, Pull, If You Can't Pull, Please Get Out of the Way': The Phyllis Wheatley Club and Home in Chicago, 1896 to 1920," *Journal of Negro History* 82, no. 2 (spring 1997): 223; Flint-Goodridge Hospital and Nurse Training School, First Annual Report, 1916, Joseph Hardin Papers, Box 1, Amistad Research Center, Tulane University, New Orleans.

18. Knupfer, "If You Can't Push, Pull," 223; Flint-Goodridge Hospital and Nurse Training School, First Annual Report, 1916, Joseph Hardin Papers, Box 1, Amistad Research Center; A. E. Perkins, ed., *Who's Who in Colored Louisiana* (Baton Rouge: Douglas Loan Co, 1930), 149; New Orleans NAACP membership lists, Selected Branch Files, 1913–1939, Reels 14 and 15, Papers of the NAACP; in 1935 the Nurses Alumni contributed $5 to branch coffers.

19. Louis Martinet to Albion W. Tourgee, December 7, 1891, cited in Otto H. Olsen, ed., *The Thin Disguise:* Plessy v. Ferguson, *A Documentary Presentation* (New York: Humanities Press, 1967), 12; Martinet to Tourgee, October 5, 1891, ibid., 56; the significance of *Plessy v. Ferguson* and the "separate but equal" ruling of the Supreme Court reinforced segregation in the United States and gave it legal standing. The NAACP was to fight in principle against this decision until it reversed it with *Brown v. Board of Education* in 1954.

20. Terborg-Penn, *African American Women in the Struggle for the Vote*, 23; Brown, "Negotiating and Transforming the Public Sphere," 123, 124; Jones, "Mary Church Terrell," 27–29; White, *Too Heavy a Load*, 52.

21. Gehman, *Women and New Orleans*, 99; Terborg-Penn, *African American Women in the Struggle for the Vote*, 36, 82.

22. Linda Sharon Bachman, "Uncompromising Sisters: The Women's Suffrage Movement in Louisiana, 1900–1921" (Honors Thesis, Department of American Studies, Newcomb College, 1981), Jones-Hall Louisiana Collection, Tulane University, 13, 31, 33; women who owned property (and therefore paid tax) were eligible to vote in Louisiana on bond issues as early as 1879, although it seems few did so. This was an extension of the old French laws that gave women legal rights to possess property entitlements and to have control over their own estates and inheritances separate from men. In 1898, when white suffragist Kate Gordon investigated New Orleans women of property, she discovered 15,000 such cases. Tellingly, two-thirds were white and thus eligible to vote, Gehman, *Women and New Orleans*, ii, 101.

23. Mrs. Wilton McHenry, leader of the Louisiana Suffrage Party in Ouachita Parish, *Monroe News Star*, May 11, 1914, cited in Bachman, "Uncompromising Sisters," 13–14, 39; William Ivy Hair, *The Kingfish and His Realm: The Life and Times of Huey Long* (Baton Rouge: Louisiana State University Press, 1991), 114.

24. Terborg-Penn, *African American Women in the Struggle for the Vote*, 91–92.

25. Sylvanie Francaz Williams, "The Social Status of the Negro Woman," *Voice* 7, no. 1 (1904), cited in White, *Too Heavy a Load*, 69; ibid., 93, 70; Robin D. G. Kelley, "We Are

Not What We Seem": Rethinking Black Working-Class Opposition in the Jim Crow South," *Journal of American History*, 80 (June 1993): 80; Sylvanie Williams (sometimes Sylvania) was an influential educator in New Orleans and later had several schools named after her, Gehman, *Women and New Orleans*, 86, and was mentioned as an important black woman of the city in the "New Orleans Number," *The Crisis: A Record of the Darker Races*, February 1916. Under the title "Men of the Month" it stated, simply, "Mrs. Williams is principal of one of the largest colored schools," 171.

26. White, *Too Heavy a Load*, 112, 134, 147; Lynne Olson, *Freedom's Daughters: The Unsung Heroines of the Civil Rights Movement from 1830 to 1970* (New York: Scribner, 2001), 43.

27. Terborg-Penn, *African American Women in the Struggle for the Vote*, 115; W. E. B. Du Bois editorial, *Crisis*, February 1921, 200.

28. Walter White, NAACP assistant executive secretary, to Dr. George Lucas, New Orleans branch president, March 9, 1921, Selected Branch Files, 1913–1939, Reel 14, Papers of NAACP; identical letters were sent to all branch presidents in the state on this date: Baton Rouge (Mr. J. H. Smith), Alexandria (Rev. H. R. Norris), Shreveport (P. L. Blackman), and St. Rose (Rev. Berry Bell).

29. Jacquelyn Grant, "Civil Rights Women: A Source for Doing Womanist Theory," in Vicki L. Crawford, J. A. Rouse, and Barbara Woods, eds., *Women in the Civil Rights Movement: Trailblazers and Torchbearers, 1941–1965* (Bloomington: Indiana University Press, 1993), 43.

30. 11th Annual Report of the NAACP, 1920, 25–27, Spingarn Collection, Howard-Tilton Memorial Library, Tulane University.

31. Brown, "Negotiating and Transforming the Public Sphere," 123–124.

32. Anne Standley, "The Role of Black Women in the Civil Rights Movement," in Crawford et al., *Women in the Civil Rights Movement*, 184.

33. Fairclough, *Race and Democracy*, 18; Gayle was on the branch executive committee (1918, 1920), secretary (1921), while Dunn was secretary (1918), president (1920), and chairman of the finance committee (1921); Selected Branch Files, 1913–1939, Reel 14, Papers of NAACP.

34. Baton Rouge NAACP branch membership lists, Selected Branch Files, 1913–1939, Reel 13, Papers of NAACP; O. Richardson, Baton Rouge branch secretary, to James Weldon Johnson, NAACP executive secretary, February 14, 1919, ibid.; the 1929 membership lists contained eleven women out of sixty-seven members: eight housewives, two teachers, and a real estate businesswoman.

35. *The Vindicator*, September 3, 1918, 3, Selected Branch Files, 1913–1939, Reel 14, Papers of NAACP; *The Vindicator*, August 20, 1918, 4; women were exclusively called on to make clothing for U.S. soldiers in Europe via the Red Cross, even though Charles Byrd advertised himself as a "First Class Taylor" in the same issue of the newspaper (p. 2). Apparently, men, especially professional tailors, were not pressed into service in such a feminine campaign.

36. *The Vindicator*, September 3, 1918, 4–5.

37. *The Vindicator*, August 20, 1918, 1; "Give White man credit for what good he does . . . Don't fight the good man for what the bad one does. There are some white men who believe in a square deal and who are trying to help us get a square deal. Have sense enough not to kill your friends." *The Vindicator*, September 3, 1918, 4.

38. Daniel C. Thompson, *The Negro Leadership Class* (Englewood Cliffs, NJ: Prentice-Hall, 1963), 68–70.
39. *The Vindicator*, August 20, 1918, 1; W. A. Lewis, "The Present Necessity of Vocational Training," ibid., 2.
40. "Social Worker Delivers Address to Colored Citizens of N.O.," ibid.
41. "War on Joints," *The Vindicator*, September 12, 1918, 1; "A Necessity for Social Workers," ibid., 4.
42. H. George Davenport, New Orleans branch secretary, to Roy Nash, NAACP executive secretary, March 25, 1917, Selected Branch Files, 1913–1939, Reel 14, Papers of NAACP; Davenport's enthusiasm soon waned and he left the South and headed for Chicago: "Am tired of the South, protest has failed here so far," Davenport to Nash, May 5, 1917, ibid.
43. William J. Breen, "Black Women and the Great War: Mobilization and Reform in the South," *Journal of Southern History* 44, no. 3 (August 1978): 432, 434–439; black and white women worked in parallel on similar work in their respective communities. The committee held a meeting at the City Council Chamber in August 1918, which was the first time in the building's history that a white and black audience had sat together.
44. *The Vindicator*, August 20, 1918, 4; Breen, "Black Women and the Great War," 438.
45. Breen, "Black Women and the Great War," 431–432; Dr George W. Lucas, New Orleans branch president (1921–1930) and member of the NAACP national board, stated, "When . . . investigating a criminal case . . . in New Orleans, I am as safe as I would be in New York. When . . . [I] . . . go into the country, that is another matter. But . . . I go." Cited in Mary White Ovington, *The Walls Come Tumbling Down* (New York: Arno Press, 1969), 227.

THREE

DESTINED TO BRING SPLENDID RESULTS

Epigraph: 20th Annual Report of the National Association for the Advancement of Colored People for the year 1925, Spingarn Collection, Howard-Tilton Memorial Library, Tulane University, New Orleans, 60.

1. Christopher Robert Reed, *The Chicago NAACP and the Rise of the Black Professional Leadership, 1910–1966* (Bloomington: Indiana University Press, 1997), 79; Mary Jacqueline Hebert, "Beyond Black and White: The Civil Rights Movement in Baton Rouge, Louisiana, 1945–1972" (Ph.D. diss., Louisiana State University and Agricultural and Mechanical College, 1999), 8; Papers of the NAACP: Part 12: Selected Branch Files, 1913–1939, Series A: The South, Louisiana, Reels 13–15, microfilm, Cambridge University Library; Papers of the NAACP: Part 16: Selected Branch Files, 1940–55, Series B: The South, Louisiana, Reels 17 and 18.
2. H. Viscount "Berky" Nelson, *The Rise and Fall of Modern Black Leadership: Chronicle of a Twentieth-Century Tragedy* (New York: University Press of America, 2003), 111, 115; Harvard Sitkoff, "African American Militancy in the World War II South: Another Perspective," in Neil R. McMillen, ed., *Remaking Dixie: The Impact of World War II on the American South* (Jackson: University Press of Mississippi, 1997), 77, 79, 84; Neil R. McMillen, "Fighting for What We Didn't Have: How Mississippi's Black Veterans Remember World War II," ibid., 109.

3. FBI Report on the New Orleans Branch of the NAACP, May 14, 1945, FBI File on the NAACP, New Orleans Public Library; *Louisiana Weekly*, April 28, 1945, Amistad Research Center, Tulane University, New Orleans, LA; Adam Fairclough, *Race and Democracy: The Civil Rights Struggle in Louisiana, 1915–1972* (Athens: University of Georgia Press, 1995), 8, 20, 75, 85; Hebert, "Beyond Black and White," 12; Daniel C. Thompson, *The Negro Leadership Class* (Englewood Cliffs, NJ: Prentice-Hall, 1963), 63, 68–70; Sheldon Avery, *Up from Washington: William Pickens and the Negro Struggle for Equality, 1900–1954* (Newark: Associated University Press, 1989), 92; Shreveport, despite being one of the earliest NAACP branches in the South in 1914, was also the Ku Klux Klan's most fertile recruiting ground in Louisiana. In 1922 the local sheriff and deputies broke up an NAACP meeting that had been attended by field secretary William Pickens in Shreveport; Appendix 3.

4. Selected Branch Files, 1913–1939, Reels 13–15, Papers of NAACP; Dorothy Autrey, "'Can These Bones Live?': The National Association for the Advancement of Colored People in Alabama, 1918–1930," *Journal of Negro History* 82, no. 1 (winter 1997): 1, 4.

5. Robert Bagnall, director of branches, to S. B. Smith, March 14, 1927, Selected Branch Files, 1913–1939, Reel 13, Papers of NAACP; "Platform," Branch Constitution and By-Laws of the National Association for the Advancement of Colored People, 1917, amended 1919, 1924, 1931, 18.

6. E. M. Dunn, New Orleans branch secretary, to John R. Shillady, executive secretary of national office, May 22, 1918, Selected Branch Files, 1913–1939, Reel 14, Papers of NAACP; B. J. Stanley, Baton Rouge branch president, to Walter White, executive secretary of national office, June 12, 1936, Papers of the NAACP: Part 8: Legal, 1910–1955, Series A, Reel 8.

7. Deborah Gray White, *Too Heavy a Load: Black Women in Defense of Themselves, 1894–1994* (New York: W. W. Norton, 1999), 112, 134, 147; Rosalyn Terborg-Penn, *African American Women in the Struggle for the Vote, 1850–1920* (Bloomington: Indiana University Press, 1998), 115; W. E. B. Du Bois editorial, *The Crisis: A Record of the Darker Races*, February 1921, 200.

8. 20th Annual Report of the NAACP, 1929, 17–18; Walter White, NAACP assistant executive secretary, to George Lucas, New Orleans branch president, March 29, 1929, Selected Branch Files, 1913–1939, Reel 14, Papers of NAACP.

9. 20th Annual Report of the NAACP, 1929, 18.

10. Ibid., 17–18.

11. Robert L. Zangrando, *The NAACP Crusade Against Lynching, 1909–1950* (Philadelphia: Temple University Press, 1980), 4; Shirley J. Carlson, "Black Ideals of Womanhood in the Late Victorian Era," *Journal of Negro History* 77, no. 2 (1992): 61–62; Glenda Elizabeth Gilmore, *Gender and Jim Crow: Women and the Politics of White Supremacy in North Carolina, 1896–1920* (Chapel Hill: University of North Carolina Press, 1996), 63, 75; Peter J. Ling and Sharon Monteith, "Introduction," *Gender in the Civil Rights Movement* (London: Garland, 1999), 1; Appendix 5.

12. Fairclough, *Race and Democracy*, 26–28; Adam Fairclough, "Forty Acres and a Mule: Horace Mann Bond and the Lynching of Jerome Wilson," *Journal of American Studies* 31 (1997): 2; 26th Annual Report of the NAACP, 1935, 26; for a full documented description of the case, see Horace Mann Bond and Julia W. Bond, *The Star Creek Papers*, ed. Adam Fairclough (Athens: University of Georgia Press, 1997).

13. "The Story of Isom Wilson," 1935, George Longe Papers, Box 6, Amistad Research Center; James E. Gayle, president, and Oneida M. Brown, secretary, to New Orleans branch members, November 11, 1935, NAACP Correspondence, A. P. Tureaud Papers, Roll 7, Amistad Research Center; Jacquelyn Dowd Hall, *Revolt Against Chivalry: Jessie Daniel Ames and the Women's Campaign Against Lynching* (New York: Columbia University Press, 1979), 165–167; the committee was made up of prominent black New Orleans citizens (mainly NAACP members such as Gayle and Merlin Hayes, president of the New Orleans NAACP youth council). The only woman was Mrs. M. O. Brown, editor of the *Louisiana Weekly*, who joined the NAACP in the 1930s and was secretary for the NAACP Birthday Ball committee in New Orleans, *Louisiana Weekly*, February 11, 1939, 4.

14. George Lucas, New Orleans branch president, to Walter White, NAACP assistant executive secretary, February 21, 1930, Selected Branch Files, 1913–1939, Reel 14, Papers of NAACP; "McCrary Defense Fund," *Louisiana Weekly*, March 1, 1930, 1; *Louisiana Weekly*, March 8, 1930, 1; "Civic Leagues," *Louisiana Weekly*, June 30, 1934; Fairclough, *Race and Democracy*, 19; Guerand's conviction was eventually upheld.

15. Gilmore, *Gender and Jim Crow*, 63, 75, 101; Anne Standley, "The Role of Black Women in the Civil Rights Movement," in Vicki L. Crawford, J. A. Rouse, and Barbara Woods, eds., *Women in the Civil Rights Movement: Trailblazers and Torchbearers, 1941–1965* (Bloomington: Indiana University Press, 1990), 183; White, *Too Heavy a Load*, 178–179; Lynne Olson, *Freedom's Daughters: The Unsung Heroines of the Civil Rights Movement from 1830 to 1970* (New York: Scribner, 2001), 16; *Louisiana Weekly*, January 7, 1939, 9.

16. *Louisiana Weekly*, February 15, 1930, 5; *Louisiana Weekly*, March 22, 1930, 1; *Louisiana Weekly*, May 17, 1930, 1.

17. *Louisiana Weekly*, February 22, 1930, 5; *Louisiana Weekly*, December 7, 1929, 4, 5.

18. Marisa Chappell, Jenny Hutchinson, and Brian Ward, "'Dress Modestly, Neatly . . . As If You Were Going to Church': Respectability, Class and Gender in the Montgomery Bus Boycott and the Early Civil Rights Movement," in Ling and Monteith, *Gender in the Civil Rights Movement*, 73; Cathy Thurlkill, "A Woman's Place Is in the War: North Louisiana Women's Contributions to World War II, 1941–45," *North Louisiana Historical Association Journal* (winter 1997): 49; Julia Kirk Blackwelder, "Women in the Work Force: Atlanta, New Orleans, and San Antonio, 1930–1940," *Journal of Urban History* 4 (May 1978): 332, 335–336, 339, 341, 350, 355; Senator Huey Long saw the role of black women as being integral to white family life: "Got to give 'em clinics and hospitals . . . That's fair and it's good sense . . . [Y]ou wouldn't want a colored woman . . . watching over your children if she had pyorrhea, would you?" Roy Wilkins, "Huey Long Says—An Interview with Louisiana's Kingfish," *Crisis*, February 1935, 52.

19. Mary Gehman, *Women and New Orleans: A History* (New Orleans: Margaret Media, 1988), 101; YWCA flyer, 1945, Longe Papers, Box 6.

20. Robert Bagnall, director of branches, to Mrs. D. Guidry, New Orleans branch secretary, May 12, 1926, Selected Branch Files, 1913–1939, Reel 14, Papers of NAACP.

21. Miss A. V. Dunn, New Orleans branch secretary, to Robert Bagnall, director of branches, November 12, 1924, ibid.

22. William Pickens, field secretary, to George Lucas, New Orleans branch president, July 17, 1925, ibid.; William Pickens, field secretary, to George Lucas, New Orleans branch president (copy also sent to secretary, Miss. A. V. Dunn), January 23, 1926, ibid.

23. George Lucas, New Orleans branch president, to William Pickens, field secretary, January 20, 1926, ibid.

24. Middle-class black women organized a "Better Baby Contest" during 1928 for poor black women to encourage regular child health check-ups. In 1932 "first place was awarded to a baby with umbellical [sic] hernia," Harriett Elsa Wiedman, "The Sylvania F. Williams Community Center" (M.A. diss., Tulane University, 1933), 72–73; Miss A. V. Dunn, New Orleans branch secretary, to Robert Bagnall, director of branches, November 12, 1924, Selected Branch Files, 1913–1939, Reel 14, Papers of NAACP.

25. "NAACP Has Installation," [ca. 1927], Joseph A. Hardin Papers, Box 1, Amistad Research Center; unsigned letter, November 15, 1927, Tureaud Papers, Roll 7; E. B. Bailey, president of Lima branch, Ohio, to George Lucas, New Orleans branch president, June 25, 1927, Selected Branch Files, 1913–1939, Reel 14, Papers of NAACP; Chief accountant of Women's League, St. Harford, Connecticut, to New Orleans NAACP branch, July 5, 1927, ibid.; George Lucas, New Orleans branch president, to William Pickens, field secretary, March 22, 1928, ibid.; Lucas to James Weldon Johnson, NAACP executive secretary, May 13, 1927, ibid.; Roy Wilkins with Tom Mathews, *Standing Fast: The Autobiography of Roy Wilkins* (New York: Da Capo Press, 1994), 119–125.

26. C. H. Myers, Monroe branch president, to Robert Bagnall, director of branches, March 15, 1932, Selected Branch Files, 1913–1939, Reel 13; Bagnall to Myers, March 19, 1932, ibid.; Robert Bagnall, director of branches, to Mrs. H. W. Johnson, chair of emergency committee, October 21, 1932, ibid.; an identical letter was sent to the chair of the emergency committee in Baton Rouge, Mrs. M. R. Lawless, also dated the October 21, 1932, ibid.

27. William Pickens, field secretary, to B. J. Stanley, Baton Rouge branch president, August 31, 1934, ibid.; Mrs. D. J. Dupuy, Baton Rouge branch secretary, to Walter White, NAACP executive secretary, October 10, 1938, ibid.; White to Stanley, November 18, 1935, ibid.; Stanley to White, November 12, 1935, ibid.

28. Robert Bagnall, director of branches, to Mrs. M. R. Lawless, Baton Rouge, June 27, 1932, ibid.; William Pickens, field secretary, to W. F. Sherman, Monroe branch secretary, June 13, 1932, ibid.

29. Dr. A. W. Brazier, New Orleans branch president, to Frederick Morrow, coordinator of branches, March 17, 1939, Selected Branch Files, 1913–1939, Reel 15, Papers of NAACP; *Louisiana Weekly*, February 11, 1939, 4.

30. Louisiana Weekly, December 5, 1931; the pictures changed annually. The first noted chair responsible for the seals was in 1938 in Baton Rouge (unfortunately the name is illegible); C. H. Myers, Monroe branch president, to Roy Wilkins, assistant NAACP executive secretary, December 6, 1932, Selected Branch Files, 1913–1939, Reel 13, Papers of NAACP; Myers to Walter White, NAACP executive secretary, December 4, 1935, ibid.

31. New Orleans, Baton Rouge, and Monroe NAACP membership lists, Selected Branch Files, 1913–1939, Reels 13–15 and Selected Branch Files, 1940–1955, Reels 17 and 18 , Papers of NAACP; notable branch treasurers were Johnson Lockett, New Orleans, 1927–1932, A. Washington, Baton Rouge, 1929–1941, S. L. Pierce, Monroe, 1931–1943.

32. The "Colored Delinquent Association" helped around 200–300 children celebrate holidays, such as organizing a Thanksgiving Day festivity "for these urchins," *Louisiana Weekly*, December 7, 1929, 6; A. E. Perkins, ed., *Who's Who in Colored Louisiana* (Baton

Rouge: Douglas Loan Co., Inc., 1930), 115; Robert Bagnall, director of branches, to George Lucas, New Orleans branch president, March 15, 1928, Selected Branch Files, 1913–1939, Reel 14, Papers of NAACP; Lucas to William Pickens, field secretary, March 22, 1928, ibid.; by March 22, six candidates had declared their involvement in the membership drive competition, only one being male: A. M. Trudeau, Mrs. T. W. Gottschalk, Miss V. D. Holt, Miss Zenobia Lockett, Miss Viola Conerly, and Mrs. M. M. Landix.

33. William Pickens, field secretary, to Dr A. W. Brazier, New Orleans branch president, January 16, 1939, Selected Branch Files, 1913–1939, Reel 15, Papers of NAACP; C. H. Myers, Monroe branch president, to Robert Bagnall, director of branches, May 17, 1932, Selected Branch Files, 1913–1939, Reel 13, Papers of NAACP; the judge was Chas Schultz, who, according to Myers, was considered "already a 'negro lover' on account of fair mindedness."

34. Fairclough, *Race and Democracy*, 46; New Orleans, Baton Rouge, and Monroe NAACP membership lists; 27th Annual Report of the NAACP, 1936, 25; Appendix 3.

35. James Gayle, New Orleans branch president, to New Orleans ministers, March 2, 1934, Selected Branch Files, 1913–1939, Reel 15, Papers of NAACP; Darlene Clark Hine, ed., *Black Women in America: An Historical Encyclopaedia* (New York: Carlson Publishing, 1993), 1:690–693; Special assistant to the secretary, New York, to Fannie Williams, New Orleans, March 15, 1937, Selected Branch Files, 1913–1939, Reel 15, Papers of NAACP; Dr. A. W. Brazier, New Orleans branch president, to Daisy Lampkin, regional field secretary, March 3, 1938, ibid.; Brazier to Walter White, NAACP executive secretary, March 17, 1939, ibid.; Brazier to White, October 5, 1939, ibid.; memorandum from William Pickens, field secretary, to White, November 21, 1938, ibid.

36. The ten women were Miss Leona Bauduit, Mrs. C. H. D. Bowers, Mrs. A. L. Brown, Miss Mary Coghill, Miss Ethel Davis, Miss M. R. Harris, Mrs. Susie Heater, Mrs. Mathilde LeBeau, Miss Eola Lyons, and Miss Daphne Toppins, Selected Branch Files, 1913–1939, Reel 15, Papers of NAACP.

37. Juanita Jackson, special assistant to the secretary, to Miss Fannie Williams, New Orleans, March 15, 1937, ibid.; especially singled out were Miss Camille Harrison (assistant secretary 1936–1939), Mrs. C. C. Dejoie, and Miss Anna Mae Berhol (director of Wicker School); spring membership campaign, Monroe, May 1–31, 1936, Selected Branch Files, 1913–1939, Reel 13, Papers of NAACP; "The Southern Broadcast," meeting at Knights of Pythias on Desmond Street, Monroe, November 16, 1935, ibid.

38. D. J. Dupuy, Baton Rouge branch secretary, to Walter White, NAACP executive secretary, June 28, 1936, Selected Branch Files, 1913–1939, Reel 13, Papers of NAACP; Baton Rouge was the only branch in Louisiana to officially record white members on its rolls up to this date: "We are proud to get *two* white members," Dupuy to White, July 14, 1937, ibid.; Monroe did have visits during the early 1930s by field secretary, William Pickens, although these were mainly lecture-based tours, C. H. Myers, Monroe branch president, to William Bagnall, director of branches, May 17, 1932, ibid.; Monroe NAACP flyer of William Pickens' address, June 12, 1934, ibid.

39. The university itinerary was Dillard (New Orleans), Southern (State Supported Black university at Scotlandville), and Xavier (Catholic); Roy Wilkins, NAACP assistant executive secretary, to Judge Jane Bolin, New York, December 4, 1945, Selected Branch Files, 1940–1955, Reel 18, Papers of NAACP.

40. Daniel Byrd, New Orleans branch executive secretary, to Roy Wilkins, NAACP assistant executive, December 1, 1945, ibid.

41. Roy Wilkins, NAACP assistant executive secretary, to Daniel E. Byrd, executive secretary of New Orleans branch, December 4, 1945, ibid.; Wilkins memorandum, January 14, 1946, ibid.

42. Executive secretary's report to the New York office for September 1945, Tureaud Papers, Roll 10; Annual Report of Branch Activities, Baton Rouge, 1943, Selected Branch Files, 1940–1955, Reel 17, Papers of NAACP; men's groups on the membership and fundraising drives were organized but women's groups were given preeminence on the report and assumed the frontline of the campaign.

43. Annual Report of Branch Activities, Lake Charles, 1944, Selected Branch Files, 1940–1955, Reel 17, Papers of NAACP; Annual Report of Branch Activities, Alexandria, 1944, ibid.; Annual Report of Branch Activities, Shreveport, 1948 and 1951, ibid.; Donaldsonville, NAACP Branch Files; Annual Report of Branch Activities, Bastrop, 1947, ibid.; Annual Report of Branch Activities, Lake Charles, 1953, ibid.; Annual Report of Branch Activities, St. Charles Parish, 1955, ibid.; Annual Report of Branch Activities, Farmerville, 1949, ibid.

44. Stephanie J. Shaw, *What a Woman Ought to Be and to Do: Black Professional Women Workers During the Jim Crow Era* (Chicago: University of Chicago Press, 1996), 213.

45. Perkins, *Who's Who in Colored Louisiana*, 75, 123; Joseph J. Boris, ed., *Who's Who in Colored America: A Biographical Dictionary of Notable Living Persons of Negro Descent in America* (New York: Who's Who in Colored America, 1927), 1:149.

46. Avery, *Up from Washington*, 54; A'Lelia Bundles, *On Her Own Ground: The Life and Times of Madam C. J. Walker* (New York: Scribner, 2001), 15–16, 264; Perkins, *Who's Who in Colored Louisiana*, 118, 136; Willard B. Gatewood, *Aristocrats of Color: The Black Elite, 1880–1920* (Bloomington: Indiana University Press), 334.

47. Perkins, *Who's Who in Colored Louisiana*, 136; Fairclough, *Race and Democracy*, 15, 42; Ella Dejoie died in August 1929.

48. Perkins, *Who's Who in Colored Louisiana*, 73–73, 106–107; Boris, *Who's Who in Colored America*, 73–74; "New Orleans Number," *Crisis*, February 1916, 171; Willis was twice married and used both husbands' names in her title: Gertrude Pocte (maiden name) Geddes (first marriage) Willis (second). It was from Joseph Geddes that Willis inherited the funeral director's business. He was a native of New Orleans, educated at Tuskegee, Alabama, was vice-president of the Unity Industrial Life Insurance Company, member of the National Negro Business League, involved in various Masonic lodges (the Elks and the Knights of Pythias) and was politically inclined to the Republican Party.

49. Paula Giddings, *When and Where I Enter: The Impact of Black Women on Race and Sex in America* (New York: William. Morrow & Co., 1984), 112; "As wife of an activist . . . (Lula White) found it easier to create her space within the . . . [Houston, Texas] branch . . . and gain access to important people who would help to implement changes in the black community." Merline Pitre, *In Struggle Against Jim Crow: Lula B. White and the NAACP, 1900–1957* (College Station: Texas A&M University Press, 1999), 25.

50. In some references S. G. Green is prefixed with *Sir* or *Professor*, and his title extended worldwide as Supreme Chancellor of the Colored Knights of Pythias of North America, South America, Europe, Asia, Africa, and Australia; see "New Orleans Number,"

Crisis, February 1916, 169, 171; Boris, *Who's Who in Colored America*, 79; New Orleans, NAACP Branch Files; Perkins, *Who's Who in Colored Louisiana*, 141; Bundles, *On Her Own Ground*, 57; other Greens included Miss L. Green, NAACP member in 1926, and Miss Mercedes I. Green, 1935.

51. Fairclough, *Race and Democracy*, 47.

52. There were sixty-seven people present at the Baton Rouge NAACP inaugural meeting. Housewives: Alzens Germany (husband, William, laborer), Florida Williams (either Chas. or Thomas, laborers), Helen A. Nelson (A. A. Nelson, laborer), Mrs. L. M. Nelson (Mr. L. M. Nelson, secretary), Mrs. L. D. Walker (Rev. M. R. Walker), Mrs. A. R. Stanley (Benjamin Stanley, general agent), Mrs. Cassie Fields, Lizzie Mack (George Mack, brakeman), Tama Williams (either Chas. or Thomas, laborers), and Katie Riley, Baton Rouge and New Orleans NAACP membership lists; "Mrs. Nixon would come to a meeting, but I think she just kept up with the meetings because he [Mr. Nixon, head of the Montgomery NAACP Branch] was on the scene." Rosa Parks, with Jim Haskins, *Rosa Parks: My Story* (London: Puffin Books, 1999), 82.

53. George Lucas, New Orleans branch president, to Walter White, NAACP executive secretary, February 21, 1930, Selected Branch Files, 1913-1939, Reel 14, Papers of NAACP; Lucas to Robert Bagnall, director of branches, June 5, 1930, ibid.; Pitre, *In Struggle Against Jim Crow*, 25; in 1932 A. P. Tureaud, NAACP attorney for the NAACP in Louisiana, carried this trend to its ultimate level and recruited his wife, Lucille A. Dejoie, from the ranks of the New Orleans NAACP.

54. Rosa Parks, with Gregory J Reed, *Quiet Strength: The Faith, the Hope, and the Heart of a Woman Who Changed a Nation* (Grand Rapids, MI: Zondervan, 1994), 46-49; Miss A. Hart had asked the branch for action over the Hattie McCrary case.

55. *Louisiana Weekly*, December 7, 1929.

56. Flint-Goodridge Hospital and Nurse Training School, 5th Annual Report, Year ending December 31, 1921, Hardin Papers, Box 1; Annual Meeting YWCA branch, May 11, 1948, Fannie C. Williams Papers, Box 1, Series 2, Amistad Research Center, Tulane University, New Orleans, Louisiana; Education committee of the YMCA, January 20, 1937, Longe Papers, Box 5; Gilmore, *Gender and Jim Crow*, 192-193.

57. Cyprian Davis, *The History of Black Catholics in the United States* (New York: Crossroad, 1990), 236-237; Fairclough, *Race and Democracy*, 14; New Orleans, NAACP Branch Files; *Louisiana Weekly*, February 8, 1930, 4; *Louisiana Weekly*, January 11, 1930, 3; *Louisiana Weekly*, July 19, 1930, 6; *Louisiana Weekly*, March 1, 1930, 7.

58. "How the Chest Works for Us," 1935 Community Chest Campaign (Colored Division), Longe Papers, Box 6; New Orleans, NAACP Branch Files.

59. Other general workers of the Community Chest campaigns who held NAACP membership included Mrs. Evelyn Easter, Mrs. J. A. Barnes, Mrs. L. T. Galleaud, Miss Lillian Loeb, Miss Frances Lawless, Miss Lillian Lockett, Mrs. Corinne Azamore, Miss Eola Lyons, and Miss Mary D. Coghill, Longe Papers, Box 6; New Orleans NAACP membership lists.

60. Program of the Valena C. Jones pageant dedicated to Fannie C. Williams, May 5, 1966, Williams Papers, Box 1, Series 1.

61. Adam Fairclough, *Teaching Equality: Black Schools in the Age of Jim Crow* (Athens: University of Georgia Press, 2001), 5, 47; Adam Fairclough, *Better Day Coming: Blacks and Equality, 1890-2000* (London: Penguin Books, 2001), 161-162.

62. George Lucas, New Orleans branch president, to Robert Bagnall, director of branches, December 14, 1926, Selected Branch Files, 1913–1939, Reel 14, Papers of NAACP; Bagnall to Lucas, December 31, 1926, ibid.; evidently this was a recurring problem for many of the branches: "[Do] not permit a short-sighted viewpoint to prevail which will cause the Branch to think of local matters and not to realize its responsibility to support the great national work," Bagnall to George Labat, New Orleans branch president, March 13, 1931, ibid.

63. New Orleans Urban League flyer, March 4, 1938, Longe Papers, Box 1; Fairclough, *Race and Democracy*, 56; Nancy J. Wiess, *The National Urban League 1910–1940* (New York: Oxford University Press, 1974), 50, 164; *Louisiana Weekly*, January 21, 1939, 3; *Louisiana Weekly*, July 1, 1939, 2; *Louisiana Weekly*, July 8, 1939; crossover membership also included Mrs. Eva Jones and Mrs. E. C. Thornhill.

64. George Lucas, New Orleans branch president, to Robert Bagnall, director of branches, December 11, 1929, Selected Branch Files, 1913–1939, Reel 14, Papers of NAACP; "Seventh Ward Civic League, 1930," Hardin Papers, Box 1; Program of the New Orleans Federation of Civic Leagues, February 19, 1933, Tureaud Papers, Roll 15; Federation of Civic Leagues, Meeting at Grace Methodist Church, New Orleans, April 28, 1935, ibid.; Brief of the Schools and Playgrounds Committee of the Federation of Civic Leagues, January 12, 1934, ibid., Rolls 10, 15; "Federation of Civic Leagues," *Louisiana Weekly*, March 4, 1933, 6; Mrs. A. M. Trudeau was second vice-president of the 7th Ward Civic League and her husband was to be the plaintiff in the NAACP test case of the Louisiana registration laws, *Trudeau v. Barnes* (1933). Other women in both organizations included Miss Lillian C. Lockett, Miss Lillian Mason, Miss Beulah Laurent, Miss Elenore White, Miss Emily Watts, and Mrs. Lola Dixon.

65. Lee Finkle, "The Conservative Aims of Militant Rhetoric: Black Protest during World War II," *Journal of American History* 60 (1974): 694, 699, 705; Jerry Pervis Sanson, *Louisiana During World War II: Politics and Society, 1939–1945* (Baton Rouge: Louisiana State University Press, 1999), 246, 265.

66. 4th Ward Loan Orleans Parish 1944, Longe Papers, Box 6.

67. Autrey, "Can These Bones Live?" 8.

68. Sitkoff, "African American Militancy in the World War II South," 84.

FOUR
GOD'S VALIANT MINORITY

Epigraph: William Pickens, director of branches, to Mrs. D. J. Dupuy, Baton Rouge branch secretary, July 15, 1937, Papers of the NAACP: Part 12: Selected Branch Files, 1913–1939, Series A, The South, Louisiana, Reel 13, microfilm, Cambridge University Library.

1. Adam Fairclough, *Race and Democracy: The Civil Rights Struggle in Louisiana 1915–1972* (Athens: University of Georgia Press, 1995), 61–62; Adam Fairclough, "'Being in the Field of Education and Also a Negro . . . Seems . . . Tragic': Black Teachers in the Jim Crow South," *Journal of American History* 87, no. 1 (June 2000): 13; Merline Pitre, *In Struggle Against Jim Crow: Lula B. White and the NAACP, 1900–1957* (College Station: Texas A&M University, 1999), 57; Darlene Clark Hine, "Black Professionals and Race Consciousness: Origins of the Civil Rights Movement, 1890–1950," *Journal of American History* 89,

no. 4 (March 2003): 1279–1280; Monica A. White, "Paradise Lost? Teachers' Perspectives on the Use of Cultural Capital in the Segregated Schools of New Orleans, Louisiana," *Journal of African American History* 88, no. 4 (March 2002): 270, 279–280; Selected Branch Files, 1913–1939, Reels 13–15, Papers of NAACP; Papers of the NAACP: Part 16: Selected Branch Files, 1940–1955, Series B: The South, Louisiana, Reels 17 and 18.

2. Fairclough, "Being in the Field of Education," 17, 20; Mark V. Tushnet, *The NAACP's Legal Strategy against Segregated Education, 1925–50* (Chapel Hill: University of North Carolina Press, 1987), 42, 45; Fairclough, *Race and Democracy*, 100–101; Annual Report of Branch Activities, Baton Rouge, 1944, Selected Branch Files, 1940–1955, Reel 17, Papers of NAACP; Stephanie J. Shaw, *What a Woman Ought to Be and to Do: Black Professional Women Workers During the Jim Crow Era* (Chicago: University of Chicago Press, 1996), 179, 183; Aaron Henry with Constance Curry, *The Fire Ever Burning* (Jackson: University Press of Mississippi, 2000), 41; Waldo E. Martin Jr., ed., *Brown v. Board of Education: A Brief History with Documents* (New York: Bedford/St. Martin's, 1998), 13–14, 23.

3. Mrs. D. J. Dupuy, Baton Rouge branch secretary, to A. P. Tureaud, New Orleans attorney, August 18, 1944, NAACP Correspondence, A. P. Tureaud Papers, Roll 7, Amistad Research Center, Tulane University, New Orleans, LA; Edward R. Dudley, assistant special counsel, NAACP Legal Defense and Educational Fund Inc., to Tureaud, August 29, 1944, ibid.; 34th Annual Report of the National Association for the Advancement of Colored People for the year 1943, 34, Spingarn Collection, Howard-Tilton Memorial Library, Tulane University, New Orleans, LA; Annual Report of Branch Activities, Scotlandville, 1943; memorandum to New York office from Thurgood Marshall, NAACP special counsel, New Orleans, September 11, 1945, Papers of the NAACP: Part 4: Louisiana Voting, 1942–1947, Reel 8; *The Crisis: A Record of the Darker Races*, September 1935, 279; Mary Lee Muller, "New Orleans Public School Desegregation," *Louisiana History* 42, no. 1 (winter 1976): 69; "History of Macarty School," George Longe Papers, Box 1, Amistad Research Center; John H. Scott with Cleo Scott Brown, *Witness to the Truth: My Struggle for Human Rights in Louisiana* (Columbia: University of South Carolina Press, 2003), 111, 115–119, Adam Fairclough, "The Costs of *Brown*: Black Teachers and School Integration," *Journal of American History* 91, no.1 (June 2004): 48–50.

4. Adam Fairclough, *Teaching Equality: Black Schools in the Age of Jim Crow* (Athens: University of Georgia Press, 2001), 62–63; Adam Fairclough, *Better Day Coming: Blacks and Equality, 1890–2000* (London: Penguin, 2001), 174, Fairclough, *Race and Democracy*, 107; Leon F. Litwack, *Trouble in Mind: Black Southerners in the Age of Jim Crow* (New York: Vintage, 1998), 64–65, 107–108; Henry, *Fire Ever Burning*, 35–36, 41–42; Harvard Sitkoff, "African American Militancy in the World War II South: Another Perspective," in Neil R. McMillen, ed., *Remaking Dixie: The Impact of World War II on the American South* (Jackson: University Press of Mississippi, 1997), 79.

5. Scott, *Witness to the Truth*, 29; Fairclough, *Race and Democracy*, 100; Fairclough, "Being in the Field of Education," 11; White, "Paradise Lost?" 271; New Orleans NAACP branch membership lists, Selected Branch Files, 1913–1939, Reel 14, Papers of NAACP.

6. Julia Kirk Blackwelder, "Women in the Work Force: Atlanta, New Orleans, and San Antonio, 1930–1940," *Journal of Urban History* 4 (May 1978): 335, 345, 349; Fairclough, *Teaching Equality*, 5; History of Macarty School," Longe Papers, Box 1; NAACP Programs 1930–1944, Tureaud Papers, Roll 13; "Report of the Committee on Teachers in the Colored

Public Schools Co-Operating with the Poll Tax Committee of the New Orleans Association of Commerce for the year 1932," Longe Papers, Box 1; the poll tax was abolished in Louisiana in 1934.

7. "Report of the Committee on Teachers in the Colored Public Schools Co-Operating with the Poll Tax Committee of the New Orleans Association of Commerce for the year 1932," Longe Papers, Box 1.

8. Harriett Elsa Wiedman, "The Sylvania F. Williams Community Center" (M.A. diss., Tulane University, 1933), 2, 10.

9. White, "Paradise Lost?," 271; Wiedman, "The Sylvania F. Williams Community Center," 24–25, 27, 46.

10. Ibid., 36, 39–43, 55, 65, 72–73, 70; Shaw, *What a Woman Ought to Be and to Do*, 95–95; New Orleans NAACP branch member lists.

11. "East Baton Rouge Parish PTA," *Louisiana Weekly*, March 11, 1933, 2, Amistad Research Center, Tulane University, New Orleans, Louisiana; Mrs. O. A. Powell, "Life in the Home," *Louisiana Weekly*, January 17, 1931.

12. "Miss Myrtle Banks Is Emancipation Speaker," *Louisiana Weekly*, January 7, 1939, 1; *Louisiana Weekly*, January 21, 1939, 4; Hine, "Black Professionals and Race Consciousness," 1280; White, "Paradise Lost?," 276–278; Ernest J. Middleton, "The Louisiana Education Association, 1901–1970," *Journal of Negro Education* (fall 1978): 366–367; Scott, *Witness to the Truth*, 27; Louisiana was the only state in the Union that had a different course of study in black schools than in whites, a flagrant disregard of the "separate but equal" pretense.

13. Marisa Chappell, Jenny Hutchinson, and Brian Ward, "'Dress Modestly, Neatly . . . as If You Were Going to Church': Respectability, Class, and Gender in the Montgomery Bus Boycott and the Early Civil Rights Movement," in Peter J. Ling and Sharon Monteith, eds., *Gender in the Civil Rights Movement* (London: Garland, 1999), 73; *Louisiana Weekly*, January 21, 1939, 4; *Louisiana Weekly*, February 4, 1939, 1; *Louisiana Weekly*, February 25, 1939, 7.

14. "List of Material for Exhibit Purposes from New Orleans, Louisiana, 1937," Texas Centennial Exposition, Longe Papers, Box 5.

15. "A Tentative Approach to Negro History," March 13, 1936, Longe Papers, Box 2.

16. Pearl C. Tasker, primary supervisor, "A Tentative Approach to Negro History," Longe Papers, Box 2; Mrs. M. D. Huggins, "Address of President of the Louisiana Congress of Parents and Teachers," *Louisiana Colored Teachers Journal* 12, no. 2 (January 1940): 18, Longe Papers, Box 4; Henry, *Fire Ever Burning*, 41–44.

17. "A Tentative Approach to Negro History," Longe Papers, Box 2; Adam Fairclough, "Being in the Field of Education and Also a Negro," 13; Fairclough, *Teaching Equality*, vii–viii; Middleton, "The Louisiana Education Association," 364.

18. *Louisiana Colored Teachers' Journal* 13, no. 2 (January 1940): 3, 15, 18, 22.

19. Joseph A. Hardin, educator, to Mr. Lionel J. Bourgeois, superintendent of New Orleans Public Schools, September 20, 1946, Joseph A. Hardin Papers, Box 1, Amistad Research Center.

20. *American Missionary* 87, no. 2 (February 2, 1933), Fannie C. Williams Papers, Box 1, Series 1, Amistad Research Center; *Louisiana Colored Teachers' Journal* 13, no. 2 (January 1940): 18.

21. *Louisiana Weekly*, June 21, 1980; program of the Valena C. Jones School pageant

dedicated to Fannie C. Williams, May 5, 1966; Williams Papers, Box 1, Series 1; Program of the Golden Anniversary May Pageant of the Valena C. Jones School, May 7, 1970, Williams Papers, Box 2, Series 3; Andrew Young, *An Easy Burden: The Civil Rights Movement and the Transformation of America* (New York: HarperCollins, 1996), 19; Fairclough, *Teaching Equality*, 43; "Local Teacher Receives National Recognition," *Louisiana Weekly*, February 1, 1930; Henry, *Fire Ever Burning*, 44.

22. Fairclough, *Teaching Equality*, 56; Juanita Jackson, special assistant to the secretary, to Fannie Williams, New Orleans, March 15, 1937, Selected Branch Files, 1913–1939, Reel 15, Papers of NAACP; "East Baton Rouge Teachers Meet," *Louisiana Weekly*, October 4, 1930; A. E. Perkins, ed., *Who's Who in Colored Louisiana* (Baton Rouge: Douglas Loan Co., 1930), 122; *Louisiana Weekly*, March 18, 1939; Baton Rouge NAACP branch membership lists, Selected Branch Files, 1913–1939, Reel 13, Papers of NAACP.

23. "Foreword," Sarah E. Gardner, in Fairclough, *Teaching Equality*, vii–viii; Daisy Lampkin, "On the N.A.A.C.P. Southern Front," *Crisis*, May 1935, 153; Program Book for NAACP Branches: Education for Negroes, 1935, 20, Tureaud Papers, Roll 10; 12th Annual Report of the NAACP, 1921, 88; Branch Constitution and By-Laws of the NAACP, 1917 (amended 1919, 1924, 1931), 16; Henry, *Fire Ever Burning*, 40–41, 44; Mrs. D. J. Dupuy, Baton Rouge branch secretary, to Roy Wilkins, NAACP assistant executive secretary, April 20, 1942, NAACP Papers, Youth File, 1940–1955, Part 19, Series C, Reel 23; Dupuy to Walter White, NAACP executive secretary, June 17, 1935, Selected Branch Files, 1913–1939, Reel 13, Papers of NAACP; Rosa Parks, with Jim Haskins, *Rosa Parks: My Story* (London: Puffin Books, 1992), 94.

24. Baton Rouge youth council charter, June 21, 1938, Papers of NAACP, Youth Councils, Louisiana, 1938–1939, Part 19, Series C, Reel 4; Mrs. D. J. Dupuy, Baton Rouge branch secretary, to Walter White, NAACP executive secretary, August 29, 1938, ibid.; Miss Lillian B. Carline, Lake Charles youth council supervisor, to A. P. Tureaud, New Orleans attorney, March 10, 1942, Tureaud Papers, Roll 7; Miss Hazel A. Augustine, New Orleans youth council advisor, to E. Frederic Morrow, branch coordinator, March 7, 1939, Youth Council, Louisiana, 1938–1939, Reel 4, Papers of NAACP; Annual Meeting YWCA New Orleans branch, May 11, 1948, Williams Papers, Box 1.

25. Spring membership campaign, Monroe, May 1–31, 1936, Selected Branch Files, 1913–1939, Reel 13, Papers of NAACP; "The Southern Broadcast," meeting at Knights of Pythias on Desmond Street, November 16, 1935, Monroe, ibid.; Juanita Jackson, national youth director, to Mrs. H. L. McClanahan, Monroe youth council adviser, June 4, 1936, ibid.; Jackson to McClanahan, June 4, 1936, ibid.

26. Miss Maude Kane, Lake Charles youth council president, to Juanita Jackson, national youth director, June 25, 1938, Youth Council, Louisiana, 1938–1939, Reel 4, Papers of NAACP; Constitution and By-Laws for the Branches of the NAACP, 1937, 10.

27. FBI Report on the New Orleans branch of the NAACP, February 7, 1945, FBI File on the NAACP, New Orleans Public Library, Louisiana; FBI Report on the New Orleans branch of the NAACP, May 14, 1945; New Orleans NAACP branch membership lists, Selected Branch Files, 1940–1955, Reel 18, Papers of NAACP; it can be reasonably assumed that the second suspected communist was Ernest J. Wright, who had once been active in the Communist Party, was a strong advocate of interracial cooperation, and had been vice-president of the People's Defense League, which argued for the ballot for African Americans.

28. John Whiteclay Chambers II, *The Tyranny of Change: America in the Progressive*

Era, 1890–1920 (New York: St. Martin's Press, 1992), 102; for a full description of John Dewey's theories on education, see S. Alexander Rippa, *Education in a Free Society: An American History* (New York: Longman, 1997), 164–172.

29. Daniel Byrd, president of NAACP Louisiana state conference, to Ella Baker, director of branches, December 5, 1945, Selected Branch Files, 1940–1955, Part 26, Series A, Reel 12, Papers of NAACP; "The Right to Vote Means," Citizens Committee flyer, September 1945, ibid.; Byrd to Thurgood Marshall, NAACP special counsel, October 16, 1944, Tureaud Papers, Roll 7; *Making Civil Rights Law: Thurgood Marshall and the Supreme Court, 1936–1961* (Oxford: Oxford University Press, 1994), 31; Fairclough, "Being in the Field of Education," 5–6, 8, 18; White, "Paradise Lost?" 272, 277; Raphael Cassimere, "Equalizing Teachers' Pay in Louisiana," *Integrated Education* 15 (July/August 1977): 4, 5; Fairclough, *Race and Democracy*, 36; Scott, *Witness to the Truth*, 120.

30. *Louisiana Weekly*, January 7, 1939, 9; Tushnet, *Making Civil Rights Law*, 119; Fairclough, *Race and Democracy*, 99–102; *Louisiana Weekly*, April 1, 1939.

31. 32nd NAACP Annual Report, 1941, 16–17; 33rd NAACP Annual Report, 1942, 17; Cassimere, "Equalizing Teachers' Pay in Louisiana," 5; Fairclough, *Race and Democracy*, 63; Scott Baker, "Testing Equality: The National Teacher Examination and the NAACP's Legal Campaign to Equalize Teachers' Salaries in the South, 1936–63," *History of Education Quarterly* 35, no. 1, (spring 1995): 56–57; Jerry Pervis Sanson, *Louisiana During World War II: Politics and Society, 1939–1945* (Baton Rouge: Louisiana State University Press, 1999), 187–188.

32. Baker, "Testing Equality," 50; Sanson, *Louisiana During World War II*, 74, 188; Cassimere, "Equalizing Teachers' Pay in Louisiana," 4.

33. 34th NAACP Annual Report, 1943, 13; A. P. Tureaud, New Orleans attorney, to Jefferson Parish School Board, January 4, 1943, Tureaud Papers, Roll 29; L. W. Higgins, superintendent of Jefferson Parish School Board, to Tureaud, January 5, 1943, ibid.; J. K. Haynes, president of LCTA, to Sam Jones, Louisiana Governor, June 14, 1943, ibid.; Middleton, "The Louisiana Education Association," 368.

34. Sanson, *Louisiana During World War II*, 187.

35. Donald Jones, field secretary, to Walter White, NAACP executive secretary, April 14, 1943, Papers of NAACP: Part 17, National Staff Files, 1940–1955, Reel 7; L. W. Higgins, superintendent of Jefferson Parish School Board; to Eula Mae Lee, August 27, 1943, Tureaud Papers, Roll 29; Higgins to Lee, October 15, 1943, ibid.

36. Louis Berry, Alexandria attorney, to A. P. Tureaud, New Orleans attorney, November 14, 1946, ibid., Roll 16; Annual Report of Branch Activities, Alexandria, 1941, Papers of the NAACP: Part 25: Branch Department Files, Regional Files 1941–1955, Series A: Reel 17; memorandum to New York office from Thurgood Marshall, NAACP special counsel, New Orleans, September 11, 1945, Louisiana Voting, 1942–1947, Reel 8, Papers of NAACP.

37. A. P. Tureaud, New Orleans attorney, to Thurgood Marshall, NAACP special counsel, September 29, 1944, ibid.; Tureaud to Eula Mae Lee, August 24, 1945, Tureaud Papers, Roll 29; Lee to Tureaud, October 10, 1946, ibid.; Tureaud to Marshall, July 30, 1948, ibid.; Tureaud to Mrs. Eula Mae Lee Brown, July 30, 1948, ibid.

38. Sanson, *Louisiana During World War II*, 188; Adam Fairclough, "The Civil Rights Movement in Louisiana," in Brian Ward and Tony Badger, eds., *The Making of Martin Luther King and the Civil Rights Movement* (London: Macmillan Press, 1996), 17; Cas-

simere, "Equalizing Teachers' Pay in Louisiana," 7; Middleton, "The Louisiana Education Association," 370–371.

39. 27th Annual Report of the NAACP, 1936, 25.

40. White, "Paradise Lost?," 271; Daniel E. Byrd, assistant field secretary, to Viola Johnson, Maharry Medical College, Nashville, Tennessee, February 3, 1948, Tureaud Papers, Roll 50.

FIVE
LEADERS WHO PERSEVERE

Epigraph: E. Frederick Morrow, coordinator of branches, to Horatio Thompson, Baton Rouge NAACP branch secretary, March 5, 1940, cited in Charles M. Payne, *I've Got the Light of Freedom: The Organizing Tradition and the Mississippi Freedom Struggle* (Berkeley: University of California Press, 1995), 276.

1. Papers of the NAACP: Part 12: Selected Branch Files, 1913–1939, Series A: The South, Louisiana, microfilm, Cambridge University Library; Papers of the NAACP: Part 16: Selected Branch Files, 1940–55, Series B: The South, Louisiana; Appendix 4.

2. Johnson was the longest serving and most active woman on the rolls during this period 1928, 1932, 1934, 1936–1939, Monroe NAACP branch membership lists, Selected Branch Files, 1913–1939, Reels 13 and 14.

3. History of Macarty School," George Longe Papers, Box 1, Amistad Research Center, Tulane University, New Orleans, LA; NAACP Programs 1930–1944, A. P. Tureaud Papers, Roll 13, Amistad Research Center; "Report of the Committee on Teachers in the Colored Public Schools Co-Operating with the Poll Tax Committee of the New Orleans Association of Commerce for the year 1932," Longe Papers, Box 1; New Orleans NAACP branch membership lists. Selected Branch Files, 1913–1939, Reel 14 and Selected Branch Files, 1940–1955, Reel 18, Papers of NAACP; Lewis retired to Florida to live with relatives in 1944; see Chapter 4 for more on Lewis and teachers' professional and social networks.

4. Article II, Section 3, Branch Constitution and By-Laws of the NAACP, 1917 (amended 1919, 1924), 4, New Orleans NAACP branch membership lists.

5. The four secretaries were Miss A. V. Dunn (1925), Mrs. D. J. Guidry (1925–1932), Mrs. Oneida Brown (1934–1935), Miss Edna St. Cyr (1944); the four assistant secretaries were Miss A. V. Dunn (1921), Irene A. Williams (1927–1930, 1932), Miss O. M. Brown (1935), Miss Camille Harrison (1936–1939); New Orleans NAACP branch membership lists; see Appendix 4.

6. James E. Gayle was on the New Orleans executive committee in 1918, 1925, 1931, 1936, New Orleans NAACP branch membership lists.

7. "History of Macarty School," Longe Papers, Box 1; Adam Fairclough, *Teaching Equality: Black Schools in the Age of Jim Crow* (Athens: University of Georgia Press, 2001), 47, 56; "Society Notes," *The Vindicator,* September 12, 1918, 3, Selected Branch Files, 1913–1939, Reel 14, Papers of NAACP; Miss A. V. Dunn's father, E. M. Dunn, was secretary of the New Orleans branch, 1917–1918, and president in 1920.

8. Robert Bagnall, director of branches, to Mrs. D. J. Guidry, New Orleans branch secretary, February 5, 1926, Selected Branch Files, 1913–1939, Reel 14, Papers of NAACP; Constitution and By-Laws for the Branches of the NAACP, 1937, Article II, Section 4 (g), 5–6.

9. Public Meeting of NAACP at Piron's Garden of Joy at the Pythian Temple, report

from Los Angeles Conference, September 25, 1928, NAACP Correspondence, Tureaud Papers, Roll, 7; NAACP Programs 1930-1944, Tureaud Papers, Roll 15; New Orleans, NAACP Branch Files.

10. "Knights of Peter Claver," Rolls 4 and 5, Tureaud Papers; Cyprian Davis, *The History of Black Catholics in the United States* (New York: Crossroad, 1990), 236-237; Adam Fairclough, *Race and Democracy: The Civil Rights Struggle in Louisiana 1915-1972* (Athens: University of Georgia Press, 1995), 14; the Junior Knights was established in 1917 and the Junior Daughters in 1930.

11. Charter, Constitutional, and By-Laws of the Ladies Auxiliary of the Knights of Peter Claver, August 1956, Tureaud Papers, Roll 4; New Orleans NAACP branch membership lists; New Orleans NAACP Campaign Literature, June 17, 1934, Selected Branch Files, 1913-1939, Reel 15, Papers of NAACP; Robert Bagnall, director of branches, to O. M. Brown, New Orleans branch secretary, June 5, 1934, ibid.

12. Claude F. Jacobs, "Benevolent Societies of New Orleans Blacks During the Late Nineteenth and Early Twentieth Centuries," *Louisiana History* 29, no. 1 (winter 1988): 21.

13. FBI Report on the New Orleans branch of the NAACP, February 7, 1945, FBI File on the NAACP, New Orleans Public Library, Louisiana; Annual Reports of Branch Activities, New Orleans, 1942-1943, Tureaud Papers, Roll 10; Adam Fairclough, *Better Day Coming: Blacks and Equality, 1890-2000* (London: Penguin, 2001), 183-184; FBI Report on the New Orleans Branch of the NAACP, November 11, 1944; Appendix 4.

14. Mrs. M. T. Wells was an occasional speaker for the branch, particularly as its spokesperson within the Mount Zion M. E. Church, NAACP Programs 1930-1944, Tureaud Papers, Roll 15; Mrs. Ida Tropez (cited also as Tropez King) was active in various charities, not least as a member of the colored committee bringing "Santa to N[ew] O[rleans] children" (along with various other NAACP members), *Times-Picayune*, January 3, 1935; Longe Papers, Box 6. Tropez King was also second vice-president of the Crescent Undertaking and Embalming Company, a Methodist, a civic worker, and a member of the Grand Household Ruth no. 26, Grand United Order Odd Fellows: A. E. Perkins, ed., *Who's Who in Colored Louisiana* (Baton Rouge: Douglas Loan Co., 1930), 135; Appendix 4.

15. New Orleans NAACP branch membership lists; the height of pre-1945 female membership of the executive committee in New Orleans was five in 1944. The State Conference was first organized in January 1943 so that "a state wide NAACP . . . could pool all our efforts and bring pressure to get results." A. P. Tureaud, New Orleans attorney, to Mr. C. A. Williams, Baton Rouge, October 13, 1942, Tureaud Papers, Roll 7; Tureaud to Georgia M. Johnson, January 24, 1943, ibid.; Appendix 4.

16. Mark Robert Schneider, *"We Return Fighting": The Civil Rights Movement in the Jazz Age* (Boston: Northeastern University Press, 2002), 49.

17. Papers of NAACP; Papers of the NAACP: Part 25: Branch Department Files, Regional Files 1941-1955, Series A: Reel 17; "Protest," Alexandria NAACP Branch to the National Executive Committee of the NAACP, January 3, 1945, Tureaud Papers, Roll 7; for more on organizational history of local branches, see Chapter 1.

18. Selected Branch Files, 1913-1939, Reel 13 and Selected Branch Files, 1940-1955, Reel 17.

19. Daniel C. Thompson, *The Negro Leadership Class* (Englewood Cliffs, NJ: Prentice-

Hall, 1963), 26; Belinda Robnett, *How Long? How Long? African-American Women in the Struggle for Civil Rights* (Oxford: Oxford University Press, 1997), 19–21, 191.

20. Baton Rouge NAACP branch membership lists, Selected Branch Files, 1913–1939, Reel 13, and Selected Branch Files, 1940–1955, Reel 17, Papers of NAACP; Mary Jacqueline Hebert, "Beyond Black and White: The Civil Rights Movement in Baton Rouge, Louisiana, 1945–1972" (Ph.D. diss., Louisiana State University and Agricultural and Mechanical College, 1999), 8; *Louisiana Weekly*, January 17, 1931, Amistad Research Center; the death of the New Orleans NAACP branch president, George W. Lucas, in 1931 was the catalyst for a decade of dissension, personality politics, and muted civil rights campaigning. New Orleans had four presidents during the 1930s after Lucas's demise. Conversely, the president of the Monroe branch, Mr. C. H. Myers, held his post for seventeen years (1930–1947). The presidents were George Labat (1931–1933), James E. Gayle (1934–37), Dr. A. W. Brazier (1938–1939), and Mr. J. E. "Chummy" Wilkens (1940); Dorothy Autrey, "'Can These Bones Live?': The National Association for the Advancement of Colored People in Alabama, 1918–1930," *Journal of Negro History* 82, no. 1 (winter 1997), 4.

21. Mrs. D. J. Dupuy, Baton Rouge branch secretary, to A. P. Tureaud, New Orleans attorney, August 18, 1944, Tureaud Papers, Roll 7; Tureaud to Edward R. Dudley, assistant special counsel, NAACP Legal Defense and Educational Fund Inc., n.d. [September 1944], ibid.; Douglas Brinkley, *Mine Eyes Have Seen the Glory: The Life of Rosa Parks* (London: Weidenfeld & Nicolson, 2000), 48; in turn this may reflect negatively on women's role as initiators of protest in the New Orleans NAACP branch.

22. William Pickens, field secretary, to Mrs. Dupuy, Baton Rouge branch secretary, July 15, 1937, Selected Branch Files, 1913–1939, Reel 13, Papers of NAACP.

23. Robert Bagnall, director of branches, to D. J. Dupuy, Baton Rouge branch vice-president, June 14, 1929, ibid.

24. Mrs. D. J. Dupuy, Baton Rouge branch secretary, to Walter White, NAACP executive secretary, May 25, 1939, ibid.; Baton Rouge NAACP branch membership lists; Hebert, "Beyond Black and White," 5, 8–13, 28, 74; membership numbers: 1938, 123; 1939, 254.

25. H. H. Huggins, New Orleans, to Walter White, NAACP executive secretary, June 26, 1939, Selected Branch Files, 1913–1939, Reel 13, Papers of NAACP.

26. Branch Constitution and By-Laws of the NAACP, 1917 (amended 1919, 1924, 1931), Article II, Section 4 (e), 5; Branch Constitution, 1937, Article IX, Section 1, and Article II, Section 4 (d) and (g), 5–6.

27. A. P. Tureaud, New Orleans attorney, to Robert Bagnall, director of branches, October 24, 1931, Tureaud Papers, Box 8; *Louisiana Weekly*, November 7, 1931; Fairclough, *Race and Democracy*, 18; Tureaud to Roy Wilkins, NAACP assistant executive secretary, either October or November 1933, Selected Branch Files, 1913–1939, Reel 15, Papers of NAACP; James B. LaFourche was branch secretary in 1936 and on its executive committee; LaFourche to Walter White, NAACP executive secretary, January 4, 1932, ibid.; LaFourche to William Pickens, field secretary, December 2, 1937, ibid.; LaFourche to White, November 27, 1937, ibid.; Dr. A. W. Brazier, New Orleans branch president, to White, November 17, 1938, ibid.; LaFourche to White, November 18, 1938, ibid.; Pickens to Brazier, 13th November 1938, ibid.; Annual Report of Branch Activities, Baton Rouge, 1943, Selected Branch Files, 1940–1955, Reel 17, Papers of NAACP.

28. Annual Report of Branch Activities, Baton Rouge, 1941, ibid.; 34th Annual Report

of the National Association for the Advancement of Colored People for the year 1943, 34, Spingarn Collection, Howard-Tilton Memorial Library, Tulane University; Mrs. D. J. Dupuy, Baton Rouge, to Lucille Baker, NAACP regional field secretary, April 14, 1945, cited in Hebert, "Beyond Black and White," 57; Daisy Lampkin, "On the N.A.A.C.P. Southern Front," *The Crisis: A Record of the Darker Races*, May 1935, 153.

29. Hebert, "Beyond Black and White," 5, 84.

30. Thompson, *The Negro Leadership Class*, 63, 68–70.

31. FBI Report on the New Orleans Branch of the NAACP, May 14, 1945, FBI File on the NAACP, New Orleans Public Library, Louisiana; *Louisiana Weekly*, April 28, 1945; Fairclough, *Race and Democracy*, 75, 85; Hebert, "Beyond Black and White," 12, 75; Annual Report of Branch Activities, Baton Rouge, 1941, Selected Branch Files, 1940–1955, Reel 17, Papers of NAACP; Jerry Pervis Sanson, *Louisiana During World War II: Politics and Society 1939–1945* (Baton Rouge: Louisiana State University Press, 1999), 286.

32. Baton Rouge NAACP branch membership lists; *Louisiana Weekly*, April 18, 1943; Hebert, "Beyond Black and White," 5, 84; so prevalent was the use of initials rather than full names, so as to prevent white people from disrespecting with being overly familiar, that it is often difficult to acquire a person's first or middle names. Dupuy's first name may have been Delphine, but this was only surmised through extensive research of local African American newspapers; it was never recorded in any NAACP files.

33. Mrs. D. J. Dupuy, Baton Rouge branch secretary, to Walter White, NAACP executive secretary, January 31, 1935, Selected Branch Files, 1913–1939, Reel 13, Papers of NAACP; Dupuy underlined much of her correspondence to express her particular indignation or passions. There were two lynchings in Louisiana in 1935, Jerome Wilson in Franklington and Anderson Ward of Maringouin. Dupuy was probably referring to the Wilson Case, which was a major affair for the branches in the state. In March 1935 the branch sent five dollars to the New York office for the national anti-lynching campaign; 26th Annual Report of the NAACP, 1935, 26.

34. Roy Wilkins, NAACP assistant executive secretary, to B. J. Stanley, Baton Rouge branch president, October 12, 1936, Selected Branch Files, 1913–1939, Reel 13, Papers of NAACP; *State of Louisiana v. Walter Ferguson*, ibid.

35. D. J. Dupuy, Baton Rouge branch secretary, to Walter White, NAACP executive secretary, June 28, 1936, ibid.

36. D. J. Dupuy, Baton Rouge branch secretary, to Walter White, NAACP executive secretary, October 12, 1936, ibid.

37. D. J. Dupuy, Baton Rouge branch secretary, to Walter White, NAACP executive secretary, June 28, 1936, ibid.

38. William Pickens, field secretary, to B. J. Stanley, Baton Rouge branch president, October 8, 1937, ibid.; Walter White, NAACP executive secretary, to all branch officers, 8th December 1937, ibid.; Annual Report of Branch Activities, Baton Rouge, 1944, Selected Branch Files, 1940–1945, Reel 17, Papers of NAACP; Mrs. D. J. Dupuy, Baton Rouge branch assistant secretary, to Walter White, NAACP executive secretary, July 30, 1941, Papers of NAACP: Part 8, Series B: Discrimination in the Criminal Justice System, 1910–1955, Reel 18.

39. B. J. Stanley, Baton Rouge branch president, to Walter White, NAACP executive secretary, June 15, 1937, Selected Branch Files, 1913–1939, Reel 13, Papers of NAACP.

40. Mrs. D. J. Dupuy, Baton Rouge branch secretary, to Walter White, NAACP executive secretary, July 6, 1937, ibid.

41. 22nd–34th Annual Reports of the NAACP; Roy Wilkins, NAACP assistant executive secretary, to B. J. Stanley, Baton Rouge branch president, May 19, 1936, Selected Branch Files, 1913–1939, Reel 13, Papers of NAACP; D. J. Dupuy, Baton Rouge NAACP branch secretary, to Walter White, NAACP executive secretary, July 14, 1937, ibid.; Monroe was on the Honor Roll for six years over this period, while New Orleans, probably due to the more serious demands made of it, only made it on the roll four times; Appendix 6.

42. Mrs. D. J. Dupuy, Baton Rouge branch secretary, to Roy Wilkins, NAACP assistant executive secretary, April 20, 1942, NAACP Papers, Youth File, 1940–1955, Part 19, Series C, Reel 23; Dupuy to Walter White, NAACP executive secretary, June 17, 1935, Selected Branch Files, 1913–1939, Reel 13, Papers of NAACP; Rosa Parks, with Jim Haskins, *Rosa Parks: My Story* (London: Puffin Books, 1992), 94.

43. Mr. Emmett Bashful, Baton Rouge youth council president, Miss Mary Theriot, recording secretary, and Joseph Davis, treasurer, to Roy Wilkins, NAACP assistant executive secretary, n.d. [October 1938], Papers of NAACP, Youth Councils, Louisiana, 1938–1939, Part 19, Series C, Reel 4; Beth Tompkins Bates, "A New Crowd Challenges the Agenda of the Old Guard in the NAACP, 1933–1941," *American Historical Review* 102, no. 2 (April 1997): 347–350.

44. Baton Rouge youth council of the N.A.A.C.P. to "Dear Consumer," October 22, 1938, Youth Councils, Louisiana, 1938–1939, Part 19, Series C, Reel 4, Papers of NAACP.

45. Vicki L. Crawford, J. A. Rouse, and Barbara Woods, "Introduction," *Women in the Civil Rights Movement: Trailblazers and Torchbearers, 1941–1965* (Bloomington: Indiana University Press, 1990), xx.

SIX
WE ARE BUT AMERICANS

Epigraph: Miss Georgia M. Johnson, Alexandria NAACP branch, Louisiana, to Miss Ella J. Baker, director of branches, March 25, 1946, NAACP Correspondence, A. P. Tureaud Papers, Roll 7, Amistad Research Center, Tulane University, New Orleans, Louisiana.

1. Charles M. Payne, *I've Got the Light of Freedom: The Organizing Tradition and the Mississippi Freedom Struggle* (Berkeley: University of California Press, 1995), 274–276; Adam Fairclough, *Race and Democracy: The Civil Rights Struggle in Louisiana 1915–1972* (Athens: University of Georgia Press, 1995), xv–xvi; Christopher Robert Reed, *The Chicago NAACP and the Rise of Black Professional Leadership, 1910–1966* (Bloomington: Indiana University Press, 1997), 116, 144.

2. Article III, Section 1 (d), Constitution and By-Laws for the Branches of the NAACP, 1937, 9.

3. Alexandria NAACP branch membership lists, Papers of the NAACP: Part 25: Branch Department Files, Regional Files 1941–1955, Series A: Reel 17, microfilm, Cambridge University Library; Walter White, NAACP assistant executive secretary, to Rev. H. R. Norris, Alexandria branch president, March 9, 1921, Papers of the NAACP: Part 12: Selected Branch Files, 1913–1939, Series A: The South, Louisiana; *Louisiana Weekly*, May 3, 1930, Amistad Research Center; Roy Wilkins, with Tom Mathews, *Standing Fast: The Autobiography of*

Roy Wilkins (New York: Da Capo Press, 1994), 119–125; John M. Barry, *The Great Mississippi Flood of 1927 and How It Changed America* (New York: Simon & Schuster, 1997), 320–321, 328–30, 388; Gunnar Myrdal, *An American Dilemma, vol. 2: The Negro Problem and Modern Democracy* (London: Transaction Publishers, 1944), 823.

4. Annual Report of Branch Activities, Alexandria, 1941, Selected Branch Files, 1940–1955, Reel 17, Papers of NAACP; "Alexandria, La," memorandum to Walter White, NAACP executive secretary, from Madison S. Jones, NAACP branch youth director, June 21, 1942, Papers of the NAACP: Part 17: National Staff Files 1940–1955, Reel 8; Fairclough, *Race and Democracy*, 2–17, 78; Jerry Pervis Sanson, *Louisiana During World War II: Politics and Society, 1939–1945* (Baton Rouge: Louisiana State University Press, 1999), 5–6, 221–226, 238.

5. William J. Breen, "Black Women and the Great War: Mobilization and Reform in the South," *Journal of Southern History* 44, no. 3 (August 1978): 431–432; Dr. George W. Lucas, New Orleans branch president (1921–1930), cited in Mary White Ovington, *The Walls Come Tumbling Down* (New York: Arno Press, 1969), 227; Jones, "Alexandria, La," memo, 4–6; the fact that Madison Jones (youth director, 1940–1943) was in Alexandria probably means that he was trying to energize youth councils in the city. However, as the memorandum to Walter White makes no mention of youth councils or college chapters, it can be assumed that he was also being employed by the national office to report on the local conditions of a city in the Deep South that had a large black population and had problems of segregated military conditions, particularly after the Alexandria riot of January 1942.

6. Membership numbers for the branch were 152 in 1943, 181 in 1944, and 212 in 1945; Alexandria NAACP branch membership lists, Selected Branch Files, 1940–1955, Reel 17.

7. Georgia Johnson, Alexandria, to Ella Baker, director of branches, March 25, 1946, Tureaud Papers, Roll 7; Miss Mildred Morgan, Protest Committee secretary, to Baker, April 6, 1945, ibid.

8. Jones, "Alexandria, La" memo, 4–6; Annual Report of Branch Activities, Alexandria, 1948, Selected Branch Files, 1940–1955, Reel 17, Papers of NAACP; Article II, Section 4 (e and f), Constitution and By-Laws for the Branches of the NAACP, 1937, 5; Georgia Johnson, Alexandria, to Ella Baker, director of branches, April 30, 1945, Tureaud Papers, Roll 7.

9. "Protest," Alexandria NAACP Branch to the National Executive Committee of the NAACP, January 3, 1945, Tureaud Papers, Roll 7.

10. Johnson to Baker, April 30, 1945, Tureaud Papers, Roll 7; Johnson to Baker, March 25, 1946, ibid.; Georgia Johnson, chair of labor committee, to Miss Mary Jamieson, Louisiana NAACP field director, January 8, 1966, NAACP Field Director Reports (NFDR), Louisiana, Roll 1, Amistad Research Center; Johnson to Mr. Harvey Britton, Louisiana field director, November 22, 1968, ibid., Roll 4; no copies of the short-lived *Alexandria Observer* were discovered, except fragments from the NAACP Branch Files at Cambridge University Library; Fairclough, *Race and Democracy*, 72.

11. Johnson to Baker, March 25, 1946, Tureaud Papers, Roll 7; Adam Fairclough, *Better Day Coming: Blacks and Equality, 1890–2000* (New York: Penguin Books, 2002), 238–239.

12. "Protest," Alexandria NAACP Branch to the National Executive Committee of the NAACP, January 3, 1945, Tureaud Papers, Roll 7; "Alexandria Branch N.A.A.C.P.," letter by Georgia Johnson, chair of legal redress committee (addressee unknown), n.d. [ca. 1941], Selected Branch Files, 1940–1950, Reel 17, Papers of NAACP.

13. Barbara Ransby, *Ella Baker and the Black Freedom Movement: A Radical Democratic Vision* (Chapel Hill: University of North Carolina Press, 2003), 9, 139; Joanne Grant, *Ella Baker: Freedom Bound* (New York: John Wiley & Sons, 1998), 48, 69; Fairclough, *Better Day Coming*, 76–78.

14. Georgia Johnson, chair of legal redress committee, to A. P. Tureaud, New Orleans NAACP branch, October 9, 1944, Papers of the NAACP: Part 4: Louisiana Voting, 1942–1947, Reel 8.

15. "Protest," Alexandria NAACP Branch to the National Executive Committee of the NAACP, January 3, 1945, Tureaud Papers, Roll 7.

16. Johnson to Baker, April 30, 1945.

17. Johnson to Baker, March 25, 1946.

18. Ibid.; Jones, "Alexandria, La," memo, 5; A. P. Tureaud, New Orleans NAACP branch, to Georgia Johnson, chair of legal redress committee, October 5, 1944, Tureaud Papers, Roll 7.

19. Johnson to Baker, March 25, 1946; Johnson to Baker, April 30, 1945; Johnson had suffered from direct persecution before: in January 1939 her home was burnt down, "entailing a loss estimated at $500." Although the "cause was not ascertained" it was believed to be due to her civil rights stance, particularly her attempts to register to vote, *Louisiana Weekly*, January 7, 1939.

20. Johnson to Baker, April 30, 1945; Johnson to Baker, March 25, 1946.

21. Johnson to Baker, April 30, 1945; Johnson to Baker, March 25, 1946.

22. Annual Report of Branch Activities, Alexandria, 1944; "Protest," Alexandria NAACP Branch to the National Executive Committee of the NAACP, January 3, 1945, Tureaud Papers, Roll 7.

23. Johnson to Baker, April 30, 1945; Annual Report of Branch Activities, Alexandria, 1941, Regional Files, 1941–1955, Reel 17, Papers of NAACP; "Alexandria Branch of the NAACP Holds Mass Meeting," unknown newspaper clipping (probably *Alexandria Observer*), September/October 1941, ibid.; Annual Report of Branch Activities, Alexandria, 1944, ibid.; Georgia Johnson, chair of legal redress committee, to A. P. Tureaud, New Orleans NAACP branch, August 1, 1943, Tureaud Papers, Roll 7; Article III, Committees, Section 1(e), Constitution and By-Laws for Branches of the NAACP, 1937, 9; Johnson to National Legal Committee, New York, May 19, 1944, Papers of NAACP: Part 8, Series B: Discrimination in the Criminal Justice System, 1910–1955, Reel 1; Hon. J. A. Williams, white lawyer in Anderson Case, to Spencer Bradley, Alexandria branch president, June 11, 1945, ibid.

24. Annual Report of Branch Activities, Alexandria, 1941, Regional Files, 1941–1955, Reel 17, Papers of NAACP; Annual Report of Branch Activities, Alexandria, 1944, ibid.; Johnson to Tureaud, August 1, 1943; Johnson to Baker, April 30, 1945; Johnson to Baker, March 25, 1946.

25. Fairclough, *Race and Democracy*, 74–75; Harvard Sitkoff, "Racial Militancy and Interracial Violence in the Second World War," *Journal of American History* 58, no.3 (December 1971), 667–669; Jones, "Alexandria, La," memo, 3.

26. Johnson to Baker, April 30, 1945.

27. Johnson to Baker, March 25, 1946; Fairclough, *Race and Democracy*, 78; Sitkoff, "Racial Militancy and Interracial Violence in the Second World War," 667–669; for an account of the censorship of the riot, see William M. Simpson, "A Tale Untold? The Alexan-

dria, Louisiana, Lee Street Riot (January 10, 1942)," in Charles Vincent, ed., *The Louisiana Purchase Bicentennial Series in Louisiana History, vol. 11: The African American Experience in Louisiana, Part C: From Jim Crow to Civil Rights*, 191–203 (Lafayette: Center for Louisiana Studies, 2002), 191–203.

28. Johnson to Baker, April 30, 1945; Johnson to A. P. Tureaud, New Orleans NAACP branch, January 5, 1943, Tureaud Papers, Roll 7; FBI Report on the New Orleans Branch of the NAACP, November 11, 1944, FBI File on the NAACP, New Orleans Public Library, Louisiana; 34th NAACP Annual Report, 1943, 3, 10–11; Annual Report of Branch Activities, Alexandria, 1944, Regional Files, 1941–1955, Reel 17, Papers of NAACP.

29. Annual Report of Branch Activities, Alexandria, 1941, Regional Files, 1941–1955, Reel 17, Papers of NAACP; Annual Report of Branch Activities, Alexandria, 1944, ibid.; Summary Report for 1944," Annual Report of the NAACP for the year 1947, 64.

30. Johnson to Baker, March 25, 1946.

31. Ibid.; Johnson to Baker, April 30, 1945.

32. Spencer Bradley, Alexandria branch president, to Roy Wilkins, NAACP assistant executive secretary, January 17, 1945, Tureaud Papers, Roll 7; Earl V. Smith, chair of legal redress committee, to Ella Baker, director of branches, May 22, 1945, ibid.

33. A. P. Tureaud, New Orleans NAACP branch, to Ella Baker, director of branches, February 4, 1946, ibid.; Georgia Johnson, chair of legal redress committee, to Tureaud, October 1944, ibid.; "Protest," Alexandria NAACP Branch to the National Executive Committee of the NAACP, January 3, 1945; Johnson to Tureaud, March 13, 1945, ibid.

34. Johnson to Baker, March 25, 1946.

35. Freddie J. Spears, Alexandria branch vice-president, to A. P. Tureaud, New Orleans NAACP branch, April 18, 1945, Tureaud Papers, Roll 7; Earl V. Smith, chair of legal redress committee, to Ella Baker, director of branches, May 22, 1945, ibid.; Baker to Georgia Johnson, Alexandria, March 20, 1946, ibid.; the other three NAACP members arrested were on the branch executive committee: Howard Williams, Teley Jones, and William Pierre.

36. Mrs. Lenora Knight, chair of membership committee, to Ella Baker, director of branches, June 22, 1945, ibid.; Annual Report of Branch Activities, Alexandria, 1948, Regional Files, 1941–1955, Reel 17, Papers of NAACP; Rev. J. M. Murphy, Alexandria branch president, Georgia Johnson, chair of legal redress committee, and Elizabeth Williams, secretary, to Hon J. A. Blackman, Mayor of Alexandria, March 4, 1947, Papers of the NAACP: Part 15, Series A: Legal Department Files, 1940–1955, Reel 2.

37. Daniel E. Byrd, president of Louisiana State Conference, to Georgia Johnson, chair of legal redress committee, October 12, 1947, Papers of the NAACP: Part 15, Series A: Legal Department Files, 1940–1955, Reel 2; Donald Jones, regional secretary, to Rev. J. M. Murphy, Alexandria branch president, December 1, 1947, ibid.; Georgia Johnson, chair of labor committee, to Harvey Britton, Louisiana field director, March 9, 1968, NFDR, Roll 3; Britton to Johnson, March 19, 1968, ibid.; Johnson to Britton, November 22, 1968, NFDR, Roll 4; Johnson to Britton, May 31, 1968, NFDR, Roll 3.

38. Johnson to Britton, May 31, 1968, NFDR, Roll 3; Johnson to Britton, June 21, 1968, ibid.; Langston Hughes, *Fight for Freedom: The Story of the NAACP* (New York: W. W. Norton, 1962), 109.

39. Johnson to Baker, March 25, 1946; Evelyn Brooks Higginbotham, "Beyond the Sound of Silence: Afro-American Women in History," *Gender and History* 1, no. 1 (spring 1989), 54.

CONCLUSION

1. John H. Scott with Cleo Scott Brown, *Witness to the Truth: My Struggle for Human Rights in Louisiana* (Columbia: University of South Carolina Press, 2003), 125; Christopher Robert Reed, *The Chicago NAACP and the Rise of Black Professional Leadership, 1910–1966* (Bloomington: Indiana University Press, 1997), 116; Charles M. Payne, *I've Got the Light of Freedom: The Organizing Tradition and the Mississippi Freedom Struggle* (Berkeley: University of California Press, 1995), 269–271; Bernice McNair Barnett, "Invisible Southern Black Women Leaders in the Civil Rights Movement: The Triple Constraints of Gender, Race, and Class," *Gender and Society* 7, no. 2 (June 1993): 177; Gerda Lerner, ed., *Black Women in White America: A Documentary History* (New York: Pantheon Books, 1972), xvii; Paula Giddings, *When and Where I Enter: The Impact of Black Women on Race and Sex in America* (New York: William Morrow & Co., 1984), 5.

2. Gunnar Myrdal, *An American Dilemma, Vol. 2: The Negro Problem and Modern Democracy* (London: Transaction Publishers, 1944), 823.

3. Adam Fairclough, *Race and Democracy: The Civil Rights Struggle in Louisiana 1915–1972* (Athens: University of Georgia Press, 1995), 48; H. Viscount Nelson, *The Rise and Fall of Modern Black Leadership: Chronicle of a Twentieth-Century Tragedy* (New York: University Press of America, 2003), 83; Dorothy Autrey, "'Can These Bones Live?': The National Association for the Advancement of Colored People in Alabama, 1918–1930," *Journal of Negro History* 82, no. 1 (1997): 8–9; Merline Pitre, *In Struggle Against Jim Crow: Lula B. White and the NAACP, 1900–1957* (College Station: Texas A&M University Press, 1999), 25; Reed, *Chicago NAACP*, viii; for a contrary view, see Mark Robert Schneider's *"We Return Fighting": The Civil Rights Movement in the Jazz Age* (Boston: Northeastern University Press, 2002), 4.

BIBLIOGRAPHY

MANUSCRIPT COLLECTIONS

African American Resource Center, New Orleans Public Library, Louisiana

FBI Files on the NAACP ("Communist Infiltration of the National Association for the Advancement of Colored People") 1941–57.

Amistad Research Center, Tulane University, New Orleans, LA

Hardin, Joseph A., Papers.
Longe, George, Papers, 1768–1971.
NAACP Field Director Reports, Louisiana.
    Education for Negroes [program book for NAACP branches] (1935).
Papers from *Separate But (Un)Equal: The* Plessy v. Ferguson *Centennial Conference*, Harvard University, W. E. B. Du Bois Institute, April 20–21, 1996.
Tureaud, Alexander Pierre, Papers, 1783–1977.
    NAACP Statement of Southern Negroes: 1942.
Williams, Fannie C., Papers 1883–1980.

Cambridge University Library, Cambridge, UK

Papers of the NAACP, microfilm.
    Constitution and By-Laws for the Branches of the National Association for the Advancement of Colored People, 1917 (amended 1919, 1924, 1931); 1937.
    Constitution and By-Laws of the National Association for the Advancement of Colored People, February 1936; June 22 1936; 1946.

Howard-Tilton Library, Tulane University, New Orleans, LA

Spingarn, Arthur B., Collection.
    NAACP Annual Reports.

Manuscript Division, Library of Congress, Washington, DC

Lonigan, Edna. "Report of the Survey of the National Association for the Advancement of Colored People," March 22, 1932, Container 22, folder: NAACP Crisis Magazine and NAACP Finances, 1932.

Newspapers/Journals

Alexandria Observer
The American Missionary
The Baptist Advocate
The Crisis: A Record of the Darker Races
The Crusader
The Louisiana Weekly
Monroe News Star
New Orleans Tribune
Times-Picayune
The Vindicator

PUBLISHED PRIMARY SOURCES

Armstrong, Louis. *Louis Armstrong, in His Own Words: Selected Writings.* New York: Oxford University Press, 1999.

———. *Satchmo: My Life in New Orleans.* New York: Da Capo Press, 1954.

Barnard, Hollinger F., ed. *Outside the Magic Circle: The Autobiography of Virginia Foster Durr.* Tuscaloosa: University of Alabama Press, 1994.

Bates, Daisy. *The Long Shadow of Little Rock: A Memoir.* New York: David Company, 1962.

Bechet, Sidney. *Treat It Gentle.* London: Cassell & Co., 1960.

Bond, Horace Mann, and Julia W. Bond. *The Star Creek Papers.* Edited by Adam Fairclough. Athens: University of Georgia Press, 1997.

Burns, Stewart, ed. *Daybreak of Freedom: The Montgomery Bus Boycott.* Chapel Hill: University of North Carolina Press, 1997.

Cooper, Anna Julia. *A Voice from the South: By a Black Woman of the South.* Xenia, Ohio: Aldine Printing House, 1892.

Du Bois, W. E. B. *The Souls of Black Folk.* 1903. Reprint, New York: Dover Publications, 1994.

———. *Darkwater: Voices from Within the Veil.* 1920. Reprint, New York: Dover Publications, 1999.

———. *Dusk of Dawn: An Essay Toward an Autobiography of a Race Concept.* 1940. Reprint, London: Transaction Publishers, 1997.

———. *An ABC of Color: Selections Chosen by the Author from over a Half Century of His Writings.* New York: International Publishers, 1963.

———. *The Autobiography of W. E. B. Du Bois: A Soliloquy on Viewing My Life from the Last Decade of Its First Century.* 1968; Reprint, New York: International Publishers, 1991.

Foner, Philip S. *W. E. B. Du Bois Speaks: Speeches and Addresses, 1890–1919 and 1920–1963.* 1970. Reprint, London: Pathfinder, 1991.

Gaudet, Frances Joseph. *"He Leadeth Me."* New York: G. K. Hall & Co., 1996.
Henry, Aaron, with Constance Curry. *The Fire Ever Burning*. Jackson: University Press of Mississippi, 2000.
Hill, Robert A., ed. *The Marcus Garvey and Universal Negro Improvement Association Papers*. Berkeley: University of California Press, 1990.
Johnson, James Weldon. *Along This Way: The Autobiography of James Weldon Johnson*. 1933. Reprint, Harmondsworth, UK: Penguin Books, 1933.
King, Coretta Scott. *My Life with Martin Luther King Jr*. 1970. Reprint, London: Hodder & Stoughton, 1994.
Lerner, Gerder, ed. *Black Women in White America: A Documentary History*. New York: Pantheon Books, 1972.
Long, Huey P. *Every Man a King: The Autobiography of Huey P. Long*. 1933. Reprint, New York: Da Capo Press, 1996.
Martine, Waldo E., Jr., ed. Brown v. Board of Education: *A Brief History with Documents*. New York: Bedford/St. Martins, 1998.
Olsen, Otto H., ed. *The Thin Disguise: Turning Point in Negro History*, Plessy v. Ferguson, *A Documentary Presentation (1864–1896)*. New York: Humanities Press, 1967.
Ovington, Mary White. *Black and White Sat Down Together: The Reminiscences of an NAACP Founder*. Edited by Ralph E. Lukar. New York: The Feminist Press, 1995.
———. *Half a Man: The Status of the Negro in New York*. 1911. Reprint, New York: Negro Universities Press, 1969.
———. "The National Association for the Advancement of Colored People." *Journal of Negro History* 9, no. 1 (April 1924): 107–116.
———. *Portraits in Color*. New York: Viking Press, 1927.
———. *The Walls Came Tumbling Down*. 1947. Reprint, New York: Arno Press, 1969.
Parks, Rosa, with Jim Haskins. *Rosa Parks: My Story*. London: Puffin Books, 1992.
———, with Gregory J. Reed. *Quiet Strength: The Faith, the Hope, and the Heart of a Woman Who Changed a Nation*. Grand Rapids, MI: Zondervan Publishing House, 1994.
Pickens, William. *The Heir of Slaves: An Autobiography*. New York: Pilgrim Press, 1911.
Robinson, Jo Ann Gibson. *The Montgomery Bus Boycott and the Women Who Started It: The Memoir of Jo Ann Gibson Robinson*. Edited by David J. Garrow. 1987. Reprint, Knoxville: University of Tennessee Press, 1996.
Rogers, Kim Lacy. *Righteous Lives: Narratives of the New Orleans Civil Rights Movement*. New York: New York University Press, 1993.
Scott, John H., with Cleo Scott Brown. *Witness to the Truth: My Struggle for*

Human Rights in Louisiana. Columbia: University of South Carolina Press, 2003.

Terrell, Mary Church. *A Colored Woman in a White World.* Washington, DC: Ransdell, Inc., 1940.

Villard, Oswald Garrison. *Fighting Years: Memoirs of a Liberal Editor.* Rahway, NJ: Harcourt, Brace, & Company, 1939.

White, Walter. *How Far the Promised Land?* New York: Viking, 1955.

———. *A Man Called White: The Autobiography of Walter White.* 1948. Reprint, Athens: University of Georgia Press, 1995.

———. *A Rising Wind.* 1945. Reprint, Westport, CT: Negro Universities Press, 1971.

———. *Rope and Faggot: A Biography of Judge Lynch.* 1928. Reprint, Salem, NH: Ayer Company Publishers, 1992.

Wilkins, Roy. "Huey Long Says—An Interview with Louisiana's Kingfish." *The Crisis: A Record of the Darker Races* (February 1935): 41, 52.

Wilkins, Roy, and Tom Mathews. *Standing Fast: The Autobiography of Roy Wilkins.* 1948. Reprint, New York: Da Capo Press, 1994.

Wilson, Sondra Kathryn. *In Search of Democracy: The NAACP Writings of James Weldon Johnson, Walter White, and Roy Wilkins.* Oxford: Oxford University Press, 1999.

Young, Andrew. *An Easy Burden: The Civil Rights Movement and the Transformation of America.* New York: HarperCollins, 1996.

Secondary Sources
Books

Arnesen, Eric. *Waterfront Workers of New Orleans: Race, Class, and Politics, 1863–1923.* Oxford: Oxford University Press, 1993.

Avery, Sheldon. *Up from Washington: William Pickens and the Negro Struggle for Equality, 1900–1954.* Newark: Associated University Press, 1989.

Barry, John M. *Rising Tide: The Great Mississippi Flood of 1927 and How It Changed America.* New York: Simon & Schuster, 1997.

Bennett, Lerone, Jr. *The Shaping of Black America: The Struggles and Triumphs of African-Americans, 1619 to the 1990s.* 1975. Reprint, London: Penguin Books, 1993.

Berg, Manfred. *The Ticket to Freedom: The NAACP and the Struggle for Black Political Integration.* Gainesville: University Press of Florida, 2005.

Boris, Joseph J., ed. *Who's Who in Colored America: A Biographical Dictionary of Notable Living Persons of Negro Descent in America,* vol. 1: 1927. New York: Who's Who in Colored America Corp., 1927.

———. *Who's Who in Colored America: A Biographical Dictionary of Notable Living Persons of Negro Descent in America, 1930–31–32.* New York: Garrett & Massie, 1933.
Brinkley, Douglas. *Mine Eyes Have Seen the Glory: The Life of Rosa Parks.* London: Weidenfeld & Nicolson, 2000.
Bunche, Ralph J. *The Political Status of the Negro in the Age of FDR.* Chicago: University of Chicago Press, 1973.
Carter, Hodding, ed. *The Past as Prelude: New Orleans, 1718–1968.* New Orleans: Pelican Publishing House, 1968.
Chafe, William H. *The American Woman: Her Changing Social, Economic and Political Roles, 1920–1970.* 1972. Reprint, New York: Oxford University Press, 1977.
Collins, Patricia Hill. *Black Feminist Thought: Knowledge, Consciousness, and the Politics of Empowerment.* Boston: Unwin Hyman Ltd., 1990.
Cook, Robert. *Sweet Land of Liberty? The African-American Struggle for Civil Rights in the Twentieth Century.* London: Longman, 1998.
Crawford, Vicki L., J. A. Rouse, and Barbara Woods, eds. *Women in the Civil Rights Movement: Trailblazers and Torchbearers, 1941–1965.* Bloomington: Indiana University Press, 1993.
Davis, Angela. *Women, Race and Class.* London: The Women's Press, 1982.
Davis, Cyprian. *The History of Black Catholics in the United States.* New York: Crossroad, 1990.
Desdune, Rodolphe Lucien. *Our People and Our History.* Translated by Sister Dorothea Olga McCants. Baton Rouge: Louisiana State University Press, 1973.
Dominguez, Virginia R. *White by Definition: Social Classification in Creole Louisiana.* New Brunswick, NJ: Rutgers University Press, 1986.
Du Bois, Ellen Carol, and Vicki L. Ruiz. *Unequal Sisters: A Multi-Cultural Reader in U.S. Women's History.* New York: Routledge, 1990.
Ellison, Mary. *The Black Experience: American Blacks since 1865.* London: B. T. Batsford, 1974.
Fairclough, Adam. *Better Day Coming: Blacks and Equality, 1890–2000.* London: Penguin Books, 2001.
———. *Race and Democracy: The Civil Rights Struggle in Louisiana, 1915–1972.* Athens: University of Georgia Press, 1995.
———. *Teaching Equality: Black Schools in the Age of Jim Crow.* Athens: University of Georgia Press, 2001.
Finch, Minnie. *The NAACP: Its Fight for Justice.* Metuchen, N.J.: Scarecrow Press, 1981.
Fischer, Roger A. *The Desegregation Struggle in Louisiana, 1862–77.* Urbana: University of Illinois Press, 1974.

Frankel, Noralee, and Nancy S. Dye, eds. *Gender, Class, Race, and Reform in the Progressive Era.* Lexington: University Press of Kentucky, 1991.

Franklin, John Hope, and Alfred A. Moss Jr. *From Slavery to Freedom: A History of African Americans.* Boston: McGraw-Hill, 1994.

Frazier, E. Franklin. *Black Bourgeoisie: The Rise of a New Middle Class in the United States.* New York: Collier Books, 1957.

Gatewood, Willard B. *Aristocrats of Color: The Black Elite, 1880–1920.* Bloomington: Indiana University Press, 1993.

Gehman, Mary. *The Free People of Color of New Orleans: An Introduction.* New Orleans: Margaret Media, Inc, 1994.

———. *Women and New Orleans: A History.* New Orleans: Margaret Media, 1988.

Giddings, Paula. *When and Where I Enter: The Impact of Black Women on Race and Sex in America.* New York: William Morrow & Co., 1984.

Gilmore, Glenda Elizabeth. *Gender and Jim Crow: Women and the Politics of White Supremacy in North Carolina, 1896–1920.* Chapel Hill: University of North Carolina Press, 1996.

Goings, Kenneth W. *The NAACP Comes of Age: The Defeat of Judge J. Parker.* Bloomington: Indiana University Press, 1990.

Grant, Joanne. *Ella Baker: Freedom Bound.* New York: John Wiley & Sons, 1998.

Greenberg, Jack. *Crusaders in the Courts: How a Dedicated Band of Lawyers Fought for the Civil Rights Revolution.* New York: Basic Books, 1994.

Hair, William Ivy. *Carnival of Fury: Robert Charles and the New Orleans Riot of 1900.* Baton Rouge: Louisiana State University Press, 1976.

———. *The Kingfish and His Realm: The Life and Times of Huey P. Long.* Baton Rouge: Louisiana State University Press, 1991.

Hall, Jacquelyn Dowd. *Revolt Against Chivalry: Jessie Daniel Ames and the Women's Campaign Against Lynching.* New York: Columbia University Press, 1979.

Hine, Darlene Clark. *Black Victory: The Rise and Fall of the White Primary in Texas.* New York: KTO Press, 1979.

———. *Black Women in America: An Historical Encyclopaedia.* Vols. 1 and 2. New York: Carlson Publishing, 1993.

——— and Kathleen Thompson. *A Shining Thread of Hope: The History of Black Women in America.* New York: Broadway Books, 1998.

Hirsch, Arnold R., and Joseph Logsdon, eds. *Creole New Orleans: Race and Americanization.* Baton Rouge: Louisiana State University Press, 1992.

Hixson, William B., Jr. *Moorfield Storey and the Abolitionist Tradition.* New York: Oxford University Press, 1972.

Honey, Maureen, ed. *Bitter Fruit: African American Women in World War II.* Columbia: University of Missouri Press, 1999.

hooks, bell. *Ain't I a Woman: Black Women and Feminism.* 1982. Reprint, London: Pluto Press, 1992.
———. *Yearning: Race, Gender, and Cultural Politics.* London: Turnaround, 1991.
Hughes, Langston. *Fight for Freedom: The Story of the NAACP.* New York: W. W. Norton, 1962.
Hutchinson, Earl Ofari. *Blacks and Reds: Race and Class in Conflict 1919–1990.* East Lansing: Michigan State University Press, 1995.
Jack, Robert L. *History of the National Association for the Advancement of Colored People.* Boston: Meador Press, 1943.
Janken, Kenneth Robert. *White: The Biography of Walter White, Mr. NAACP.* New York: New Press, 2001.
Jonas, Gilbert. *Freedom's Sword: The NAACP and the Struggle Against Racism in America, 1909–1969.* London: Routledge, 2005.
Kein, Sybil, ed. *Creole: The History and Legacy of Louisiana's Free People of Color.* Baton Rouge: Louisiana State University Press, 2000.
Kelley, Robin D. G. *Hammer and Hoe: Alabama Communists During the Great Depression.* Chapel Hill: University of North Carolina Press, 1990.
Kellogg, Charles Flint. *NAACP: A History of the National Association for the Advancement for Colored People, vol. 1: 1909–1920.* 1967. Reprint, Baltimore: John Hopkins University Press, 1973.
Kirk, John A. *Redefining the Color Line: Black Activism in Little Rock, Arkansas, 1940–1970.* Gainesville: University Press of Florida, 2002.
Lawson, Steven F. *Black Ballots: Voting Rights in the South, 1944–1969.* New York: Columbia University Press, 1979.
Lee, Chana Kai. *For Freedoms Sake: The Life of Fannie Lou Hamer.* Urbana: University of Illinois Press, 2000.
Lewis, David Levering, ed. *W. E. B. Du Bois: A Reader.* New York: Henry Holt, 1995.
———. *W. E. B. Du Bois: Biography of a Race, 1868–1919.* New York: Henry Holt, 1993.
———. *W. E. B. Du Bois: The Fight for Equality and the American Century, 1919–1963.* New York: Henry Holt, 2000.
Ling, Peter J., and Sharon Monteith, eds. *Gender in the Civil Rights Movement.* London: Garland, 1999.
Linn, James Weber. *Jane Addams: A Biography.* Urbana: University of Illinois Press, 2000.
Litwack, Leon. *Trouble in Mind: Black Southerners in the Age of Jim Crow.* New York: Vintage Books, 1998.
Lorini, Alessandra. *Rituals of Race: American Public Culture and the Search for Racial Democracy.* Charlottesville: University Press of Virginia, 1999.

Marable, Manning. *How Capitalism Underdeveloped Black America*. Boston: South End Press, 1983.
———. *W. E. B. Du Bois: Black Radical Democrat*. Boston: Twayne, 1986.
———. *Black Leadership*. New York: Columbia University Press, 1998.
McMillen, Neil R., ed. *Remaking Dixie: The Impact of World War II on the American South*. Jackson: University Press of Mississippi, 1997.
McMurray, Linda O. *To Keep the Waters Troubled: The Life of Ida B. Wells*. Oxford: Oxford University Press, 1998.
McNeil, Genna Rae. *Groundwork: Charles Hamilton Houston and the Struggle for Civil Rights*. Philadelphia: University of Pennsylvania Press, 1983.
McPherson, James M. *The Abolitionist Legacy: From Reconstruction to the NAACP*. Princeton: Princeton University Press, 1977.
Meier, August. *Negro Thought in America, 1880–1915: Racial Ideologies in the Age of Booker T. Washington*. 1963. Reprint, Ann Arbor: University of Michigan Press, 1988.
——— and Elliott Rudwick. *Along the Color Line: Explorations in the Black Experience*. Urbana: University of Illinois Press, 1976.
Mills, Kay. *This Little Light of Mine: The Life of Fannie Lou Hamer*. 1993. Reprint, New York: Plume, 1994.
Myrdal, Gunnar. *An American Dilemma, vol. 2: The Negro Problem and Modern Democracy*. London: Transaction Publishers, 1944.
Nelson, H. Viscount. *The Rise and Fall of Modern Black Leadership: Chronicle of a Twentieth Century Tragedy*. New York: University Press of America, 2003.
Noble, Jeanne. *Beautiful, also, are the souls of my black sisters: A History of the Black Woman in America*. Englewood Cliffs, NJ: Prentice-Hall, 1978.
Obadele-Starks, Ernest. *Black Unionism in the Industrial South*. College Station: Texas A&M University Press, 2000.
Olson, Lynne. *Freedom's Daughters: The Unsung Heroines of the Civil Rights Movement from 1830 to 1970*. New York: Scribner, 2001.
Omolade, Barbara. *The Rising Song of African American Women*. New York: Routledge, 1994.
Payne, Charles M. *I've Got the Light of Freedom: The Organizing Tradition and the Mississippi Freedom Struggle*. Berkeley: University of California Press, 1995.
Perkins, A. E., ed. *Who's Who in Colored Louisiana*. Baton Rouge: Douglas Loan Co., 1930.
Pitre, Merline. *In Struggle Against Jim Crow: Lula B. White and the NAACP, 1900-1957*. College Station: Texas A&M University Press, 1999.
Ransby, Barbara. *Ella Baker and the Black Freedom Movement: A Radical Democratic Vision*. Chapel Hill: University of North Carolina Press, 2003.

Reed, Adolph L., Jr. *W. E. B. Du Bois and American Political Thought: Fabianism and the Color Line.* Oxford: Oxford University Press, 1997.
Reed, Christopher Robert. *The Chicago NAACP and the Rise of the Black Professional Leadership, 1910–1966.* Bloomington: Indiana University Press, 1997.
Reynolds, George M. *Machine Politics in New Orleans, 1897–1926.* New York: Columbia University Press, 1936.
Rippa, S. Alexander. *Education in a Free Society: An American History.* New York: Longman, 1997.
Robnett, Belinda. *How Long? How Long?: African-American Women in the Struggle for Civil Rights.* Oxford: Oxford University Press, 1997.
Rodgers-Rose, La Frances, ed. *The Black Woman.* London: SAGE, 1980.
Rohrer, John H., and Munro S. Edmonson, eds. *The Eighth Generation Grows Up: Cultures and Personalities of New Orleans Negroes.* New York: Harper Torchbooks, 1960.
Ross, B. Joyce. *J. E. Spingarn and the Rise of the NAACP, 1911–1939.* New York: Atheneum, 1972.
Ruiz, Jim. *The Black Hood of the Ku Klux Klan.* London: Austin & Winfield, 1999.
Russell, Sandi. *Render Me My Song: African-American Women Writers from Slavery to the Present.* London: Pandora Press, 1990.
Sanson, Jerry Pervis. *Louisiana During World War II: Politics and Society, 1939–1945.* Baton Rouge: Louisiana State University Press, 1999.
Sauer, Lillian Brewster. *Women's Clubs of New Orleans 1930.* New Orleans: n.p., 1930.
Schneider, Mark Robert. *"We Return Fighting": The Civil Rights Movement in the Jazz Age.* Boston: Northeastern University Press, 2003.
Schweninger, Loren. *Black Property Owners in the South, 1790–1915.* Urbana: University of Illinois Press, 1990.
Scott, Anne Firor. *The Southern Lady from Pedestal to Politics, 1830–1930.* Chicago: University of Chicago Press, 1970.
Shaw, Stephanie J. *What a Woman Ought to Be and to Do: Black Professional Women Workers During the Jim Crow Era.* Chicago: University of Chicago Press, 1996.
Sitkoff, Harvard. *A New Deal for Blacks: The Emergence of Civil Rights as a National Issue, vol. 1: The Depression Decade.* New York: Oxford University Press, 1978.
St. James, Warren D. *NAACP: Triumphs of a Pressure Group, 1909–1980.* New York: Exposition Press, 1980.
―――. *The National Association for the Advancement of Colored People: A Case Study in Pressure Groups.* New York: Exposition Press, 1958.

Sterx, H. E. *The Free Negro in Ante-Bellum Louisiana.* Cranbury, NJ: Farleigh Dickinson University Press, 1972.
Stokes, Melvyn, and Rick Halpern. *Race and Class in the American South since 1890.* Oxford: Berg Publishers, 1994.
Sullivan, Patricia. *Days of Hope: Race and Democracy in the New Deal Era.* Chapel Hill: University of North Carolina Press, 1996.
Terborg-Penn, Rosalyn. *African American Women in the Struggle for the Vote, 1850–1920.* Bloomington: Indiana University Press, 1998.
Thomas, Richard W. *Understanding Interracial Unity: A Study of U.S. Race Relations.* London: SAGE, 1996.
Thompson, Daniel C. *The Negro Leadership Class.* Englewood Cliffs, NJ: Prentice-Hall, 1963.
Tregle, Joseph G. *Louisiana in the Age of Jackson: A Clash of Cultures and Personalities.* Baton Rouge: Louisiana State University Press, 1999.
Tushnet, Mark V. *The NAACP's Legal Strategy Against Segregated Education, 1925–50.* Chapel Hill: University of North Carolina Press, 1987.
———. *Making Civil Rights Law: Thurgood Marshall and the Supreme Court, 1936–1961.* Oxford: Oxford University Press, 1994.
Vaz, Kim Marie. *Black Women in America.* London: SAGE, 1995.
Vincent, Charles, ed. *The Louisiana Purchase Bicentennial Series in Louisiana History, vol. 11: The African American Experience in Louisiana, Part C: From Jim Crow to Civil Rights.* Lafayette: Center for Louisiana Studies, 2002.
Wallace, Michele. *Black Macho and the Myth of the Superwoman.* 1979. Reprint, London: Verso, 1990.
Ward, Brian, and Tony Badger, eds. *The Making of Martin Luther King and the Civil Rights Movement.* London: Macmillan, 1996.
Wedin, Carolyn. *Inheritors of the Spirit: Mary White Ovington and the Founding of the NAACP.* New York: John Wiley & Sons, 1998.
Weiss, Nancy J. *Farewell to the Party of Lincoln: Black Politics in the Age of FDR.* Princeton: Princeton University Press, 1983.
———. *The National Urban League, 1910–1940.* New York: Oxford University Press, 1974.
White, Deborah Gray. *Too Heavy a Load: Black Women in Defense of Themselves, 1894–1994.* New York: W. W. Norton, 1999.
Williamson, Joel. *The Crucible of Race: Black-White Relations in the American South since Emancipation.* Oxford: Oxford University Press, 1984.
———. *New People: Miscegenation and Mulattoes in the United States.* New York: Free Press, 1980.
Woodward, C. Vann. *The Strange Career of Jim Crow.* 1957. Reprint, New York: Oxford University Press, 1974.

Wynn, Daniel Webster. *The NAACP Versus Negro Revolutionary Protest: A Comparative Study of the Effectiveness of Each Movement.* New York: Exposition Press, 1955.
Zangrando, Robert L. *The NAACP Crusade Against Lynching.* Philadelphia: Temple University Press, 1980.

Periodical Articles

Anderson, Karen Tucker. "Last Hired, First Fired: Black Women Workers During World War II." *Journal of American History* 69, no. 1 (June 1982): 82–97.
Autrey, Dorothy. "'Can These Bones Live?': The National Association for the Advancement of Colored People in Alabama, 1918–1930." *Journal of Negro History* 82, no. 1 (winter 1997): 61–73.
Baker, Riley E. "Negro Voter Registration in Louisiana, 1879–1964." *Louisiana Studies* 4, no.4 (winter 1965): 332–350.
Baker, Scott. "Testing Equality: The National Teacher Examination and the NAACP's Legal Campaign to Equalize Teachers' Salaries in the South." *History of Education Quarterly* 35, no. 1 (spring 1995): 49–64.
Barnett, Bernice McNair. "Invisible Southern Black Women Leaders in the Civil Rights Movement: The Triple Constraints of Gender, Race, and Class." *Gender and Society* 7, no. 2 (June 1993): 162–182.
Bates, Beth Tompkins. "A New Crowd Challenges the Agenda of the Old Guard in the NAACP, 1933–1941." *American Historical Review* 102, no. 2 (April 1997): 340–377.
Blackwelder, Julia Kirk. "Women in the Work Force: Atlanta, New Orleans, and San Antonio, 1930 to 1940." *Journal of Urban History* 4 (May 1978): 331–358.
Breen, William J. "Black Women and the Great War: Mobilization and Reform in the South." *Journal of Southern History* 44, no. 3 (1978): 421–440.
Carlson, Shirley J. "Black Ideals of Womanhood in the Late Victorian Era." *Journal of Negro History* 77, no. 2 (spring 1992): 61–73.
Cassimere, Raphael. "Equalizing Teachers' Pay in Louisiana." *Integrated Education* 15 (July–August 1977): 3–8.
Clayton, Ronnie W. "The Federal Writers' Project for Blacks in Louisiana." *Louisiana History* 19, no. 3 (summer 1978): 327–335.
Dalfiume, Richard M. "The 'Forgotten Years' of the Negro Revolution." *Journal of American History* 4 (1969): 90–106.
De Jong, Greta. "With the Aid of God and the FSA: The Louisiana Farmers' Union and the African American Freedom Struggle in the New Deal Era." *Journal of Social History* 34, no. 1 (2000): 105–139.

Eisenberg, Bernard. "Only for the Bourgeois? James Weldon Johnson and the NAACP, 1916–1930." *Phylon* 43, no. 2 (summer 1982): 110–124.

Ellis, Mark. "W. E. B. Du Bois and the Formation of Black Opinions in World War I: A Commentary on 'The Damnable Dilemma.'" *Journal of American History* 81 (March 1995): 1584–1590.

———. "'Close Ranks and Seeking Honors': W. E. B. Du Bois in World War I." *Journal of American History* 79 (June 1992): 96–124.

Fairclough, Adam. "State of the Art: Historians and the Civil Rights Movement." *Journal of American Studies* 24, no. 3 (December 1990): 387–399.

———. "'Forty Acres and a Mule': Horace Mann Bond and the Lynching of Jerome Wilson." *Journal of American Studies* 31 (1997): 1–17.

———. "'Being in the Field of Education and Also a Negro . . . Seems . . . Tragic': Black Teachers in the Jim Crow South." *Journal of American History* 87, no 1 (2000): 65–91.

———. "The Costs of *Brown:* Black Teachers and School Integration." *Journal of American History* 91, no.1 (June 2004): 43–55.

Finkle, Lee. "The Conservative Aims of Militant Rhetoric: Black Protest During World War II." *Journal of American History* 60 (1974): 692–713.

Foner, Laura. "The Free People of Color in Louisiana and St. Dominique: A Comparative Portrait of Two Three-Caste Slave Societies." *Journal of Social History* 3 (1970): 406–430.

Gordon, Linda. "Black and White Visions of Welfare: Women's Welfare Activism, 1890–1945." *Journal of American History* 78 (September 1991): 559–590.

Harley, Sharon. "For the Good of Family and Race: Gender, Work, and Domestic Roles in the Black Community, 1880–1930." *Signs* 15 (winter 1990): 336–349.

Harris, Fredrick C. "Something Within: Religion as a Mobilizer of African American Political Activism." *Journal of Politics* 56, no. 1 (February 1994): 42–68.

Helmbold, Lois Rita. "Beyond the Family Economy: Black and White Working-Class Women During the Great Depression." *Feminist Studies* 13, no. 3 (fall 1987): 629–655.

Higginbotham, Evelyn Brooks. "Beyond the Sound of Silence: Afro-American Women in History." *Gender and History* 1 (spring 1989): 50–67.

Hine, Darlene Clark. "Black Professionals and Race Consciousness: Origins of the Civil Rights Movement, 1890–1950." *Journal of American History* 89, no.4 (March 2003): 1279–1294.

Howard, Perry H. "An Analysis of Voting Behavior in Baton Rouge." *The Proceedings of the Louisiana Academy of Sciences* 25 (August 1952): 84–100.

Jacobs, Claude F. "Benevolent Societies of New Orleans Blacks During the Late Nineteenth and Early Twentieth Centuries." *Louisiana History* 29, no. 1 (winter 1988): 21–33.

Johnson, Joan Marie. "'Drill into us . . . the Rebel Tradition': The Contest over Southern Identity in Black and White Women's Clubs, South Carolina, 1898-1930." *Journal of Southern History* 66, no. 3 (August 2000): 525-562

Johnson, Kenneth R. "Kate Gordon and the Woman-Suffrage Movement in the South." *Journal of Southern History* 38, no. 2 (August 1972): 365-393.

Johnson, Phillip J. "The Limits of Interracial Compromise: Louisiana, 1941." *Journal of Southern History* 69, no. 2 (May 2003): 319-348.

Jones, Beverly W. "Mary Church Terrell and the National Association of Colored Women, 1896 to 1901." *Journal of Negro History* 67, no. 1 (Spring 1916): 20-33.

Jordan, William. "'The Damnable Dilemma': African American Accommodation and Protest During World War I." *Journal of American History* 81 (March 1995): 1562-1583.

Keith, Jeanette. "The Politics of Southern Draft Resistance, 1917-1918: Class, Race, and Conscription in the Rural South." *Journal of American History* 87, no. 4 (March 2001): 1335-1361.

Kelley, Robin D. G. "'We Are Not What We Seem': Rethinking Black Working-Class Opposition in the Jim Crow South." *Journal of American History* 80 (June 1993): 75-112.

Kerber, L. K. "Separate Spheres, Female Worlds, Women's Place: The Rhetoric of Women's History." *Journal of American History* 75 (June 1988): 9-39.

Klarman, Michael J. "How Brown Changed Race Relations: The Backlash Thesis." *Journal of American History* 81 (June 1994): 81-118.

Knupfer, Anne Meis. "'If you can't push, pull, if you can't pull, please get out of the way': The Phyllis Wheatley Club and Home in Chicago, 1896 to 1920." *Journal of Negro History* 82, no. 2 (spring 1997): 221-231.

Korstad, Robert, and Nelson Lichtenstein. "Opportunities Found and Lost: Labor, Radicals and the Early Civil Rights Movement." *Journal of American Studies* 75 (December 1988): 786-811.

Lerner, Gerder. "Early Community Work of Black Club Women." *Journal of Negro History* 59 (1974): 158-167.

Lewis, Diane K. "A Response to Inequality: Black Women, Racism, and Sexism." *Signs* 3, no.2 (Winter 1977): 339-361.

Liu, Tessie. "Teaching the Differences Among Women from a Historical Perspective: Rethinking Race and Gender as Social Categories." *Women's Studies International Forum* 14 (1991): 265-276.

Manning, Diane T., and Perry Rogers. "Desegregation of the New Orleans Parochial Schools." *Journal of Negro History* 71, nos. 1/2 (winter/spring 2002): 31-42.

Meier, August, and J. H. Bracey, Jr. "The NAACP as a Reform Movement, 1909-

1965: 'To Reach the Conscience of America.'" *Journal of Southern History* 59, no. 1 (February 1993): 3–30.
Meier, August, and Elliott Rudwick. "Attorneys Black and White: A Case Study of Race Relations Within the NAACP." *Journal of American History* 62 (1976): 913–946.
Middleton, Ernest J. "The Louisiana Education Association, 1901–1970." *Journal of Negro Education* (fall 1978): 363–378.
Muller, Mary Lee. "New Orleans Public School Desegregation." *Louisiana History* 42, no. 1 (1976): 69–88.
Norwood, Stephen H. "Bogalusa Burning: The War Against Biracial Unionism in the Deep South, 1919." *Journal of Southern History* 63, no. 3 (August 1997): 591–628.
O'Kelley, Charlotte G. "Black Newspapers and the Black Protest Movement: Their Historical Relationship, 1827–1945." *Phylon* 43, no. 1 (1982): 1–14.
O'Reilly, Kenneth. "The Roosevelt Administration and Black America: Federal Surveillance Policy and Civil Rights During the New Deal and World War II Years." *Phylon* 48, no. 1 (1987): 12–25.
Palmer, Phyllis Marynick. "White Women/Black Women: The Dualism of Female Identity and Experience in the United States." *Feminist Studies* 9, no. 1 (spring 1983): 151–170.
Pauley, Garth E. "W. E. B. Du Bois on Woman Suffrage: A Critical Analysis of His Writings." *Journal of Black Studies* 30, no. 3 (January 2000): 383–410.
Pitre, Merline. "Building and Selling the NAACP: Lula B. White as an Organizer and Mobilizer." *East Texas Historical Journal* 39, no. 1 (2001): 22–32.
Rath, Richard Cullen. "Echo and Narcissus: The Afrocentric Pragmatism of W. E. B. Du Bois." *Journal of American Studies* 84 (September 1997): 461–495.
Reich, Steven A. "Soldiers of Democracy: Back Texans and the Fights for Citizenship, 1917–1921." *Journal of American History* (March 1996): 1480–1504.
Reed, Germaine A. "Race Legislation in Louisiana, 1864–1920." *Louisiana History* 6, no. 4 (fall 1965): 379–392.
Reed, Merl E. "The FEPC, the Black Worker, and the Southern Shipyards." *South Atlantic Quarterly* 74 (autumn 1975): 446–467.
Ryan, Roderick N. "An Ambiguous Legacy: Baltimore Blacks and the CIO, 1936–1941." *Journal of Negro History* 65 (winter 1980): 18–33.
Scott, Anne Firor. "Most Invisible of All: Black Women's Voluntary Associations." *Journal of Southern History* 56 (February 1990): 3–22.
Shaw, Stephanie J. "Black Club Women and the Creation of the National Association of Colored Women." *Journal of Women's History* 3, no. 2 (fall 1991): 10–25.

Holmes Singleton, Gregory Holmes. "Birth, Rebirth, and the 'New Negro' of the 1920s." *Phylon* 43, no. 1 (March 1982): 29–45.

Sitkoff, Harvard. "Racial Militancy and Interracial Violence in the Second World War." *Journal of American History* (December 1971): 661–681.

Skotnes, Andor. "Narratives of Juanita Jackson Mitchell: The Making of a 1930s Freedom Movement Leader." *Maryland Historian* 1 (fall/winter 2001): 44–66.

Somers, Dale A. "Black and White in New Orleans: A Study in Urban Race Relations, 1865–1900." *Journal of Southern History* 40, no. 1 (February 1974): 19–42.

Sundstrom, William A. "Discouraging Times: The Labor Force Participation of Married Black Women, 1930–1940." *Explorations in Economic History* 38 (January 2001): 123–146.

Thornbrough, Emma Lou. "The National Afro-American League, 1887–1908." *Journal of Southern History* 27 (1961): 494–512.

Thurlkill, Cathy. "A Woman's Place Is in the War: North Louisiana Women's Contributions to World War II, 1941–45." *North Louisiana Historical Association Journal* 28, no. 1 (winter 1997): 49–60.

Weaver, Bill and Oscar C. Page. "The Black Press and the Drive for Integrated Graduate and Professional Schools." *Phylon* 43, no. 1 (1982): 15–28.

White, Monica A. "Paradise Lost?" Teachers' Perspectives on the Use of Cultural Capital in the Segregated Schools of New Orleans, Louisiana." *Journal of African American History* 87 (March 2002): 269–281.

Wieder, Alan. "The New Orleans School Crisis of 1960: Causes and Consequences." *Phylon* 48, no. 2 (summer 1987): 121–131.

Wingo, Barbara C. "The 1928 Presidential Election in Louisiana." *Louisiana History* 18, no. 4 (fall 1977): 405–435.

Wolters, Raymond. "Personal Connections and the Growth of the NAACP." *Reviews in American History* 2 (March 1974): 138–145.

Unpublished Theses and Dissertations

Agnes, Anthony Arthe. "The Negro Creole Community in New Orleans, 1880–1920: An Oral History." Ph.D., University of California, Irvine, 1978.

Autrey, Dorothy. "The National Association for the Advancement of Colored People in Alabama, 1913–1952." Ph.D., University of Notre Dame, 1985.

Bachman, Linda Sharon. "Uncompromising Sisters: The Women's Suffrage Movement in Louisiana, 1900–1921." Honors Thesis, Department of American Studies, Newcomb College, Tulane University 1981. Jones-Hall Louisiana Collection, Tulane University, New Orleans.

Cole, Constance. "Changing Self-Images of the Negro: A Cover Analysis of *The Crisis* (NAACP), 1910–1968." M.A., American University, 1984.

Hebert, Mary Jacqueline. "Beyond Black and White: The Civil Rights Movement in Baton Rouge, Louisiana, 1945–1972." Ph.D., Louisiana State University, 1999.

Wiedman, Harriet Elsa. "The Sylvania F. Williams Community Center." M.A., Tulane University, 1933.

Novels

Johnson, James Weldon. *The Autobiography of an Ex-Colored Man.* 1912. Reprint, New York: Dover, 1995.

Walker, Alice. *Meridian.* London: Women's Press, 1976.

INDEX

Adams, Mrs. W. R. (New Orleans), 86
Adderly, Mildred (New Orleans), 89
African American men, 1, 2–7, 9–10, 13–14, 40–43, 46–47, 48, 50–53, 58–63, 75, 107, 126, 139–40, 143, 166n35. *See also* white men
African American women: Louisiana Governor John M. Parker's view of, 48; Senator Huey Long's view of, 169n18. *See also* women's auxiliaries; women's employment; women's fundraising; women's social networks
Alexandria, 12, 55, 74; black elite, 121, 123; military bases, 121, 122; population growth during World War II, 121. *See also* Georgia M. Johnson; Alexandria NAACP
Alexandria NAACP, 112, 121, 166n28; Anderson case, 129; branch meetings, 107; campaigns, 128; committees, 72; conservative nature, 125; elected positions, 110, 123; equality of teachers' salaries case, 97; Green case, 131; membership, 122; personal disputes, 37, 112, 122, 125, 131–35, 186n35; riot (1942), 129–30, 184n5; three soldiers' case, 130. *See also Alexandria Observer*; Georgia M. Johnson; women's auxiliaries; women's fundraising
Alexandria Observer, 124, 127, 184n10
antilynching campaigns, 20, 24, 28, 38, 41, 104–5, 118, 134, 137, 182n33; Association of Southern Women for the Prevention of Lynching, 61; Costigan-Wagner anti-lynching bill, 21; Dillard University demonstration, 33; Dyer Anti-Lynching Bill, 20–21; Ferguson case, 113, 115; gender, 42–43, 60, 113–15, Wilson case, 60–61

Armstrong, Maude C. (New Orleans), 72, 88
Aubry, Mrs. A. R., 104. *See also* Masonic lodges, Ladies Auxiliary of the Knights of Peter Claver
Autrey, Dorothy, 6
Azamore, Corinne (New Orleans), 81, 173n59

Bagnall, Robert, 35, 59, 109, 174n62. *See also* women's auxiliaries
Baker, Ella, 36–37, 125; correspondence with Georgia M. Johnson of Alexandria, 125, 132, 133–34; gender issues, 8–9
Baker, Tracey E. (Baton Rouge), 91
Banks, Myrtle (New Orleans), 87, 92
Baranco, Oralee (New Orleans), 78
Barnett, Bernice McNair, 5
Baton Rouge, 12, 13; bus boycott (1953), 11, 111, 118; Daisy Lampkin visit, 69–70. *See also* Baton Rouge NAACP; NAACP local branches
Baton Rouge NAACP, 51, 58, 59, 74–76, 99, 101, 112, 116, 120, 142, 170n30; antilynching campaigns, 113–14; branch meetings, 107, 115; citizenship, 114; education, 83, 90–91, 108; elected officials, 99, 106, 109, 110–11; executive committee, 91, 106; female membership, 58, 69–70, 173n52; Ferguson case, 113–15; internal divisions, 109–10; membership, 25, 76, 138; membership campaigns, 72; police brutality cases, 115; secretaries, 51; voter registration campaigns, 111; white members, 116; World War II, 115; youth councils, 92, 116–17. *See also* Mrs. D. J. Dupuy; Daisy Lampkin; William Pickens; Horatio Thompson; women's auxiliaries; women's fundraising
Bauduit, A. L. (New Orleans), 88

Beauchamp, Agnes (New Orleans), 89
Bell, Mrs. M (New Orleans), 62
Berhol, Anna Mae (New Orleans), 85, 171n37
Bolin, Jane (New York), 71, 171n39
Borikins, Naomi (New Orleans), 81
Brazier, Dr. A. W. (New Orleans), 62, 69; Urban League membership, 80
Brown, Mayme Osby (New Orleans), 88, 169n13
Brown, Oneida (New Orleans), 77, 103, 104, 179n5. *See also* Masonic lodges, Ladies Auxiliary of the Knight of Peter Claver
Brunner, Mrs. A. L. (Monroe), 75
Burke, Mrs. E. S. (Baton Rouge), 87
Burrell, Alberta (New Orleans), 88
Byrd, Daniel E. (New Orleans), 71, 106; increasing African American militancy in 1940s, 58; on racial integration, 98
Byrd, Mildred C. (New Orleans): executive committee, 92, 106; state conference, 106; youth council, 92

Carline, Lillian B. (Lake Charles), 92
Carroll, H. M. (Monroe), 70
civil rights movement, 4, 11, 137. *See also* Martin Luther King Jr.
Coghill, Mary D. (New Orleans), 81, 171n36, 173n59
communism, 22, 24, 93, 94, 177n27; Communist Party, 22, 32, 61
Community Chest campaigns, 62, 77–78, 81, 173n59
Congress of Racial Equality (CORE), 33
Consumers League of New Orleans, 33
Cooper, Anna Julia, 43
Cornelius, V. C. (New Orleans), 86
Creuzot, Mrs. P. P. (New Orleans), 80
Crisis, 16–17, 23, 49, 85. *See also* W. E. B. Du Bois
Crowley, La., 11
Cunningham, Noelie (New Orleans), 93, 96; suspected communist sympathizer, 94. *See also* Louisiana Progressive Educational Association
Curry, Irma (Baton Rouge), 76, 87, 91; sister, Olga Curry, and mother, Mrs. M. L. Curry, 76

Daniels, Eunice (New Orleans), 86
Darrow, Clarence, 26
Davis, Angela, 41–42
Dejoie: Mrs. C. C. (New Orleans), 92, 171n37; Ella, 73, 172n47; Julia B., 81; Mrs. J. J., 80; Lucille A., 173n53; Dr. P. H., 73
Dewey, John, 93. *See also* Louisiana Progressive Educational Association
Dominique, Viola (New Orleans), 87
Du Bois, W. E. B., 13, 17, 19; critic of NAACP, 33–34, 37; editor of *Crisis*, 16, 23; Lonigan report, 23; resigns as *Crisis* editor, 19
Dunbar Nelson, Alice, 55
Dunn, Alberta V. (New Orleans), 64, 102, 104, 105, 179n5; father (E. M. Dunn), 51, 59, 166n33; father as *Vindicator* editor and manager, 52
Dupuy, Mrs. D. J. (Baton Rouge), 2, 14, 52, 66–67, 99, 101, 107–18, 141, 182n33; as community bridge leader, 107; contrast with Georgia M. Johnson (Alexandria), 142–43; Ferguson case, 113–16; William Pickens's correspondence, 109; possible family, 112–13; possible first name, 182n32; youth council, 92, 116–17. *See also* Horatio Thompson; Benjamin J. Stanley

East Carroll Parish, 84; NAACP branch, 1
Evans, Naomi K. (New Orleans), 86

Fairclough, Adam, 11–12, 40
Federation of Civic Leagues, 80, 91, 174n64. *See also* Republican Party
Flint-Goodridge Hospital (New Orleans), 46, 76, 77, 87; Nurses' Alumni Association and NAACP club membership, 46, 165n18; Phyllis Wheatley Club of New Orleans, 79
Flowers, Mrs. O. B. (New Orleans), 51

Garner, Mrs. J. (New Orleans), 106

Gayle, Mrs. James E. (New Orleans), 77; husband, 51, 68, 80, 102, 110, 115, 166n33, 169n13, 181n20; Community Chest campaign, 77
Gayle & Dunn's African American Books, 51, 102
gender and civil rights, 2, 5, 7, 9, 10, 14, 36, 49, 50, 59, 61, 72, 75, 87, 93, 101, 118, 120, 139–40, 142–43; and class, 9, 40, 59, 63, 87, 98; great depression, 58; 1920s, 58; and race, 7, 58, 86, 120, 136, 140; world war II, 52. *See also* anti-lynching campaigns; *Vindicator*
Giddings, Paula, 3, 43
Gilmore, Glenda E., 9
Goings, Kenneth W., 21
Gordon, Kate and Jean (sisters), 47; Kate, 165n22; ERA, 47
Great Depression, 24, 32, 58, 66, 162n43; decrease in NAACP membership, 57–58, 100, 121. *See also* gender and civil rights
Green, Mrs. S. W. (New Orleans), 74, 138; husband, 74, 172n50; daughters (L. Green and Mercedes I. Green), 173n51
Guidry, D. J. (New Orleans), 66, 68, 103, 141, 179n5; husband (George Guidry), 103; Federation of Civic Leagues (Republican Party), 80; W. E. & Frances Memorial Home for Colored Juvenile Delinquents, 103

Harper, Frances E. W., 47
Harrison, Camille (New Orleans), 102, 110, 171n37, 179n5
Hart, Althea (New Orleans), 76; brothers, James and Marcel, 76
Hart, Annette G. (New Orleans), 73
Haynes, J. K., 96
Hayward, Myra U. (New Orleans), 81
Henly, Mrs. A. M. (New Orleans), 51
Houston, Charles, 26
Huggins, Mrs. H. Horne, 91 (Baton Rouge); husband, 109

Jackson, Juanita, 24, 36, 37, 93; calls NAACP youth conference (1936), 32; mother, Lillie Jackson (Baltimore, Maryland), 9, 37
Jacobs, Claude F., 41
Johnson, Georgia M. (Alexandria), 2, 107, 120–36; Alexandria riot (1942), 129–30; Anderson case, 129; attempts to register to vote, 122; Christianity, 124, 127; civil rights philosophy, 123, 127; contrast with Mrs. D. J. Dupuy (Baton Rouge), 142–43; correspondence with Ella Baker, 125, 132, 133–34; employment, 123–24; factionalism of Alexandria NAACP, 132–35; family, 124, 132; gender issues, 14, 120, 126; Green case, 131; leadership concepts, 125; persecution by whites, 130, 131–32, 185n19; personal characteristics, 122, 135; three soldiers' case, 130–31; visit to Alexandria mayor, 123, 134. *See also* Alexandria; Madison S. Jones
Johnson, Mrs, H. W. (Monroe), 2, 66, 70, 99–100, 101, 102, 141, 179n2; family, 100, 138
Johnson, James Weldon, 18–19, 20; Dyer Anti-Lynching Bill, 20
Johnson, Mrs. L. M. (Baton Rouge), 73
Johnson, Nancy (New Orleans), 105
Jones, Donald, 95
Jones, Edith (Plaquemine), 94
Jones, Eva (New Orleans), 85, 174n63
Jones, Liley (Alexandria), 72
Jones, Madison S., 122, 184n5; Alexandria riot (1942), 129; visit to Alexandria mayor, 123, 126. *See also* Georgia M. Johnson
Jones, Naomi (New Orleans), 89

Kane, Maude (Lake Charles), 93
King, Hazel S. (Baton Rouge), 76, 87, 91; husband (Cornelius King), 76
King, Ida T. (New Orleans), 78, 180n14
King, Martin Luther Jr., 4, 124

Labat, L. J. (New Orleans), 75; husband (George Labat), 40, 181n20

Lake Charles NAACP, 72, 102; youth council, 92, 93; state conference, 106
Lamothe, L. E. (Monroe), 73, 75; husband (S. C. Lamothe), 73
Lampkin, Daisy, 35–37, 69–70, 163n55
Landry, Mrs. L. B. (New Orleans), 51
Lawless, Frances (New Orleans), 88, 173n59
Lee, Eula Mae (Jefferson Parish, La.), 96–97. *See also* teachers and NAACP
Lenoir, Elsie (New Orleans), 33
Lewis, Florence A. (New Orleans), 85, 88, 100, 101, 105; W. E. & Francis Memorial Home for Colored Juvenile Delinquents, 100; retires to Florida, 179n3
Logan, Adella Hunt, 17, 48
Longe, George, 81
Lonigan report, 23–24, 34–35, 161n19, 163n55
Louisiana, 11; black electorate, 11; Dillard University, 33, 88, 100; disfranchisement laws, 11, 47; history (colonial to Reconstruction), 39–41, 46; Louisiana State University, 11; University of New Orleans, 45, 86; Nineteenth Amendment, 48; William Pickens NAACP visit (1937), 115; Republican Party, 46; school conditions, 84, 94–95, 95–96, 176n12; Southern University, 109; UNIA, 25; Xavier University, 88. *See also* Alexandria; Crowley; Baton Rouge; East Carroll; Lake Charles; Monroe; NAACP; New Iberia; New Orleans; Shreveport; Transylvania
Louisiana NAACP: Alexandria (general campaigns), 128; Alexandria riot (1942), 129–30, 184n5, 185n27; Anderson case, 129; Baton Rouge bus boycott (1953), 11, 111, 118; Eros Murder case, 60; Ferguson case, 113–15; Green case, 131; Hattie McCrary shooting case, 61, 173n54; Lily Johnson case, 65; Mississippi flood (1927), 66; police brutality cases, 115; Rehabilitation of the Wilson Family, 61; three soldiers' case, 130; Wilson (Franklington) case, 60–61, 182n33; voter registration, 111. *See also* teachers and NAACP
Louisiana Progressive Educational Association, 93–94
Louisiana State Conference, 94, 106, 112, 180n15
Louisiana Weekly, 62, 77, 80, 90, 110; James B. LaFourche, editor, 110, 181n27
Lucas, Mrs. George W. (New Orleans), 75; Community Chest campaigns, 77; husband, 65, 75, 103, 122, 181n20
Lute, Atholia Ladd (Lake Charles), 106
Lyons-Taylor, Mrs. E. O. (New Orleans), 46, 76, 173n59. *See also* Flint-Goodridge Hospital

Marable, Manning, 3
Mason, Mrs. B. (New Orleans), 62
Masonic lodges, 65, 77, 78, 103, 104, 137, 138; Catholic Knights of Peter Claver, 77, 103–4; Grand Household Ruth no. 26, Grand United Order Oddfellows, 180n14; Knights of Pythias, 74, 108, 172n48, 172n50; Ladies Auxiliary of the Knights of Peter Claver, 73, 104, 137, 138; Mt. Olive Grand Chapter of the Order of the Eastern Star, 77
McClanahan, Mrs. H. L. (Monroe), 67, 106; youth council, 70, 92–93
McHenry, Mrs. Wilton, 48; leader of Louisiana Suffrage Party (Ouachita Parish), 47
McKelpin v. Orleans Parish (1942), 95–96, 97. *See also* teachers and NAACP
Meier, August, 18
Miller, Mrs. M. G. (Monroe), 75
Mississippi River flood (1927), 22, 29, 66, 121; Colored Advisory Commission, 23; President Calvin Coolidge 22; Herbert Hoover, undersecretary of commerce, 23; Women's League of St. Harford, Connecticut, 66
Monroe NAACP, 2, 57, 66, 67, 69, 73, 171n38, 183n41; 1930s, 58; elected offices, 99, 101–2, 141, 181n20; Eros murder case, 60; executive committee, 106; family linked to membership, 74–75,

138; membership, 58, 68, 69–70; racial diplomats, 112, 114; teachers' equality of pay case, 97; William Pickens's NAACP visit (1932), 68, 171n38; youth council, 93

Myers, Mrs. C. H. (Monroe), 75; husband, 57, 181n20

Myrdal, Gunnar, 141

Nance-Givens, Ida (Baton Rouge), 76, 90, 91; daughter (M. A. Givens), 76

Nash, Roy, 18

National American Women Suffrage Association, 48; New Orleans conference (1903), 48

National Association for the Advancement of Colored People (NAACP):
—Local branches: Alabama, 6, 9, 118, 120; Baltimore, 9; branch organization, 29, 30; Chicago, 6–7; elected positions, 99–108; Independence (La.), 102; Lima (Ohio), 65; organizational democracy, 26, 34, 38; St. Jackson (La.), 102; state conference, 29; women essential to, 51–52. See also Alexandria; Crowley; Baton Rouge; East Carroll; Lake Charles; Monroe; New Iberia; New Orleans; Shreveport; Transylvania; women's auxiliaries; women's fundraising; youth councils and college chapters
—National organization: Amenia conference (1916), 15; Amenia conference (1932), 24; *Birth of a Nation* (1915), 20; board of directors, 16, 18, 30, 34; *Buchanan v. Warley* (1917), 19; "The Call," 15, 17; chairman, 16; Costigan-Wagner bill, 21; Dyer Anti-Lynching Bill, 20, 21; executive secretary, 16, 18; Federal Employment Practices Committee, 25–26; founding (1909), 15; *Gaines v. University of Missouri* (1935), 28; *Guinn v. US* (1915), 19; Harris report, 24; Legal Defense and Educational Fund, 27, 95; Margold report, 26; *Moore v. Dempsey* (1923), 19; New York national office, 1, 7, 8, 12, 14, 16, 29, 34, 36, 64, 66, 113, 114, 116, 120, 123, 125, 128, 130, 131, 133, 136, 137, 141, 183n33; *Nixon v. Condon* (1932), 21; Judge J. Parker campaign, 21, 33; philosophy, 38; president, 16, 17; Scottsboro case, 22, 32, 61; silent parade 28 July 1917, 20; vice-president, 17. See also Ella Baker; Robert Bagnall; Clarence Darrow; W. E. B. Du Bois; Charles Houston; Juanita Jackson; James Weldon Johnson; Daisy Lampkin; Lonigan report; Roy Nash; Mary Childs Nerney; Mary White Ovington; William Pickens; John Shillady; Arthur Spingarn; Joel Spingarn; Moorfield Storey; William English Walling; Walter White; Roy Wilkins; women's auxiliaries; women's fundraising; youth councils and college chapters

National Association of Colored Women, 3, 17, 44–45, 48–49, 104; Phyllis Wheatley Club of New Orleans, 45. See also Mary Talbert; Mary Church Terrell; Fannie Barrier Williams

National Urban League, 37, 73, 79–80, 139

Nelson, H. Viscount, 57–58

Nerney, Mary Childs, 18

New Iberia, La., 13

New Orleans, 11; black elite, 12, 41, 65, 74, 110; civil rights advances, 11, 33; Colored Female Benevolent Society of Louisiana, 40–41; Comité des Citoyens, 46; jazz, 164n3; Joseph A. Hardin Playground Committee, 90; Daisy Lampkin's NAACP visit and correspondence, 69–70; Phyllis Wheatley Club of New Orleans, 45; William Pickens's NAACP visit (1934), 104; Société des Jeunes Amis, 41; Sylvania F. Williams Community Center, 85–88; Storyville, 54; UNIA, 25. See also NAACP local branches; New Orleans NAACP

New Orleans NAACP, 12, 13, 25, 46, 51–54, 56, 58, 99, 120, 174n62; attitudes toward citizenship, 52–54, 62; education, 83–85; Eros murder case, 60; executive committee, 105; FBI surveillance, 93,

New Orleans NAACP (cont.) 105; female membership, 58–59, 74, 76; female secretaries and assistant secretaries, 102–4, 110; female vice-presidents, 100–102; internal divisions, 37, 40, 57, 95, 109, 111–12, 181n20; Hattie McCrary shooting case, 61; Mississippi floods (1927), 66; membership crisis, 68–69; membership increase (1940s), 71–72, 112; Rehabilitation of the Wilson Family, 61; religion, 66, 77; state conference, 106; voter registration lessons, 111; World War I, 52; youth council, 33, 92. *See also Crisis*; A. P. Tureaud; *Vindicator*; Roy Wilkins; women's auxiliaries; women's fundraising

Nickerson, Camille (New Orleans), 72

Nineteenth Amendment to US Constitution, 47, 49, 59, 143; *Crisis*, 17; Louisiana's failure to ratify, 48

Ovington, Mary White, 13, 17–18, 19; "The Call", 15

Parent Teacher Associations (PTA), 83, 85, 87, 90, 91, 100

Parks, Rosa, 10, 118; husband (Raymond Parks), 10

Parnell, Naomi (New Orleans), 106

Payne, Charles, 4–5; *I've Got the Light of Freedom*, 4

Peevy, Clementine (Monroe), 97

Phyllis Wheatley Club of New Orleans, 45; black suffrage, 47; NAWSA, 48; training nurses, 45, 55, 79; Sylvanie Williams (president), 48

Pickens, William, 35–36, 68, 104, 163n55; Sheldon Avery's *Up From Washington*, 35. *See also* Mrs. D. J. Dupuy; Louisiana; Monroe; New Orleans; Shreveport; women's fundraising

Pipe, Freddye A. (Baton Rouge), 92

Pitre, Merline, 7

Plessy v. Ferguson (1896), 27, 165n19; Homer Plessy, 46

Powell, Mrs. O. A. (Baton Rouge), 87

Priestly, Helen (New Orleans), 86

Ransby, Barbara, 8

Red Cross, 52, 97, 166n35

Reed, Christopher R., 6–7, 141

Republican Party, 19, 46, 172n48; and Fannie C. Williams (New Orleans), 138; Federation of Civic Leagues (New Orleans), 80

Richards, Charlotte M. (New Orleans), 51, 102, 104. *See also* Gayle & Dunn's African American Books

Richards, Edna (New Orleans), 86

Richardson, O. P. (Baton Rouge), 51

Riley, Mrs. M. V. (New Orleans), 76

Ringgold, Maggie D. (Baton Rouge), 90

Robnett, Belinda, 5, 107

Rodgers-Rose, La Frances, 3–4

Ross, Louise J. (New Orleans), 52

Rudwick, Elliot, 18

Sartor, C. D. (New Orleans), 33

Sazon, Wylene (New Orleans) (Mrs. Samuel), 76, 78

Schneider, Mark Robert, 14

Scott, Hattie D. (Baton Rouge), 91

Scott, John H. (East Carroll), 1

Secrease, Ozenia (Monroe), 97

Shelby, Thelma S. (New Orleans), 33, 100

Shillady, John, 18

Shreveport, 12, 13, 55, 75; NAACP branch, 166n28, 168n3; schools, 84

Smith, Mrs. A. (New Orleans), 62

Spingarn, Arthur, 17

Spingarn, Joel, 15, 17, 19; commissions Lonigan report, 23

Stanley, A. R. (Baton Rouge), 75, 173n52; daughter (Sophronia Stanley), joins NAACP, 76; husband (Benjamin J. Stanley), 59, 70, 108–9, 110, 112, 142

statewide NAACP conference, 21, 55, 57, 94, 180n15; equality of black teachers' pay, 14, 57, 106, 121; teachers, 91, 96

Storey, Moorfield, 17, 26, 27

suffragist movement, 111, 165n22; African American men, 46; African American women, 43, 47–48, 49; divisions in white suffrage movement in Louisiana, 47; Equal Rights Association, 47; Fourteenth and Fifteenth Amendments to U.S. Constitution, 47, 50; white female, 47–48; Women's Suffrage Party of Louisiana, 47. *See also* Kate and Jean Gordon; Mrs. Wilton McHenry; Nineteenth Amendment; Phyllis Wheatley Club of New Orleans

Talbert, Mary, 17
teachers and NAACP, 12, 14, 51, 82, 83–84; developing notions of black history, 87–89, 94, 100, 139; equal pay campaign, 11, 14, 28, 83, 95–97, 106; Earl K. Long (governor), 97; unions, 87, 89, 90, 92; voter registration campaign, 85. *See also McKelpin v. Orleans Parish*; statewide NAACP conference
Terrell, Mary Church, 17, 44
Thompson, Daniel C., 53; racial diplomats, 111
Thompson, Mrs. E. L. (Lake Charles), 72
Thompson, Horatio (Baton Rouge), 109–10, 111, 112; bus boycott (1953), 111. *See also* Mrs. D. J. Dupuy
Thompson, Lillie R. (New Orleans), 77
Thompson, Virginia Barnes (New Orleans), 68
Thornhill, Mrs. E. C. (New Orleans), 78, 174n63
Transylvania NAACP, 1
Tregle, Joseph G., 40; *Louisiana in the Age of Jackson*, 40
Tropaz, Ida (New Orleans), 105
Trudeau, Mrs. A. M. (New Orleans), 80; husband, 171n32; *Trudeau v. Barnes* (1933), 174n64
Tureaud, A. P. (New Orleans), 62; "Alexandria Problem," 132, 133; Mrs. D. J. Dupuy (Baton Rouge), 108; criticized by G. M. Johnson, (Alexandria), 126; criticizes G. M. Johnson, (Alexandria), 126; criticizes New Orleans NAACP, 40; marries Lucille A. Dejoie, 173n53;

teachers' salary equalization cases, 96–97; war loan drives, 81

Universal Negro Improvement Association, 24–26; International Longshoremen's Union, 25. *See also* New Orleans

Vindicator, 13, 52–55

Walling, William English, 15
Walls, Mrs. R. J. (New Orleans), 51
Walker, C. J, 73
Washington, Booker T., 16, 19, 45, 160n18
Washington, Ella (New Orleans), 86
Washington, P. A. (Baton Rouge), 110, 170n31
Wells, M. T. (New Orleans), 105
Wells-Barnett, Ida B., 17
White, Deborah Gray, 48–49
White, E. W. (New Orleans), 52, 53, 73
White, Eva (New Orleans), 73
White, Lula B. (Houston, Texas), 7–8, 172n49
White, Walter, 13, 18, 19, 22, 24, 26, 35, 49, 113, 114; Costigan-Wagner bill, 21; Scottsboro boys, 22
white men, 48, 53, 59–60, 114, 166n37. *See also* African American men
Who's Who in Colored Louisiana (Perkins, ed.), 45, 73, 74
Wickham, Katie (New Orleans), 100
Wilkins, Roy, 19, 24, 29; Baton Rouge NAACP, 116; New Orleans NAACP, 71
Williams, E. (New Orleans), 62
Williams, Fannie Barrier, 48
Williams, Fannie. C. (New Orleans), 62, 63, 78–79, 90–91, 138; children's health day, 78; Community Chest, 78; Federation of Civic Leagues (Republican Party), 80; girl scouts, 90; Joseph A. Hardin Playground Committee, 90; NAACP, 63, 70; parents study group, 91; school building project, 91; teacher voter registration campaign, 85; "Tentative Approach to Negro History," 89; YWCA, 63
Williams, H. P. (Alexandria), 97

Williams, Sylvanie (Sylvania) F. (New Orleans), 39 (epigraph), 48, 166n25; president of Phyllis Wheatley Club of New Orleans, 48; Women's Committee (1918), 55
Willis, Gertrude Geddes (New Orleans), 73, 77, 138–39, 172n48
Wilson, Mrs. R. Stanley (Baton Rouge), 92
women's auxiliaries (NAACP), 31, 57, 64, 65, 66–68, 140, 171n32
women's employment, 42, 63, 97, 138–40; arts, 72, 108; beauty industry, 73, 81; business, 102, 72–74, 123–24, 132; domestic service, 42; journalism, 124, 169n13; juvenile probation enforcement, 81; insurance, 73, 74, 76, 80, 123; lost jobs due to civil rights work, 4, 95, 126; management, 74, 81, 124; nursing, 45–46, 51, 55, 76, 87; property, 165n22; real estate, 73, 166n34; social work, 15, 86, 123, 126; teaching, 42, 82, 101, 139; undertaking, 73, 75, 180n14; war jobs (World War I), 55
women's fundraising (NAACP), 2, 7, 14, 31, 57, 64, 66–67, 72, 77, 101, 140, 172n42; William Pickens, 64, 66
women's social networks, 2, 4, 5, 7, 14, 39, 57, 77, 102, 104, 137, 139–40; Bells of Joy Club (New Orleans), 62; church network (Alexandria), 132, 135; Mrs. D. J. Dupuy (Baton Rouge), 143; family, 99; middle class, 65, 105; NAACP branches, 21, 66; NAACP state conference (Louisiana), 57; Rosa Parks, 9; Primrose Art Sewing Circle (New Orleans), 62; Rose Bud Art Club (New Orleans), 62; teachers, 82, 84–85, 91, 106, 137, 139; Lula White (Houston, Tex.), 7. *See also* Masonic lodges

World War I, 12, 52, 80, 102; Committee on Women's Defense Work of the Council of National Defense (Women's Committee), 55, 167n43

World War II, 22, 58, 63, 91, 93; Louisiana military training center for US, 121, 128, 130; NAACP membership growth, 12, 16, 111–12, 137; war loans drives, 80–81

Young Men's Christian Association (YMCA), 76, 77
Young Women's Christian Association (YWCA), 63, 76, 88, 92
youth councils and college chapters (NAACP), 31–33, 92–93, 116–17. *See also* Baton Rouge NAACP; Lake Charles NAACP; Monroe NAACP; New Orleans NAACP

Zangrando, Robert, 20

Printed in the USA
CPSIA information can be obtained
at www.ICGtesting.com
LVHW031702230923
758951LV00004B/693